Research

Research

The Journey from Pondering to Publishing

EDITED BY

Serwan M.J. Baban

Canoe Press
Jamaica • Barbados • Trinidad and Tobago

Canoe Press
7A Gibraltar Hall Road   Mona
Kingston 7   Jamaica
www.uwipress.com

© 2009 by Serwan M.J. Baban

All rights reserved. Published 2009

ISBN: 978-976-8125-90-3

A catalogue record of this book is available from the National Library of Jamaica.

Set in Plantin 10/14.5 x 27
Book and cover design by Robert Harris.

Printed in the United States of America.

To my family (Daya Dora, Judith, Shereen and Zana),
for sharing their son, husband and father
with the rigours of academia.
Thank you for your understanding, support and encouragement.

Sit down before fact like a little child, and be prepared
to give up every preconceived notion, follow humbly wherever
and to whatever abyss Nature leads, or you shall learn nothing.

— *Thomas Henry Huxley*

Contents

Acknowledgements / *ix*

Introduction / *1*

Section 1 Conducting Research: The First Steps

CHAPTER 1	What Is Research? / *5*	
	Serwan M.J. Baban	
CHAPTER 2	Characteristics of Research / *8*	
	Serwan M.J. Baban	
CHAPTER 3	Types of Research / *20*	
	Patricia Mohammed	
CHAPTER 4	Originality and Thinking of Research / *32*	
	Serwan M.J. Baban	
CHAPTER 5	Strategies for Identifying Issues for Research / *39*	
	Patricia Mohammed	
CHAPTER 6	The Research Process / *44*	
	Serwan M.J. Baban	
CHAPTER 7	Developing and Articulating Persuasive Research Arguments / *61*	
	Serwan M.J. Baban	
CHAPTER 8	Research and Ethics / *72*	
	David Lloyd	

Section 2 Accomplishing Research

CHAPTER 9 Developing the Research Proposal / *93*
Bill Boyd

CHAPTER 10 Formulating and Conceptualizing the Research Problem / *121*
Bill Boyd

CHAPTER 11 Using Statistics to Effectively Capture and Analyse the Real World / *145*
Serwan M.J. Baban *and* Bruce Lauckner

CHAPTER 12 A Framework for Successful MPhil/PhD Research Projects / *167*
Serwan M.J. Baban

Section 3 Writing Up Research

CHAPTER 13 Writing a Research Proposal for Funding: A Practical Guide / *183*
Peter Baverstock

CHAPTER 14 Writing a Research Report / *195*
Serwan M.J. Baban

CHAPTER 15 Writing to Publish in a Peer-Reviewed Journal: A Practical Approach / *208*
Serwan M.J. Baban

CHAPTER 16 Writing to Publish in a Peer-Reviewed Journal: Developing a Checklist / *216*
Serwan M.J. Baban *and* Clement K. Sankat

CHAPTER 17 Introduction to the Reviewing/Refereeing Process / *236*
Serwan M.J. Baban

CHAPTER 18 A Formula for Writing a Successful MPhil/PhD Thesis / *248*
Serwan M.J. Baban

Contributors / *263*

Acknowledgements

I am grateful for the support provided by Royal Bank of Trinidad and Tobago Education Foundation, the University of the West Indies, St Augustine, Research and Publication Fund Committee, and the Office of Research. I am also indebted to a number of colleagues in the West Indies, the United Kingdom and Australia who supported this book and acted as valuable resource persons.

SERWAN M.J. BABAN

Introduction

Some universities and higher education institutions, despite having a workforce consisting of highly qualified staff, tend to suffer from a deficiency in research output and lack a research culture. This observation is backed up by the fact that a significant number of staff cannot be described as research active. This insufficiency could be due to (1) the lack of mentoring for "new" members of staff in terms of research, supervision, research proposal preparations, as well as finding and targeting funding agencies; (2) the lack of critical mass to conduct serious research in order to be recognized by international funding agencies; and (3) the lack of effective guidance for new MPhil/PhD students in terms of conceptualization, research proposal preparations and research strategies.

A way forward to enhance research in universities and higher education institutions is by providing the necessary building blocks for research excellence through encouraging staff research development by nourishing their needs through carefully designed and delivered workshops. These workshops will need to focus and provide practical guidance on the essential issues, which include defining research, critically evaluating research, research methodologies, proposal preparations and writing research reports and, most significantly, research papers. A second requirement is providing MPhil and PhD students with the necessary information, skills and guidance to successfully complete their research.

This book is designed to provide theoretical background, and the necessary training, guidance and building blocks for research excellence. The book deals with the critical issues involved, including defining research, critically evaluating research, research methodologies, proposal preparation and writing research reports and, most critically, research papers.

More specifically, the book has been designed to deliver the following objectives:

1. To provide participants (staff and postgraduate students) with the essential elements for understanding and being able to evaluate critically the quality of research.
2. To develop the necessary elementary research knowledge and skills.
3. To familiarize participants with various research approaches and methodologies.
4. To develop the necessary transferable skills.
5. To provide guidance for writing up the research.
6. To provide guidance for writing to publish in peer-reviewed journals.
7. To generate teaching material for research methodology and research seminar courses.
8. To facilitate the exchange of ideas between participants and invited guests.

In addition, the book aspires to

1. Enhance the research environment for a number of staff and postgraduate students working in universities and other higher education institutions.
2. Heighten the reputation of universities and higher education institutions as research oriented institutions.
3. Assist universities and higher education institutions with capacity building and the leadership role of providing the intellectual resources necessary for regional development processes.

The book has been divided into three sections, each containing several chapters. The first deals with the first steps, such as characterizing and defining research. The second focuses on accomplishing research through exploring various methodologies and approaches for actualizing research. The final section deals with writing research proposals for funding as well as writing to publish.

Section 1

Conducting Research: The First Steps

1

What Is Research?

▸ SERWAN M.J. BABAN

1.1   Introduction
1.2   Research Description Form
Chapter 1 Activity

1.1   Introduction

This chapter aims to explore views and perceptions regarding research and the motivation for doing research.

This process requires the completion of the Research Description Form *while* thinking about a specific research project, such as a PhD research project or a concept the reader intends to develop as a research project.

Completing the form is necessary before progressing to chapter 2.

1.2 Research Description Form

Research Description Form

Name:

Department and Faculty:

Degree programme:

Research topic/title:

The rationale for conducting the research:

The rationale for selecting/proposing methodologies and theoretical approaches:

The originality of the research:

A proposed timeline for completion:

Reasons for wanting to undertake MPhil/PhD research. Be as brief and as specific as possible.

Chapter 1 Activity

Activity 1

Individual participants should give a brief introduction to their research project, guided by the information provided on the submitted Research Description Form.

This should be followed by comparing notes within small groups and between the groups in the class.

The facilitator will intervene when necessary and will also summarize and condense the outcomes.

2

Characteristics of Research

▸ SERWAN M.J. BABAN

2.1	What Is Research?
2.1.1	A Comprehensive Philosophical Orientation
2.1.1.1	Positivism
2.1.1.2	Post-Positivism
2.1.1.3	Interpretivism
2.1.1.4	Critical
2.1.1.5	Postmodernism
2.1.2	Validity and Reliability
2.1.3	Unbiased and Objective
2.2	Drivers for Research
2.3	The Importance of Research for the Researcher
2.4	The General Process of Research
2.5	Characteristics of Research
2.5.1	Logical
2.5.2	Understandable
2.5.3	Valid, Rigorous and Verifiable
2.5.4	Controlled and Critical
2.5.5	Useful
2.5.6	Produces Outputs
References	
Chapter 2 Activities	

2.1 What Is Research?

The word *research* is composed of two syllables, *re* and *search*. The dictionary defines them as follows:

Re: a prefix meaning once more, afresh, repeated.

Search: a verb meaning to examine thoroughly for what may be found or to find something of which presence is suspected, make search or investigation.

Research: a noun describing a careful search or inquiry, endeavour to discover facts by scientific study of a subject, course of critical investigation.

There are many definitions for research, including

> Research is a multiple, systematic strategy to generate knowledge about human behaviour, human experience, and human environments in which the thought and action process of the researcher are clearly specified so that they are logical, understandable, conformable and useful. (DePoy and Gitlin 1994, 5)

> Research is a planned investigation employing recognized scientific methodology en route for explaining issues, solving problems and creating new knowledge that is generally applicable. (Grinnell 1993, 4)

Generally, research may be defined as a systematic exploration designed to advance knowledge and understanding of a subject. Therefore, it is a process employed to seek, analyse and deduce information about people, objects and nature; to revise available information in light of new information; to interpret the outcomes and to communicate that interpretation to others. Some also view research as a method of obtaining answers to questions (Baban 2006). It is important to note when a research study is undertaken to fulfil specific aims and objectives, adherence to the following criteria is essential to enable the process to be called "research".

2.1.1 A Comprehensive Philosophical Orientation

The philosophical orientation may stem from the academic discipline in which the researcher has received training and a number of research paradigms (the *isms*). These are described below.

2.1.1.1 Positivism

Positivism is a very predominant way of knowing the spatial world; what Guba and Lincoln (1994) refer to as the "received view". This can be seen by the ways in which many perceive positivist approaches to be simply a commonsense way of conducting research (Baban 2006).

The main characteristics of positivism include

- The belief that it is possible to capture "the real world" through the use of quantitative instruments, such as statistics, experiments and questionnaires.
- Objectivity and detachment from the objects of research on the part of the researcher.
- Research that aims to offer explanation leading to control and predictability.
- Research that is based on generalization and classification.

▶ **Key words:** objective view of the world, explaining

2.1.1.2 Post-Positivism

This approach developed as a response to the criticisms that have been made about positivism (Denzin and Lincoln 1994; Baban 2006).

The main characteristics of post-positivism include

- Maintaining a set of basic beliefs, as for positivism. However, post-positivists argue that it is only possible to know "the real world" imperfectly and probabilistically.
- While objectivity remains an ideal, there is an increased use of qualitative techniques in order to check the validity of findings.
- Post-positivism argues that as all investigation methods are imperfect, only partially objective accounts of the world can be formed.

▶ **Key words:** partially objective view of the world, explaining

2.1.1.3 Interpretivism

Interpretivist approaches to research in spatial sciences reflect on the problems in the real world from social and historical viewpoints. Interpretivism is often linked to the work of Max Weber (1864–1920), who indicated that the social sciences are concerned with understanding. This is in contrast to to explaining, which forms the basis of seeking causal explanations and is the hallmark of the natural sciences (Baban 2006).

The main characteristics include

- Allowing for interpretations of the real world being culturally derived and historically situated.
- Focusing on qualitative rather than quantitative approaches to research.

▶ **Key words:** understanding

2.1.1.4   Critical

This research paradigm assesses critically both positivism and interpretivism as ways of understanding the social world. Research schemes within this approach include feminist, neo-Marxist, antiracist and participatory procedures. Critical research is concerned with understanding as well as challenging.

The main characteristics include

- Taking up a view of conflict.
- Seeking to make a difference and bring about change.

▶ **Key words:** understanding, challenging, seeking change

2.1.1.5   Postmodernism

While the other paradigms offer substantial theories for understanding the world, believers in postmodernism have argued that the era of big narratives and theories is over (Flick 1998).

The main characteristics include

- Focusing on locally – temporally and situationally – limited narratives.
- Seeking to overcome the boundaries that are placed between art and the social and physical sciences.

▶ **Key words:** local and temporal narratives, no generalizations

2.1.2 Validity and Reliability

The concept of *validity* can be applied to any aspect of the research process. It ensures that in a research study, correct procedures have been applied to find answers to a question(s). *Reliability* refers to the quality of a measurement procedure.

2.1.3 Unbiased and Objective

This means that the researchers have followed the most relevant research process and drawn the most plausible conclusions without any prejudice, that is, without introducing their own vested interest. Within this context there is a distinction between bias and subjectivity. Subjectivity is an integral part of the thinking process that is conditioned by educational background, discipline, philosophy, experience and skills. Bias, on the other hand, is a deliberate attempt to either conceal or highlight something. For example, a biologist may view a piece of information differently from the way a social scientist views it.

However, the degree to which these criteria are expected to be fulfilled varies between disciplines and consequently the essence of research can differ from one academic discipline to another. For example, in the physical sciences a research endeavour is expected to be strictly controlled at each step, whereas in the social sciences rigid control cannot be enforced and sometimes is not even demanded.

Within the social sciences the level of control required also varies markedly from one discipline to another, as social scientists differ over the need for the research process to meet the above expectations. Despite these differences among disciplines, their broad approach to inquiry is similar.

2.2 Drivers for Research

Conducting research can be a hard task; therefore, success requires a clear motivation and a strong drive to achieve something. Cryer (2000) indicates that researchers need to have, at least in part, motives that are intellectual. Baban (2006) articulates that it is acceptable to have a core motivation that is not intellectual but can be fulfilled in an intellectual way. For example, an environmental campaigner may find a research degree a good way to work through strongly held ethical beliefs. Others do this by organizing campaigns or political action but researching a key issue and publicizing the results is a perfectly valid way of working through such a motivation.

There are several appropriate drivers for doing research. These include

1. Personal development
2. Desire to make a difference
3. Intellectual curiosity
4. Career progression
5. Keeping an active mind

Many researchers who start their careers with "inappropriate" drivers (such as a researcher who undertakes work on a subject that does not truly interest him or her because of the availability of a scholarship or funding, or someone who finds employment on a research project only because it is in a desirable geographical location) find it hard to complete a research degree (a PhD in particular) or to finalize a project. Personal motivation is an essential factor for success. However, the line between appropriate and inappropriate drivers is not always evident. For example, the career or job aspect can fall between categories. Perhaps the difference is whether someone is simply trying to escape from one job or is positively running towards another. Personal circumstances can play an important part and constrain available choices.

2.3 The Importance of Research for the Researcher

- Research is a crucial skill for an educated person. Researchers tend to gain habits of mind that will serve them in every endeavour.
- Learning to research promotes careful, critical, systematic thinking.
- Learning to write promotes the effective communication of the ideas and insights gained in the research process.
- Researching and research writing necessarily go together, with each building on and promoting the other.

2.4 The General Process of Research

The process begins with an observation followed by a conscious probing for a solution to the problem, a time of subconscious activity, an intuition about the solution and finally a systematic testing to verify the solution. This process may be broken into four stages that are not always clearly separated (Baban 2006):

1. Preparation:
   - This stage involves the first awareness in researchers that a problem or a question exists that needs systematic inquiry.
   - Researchers formulate the problem and begin to explore it.
   - By stating the problem in a number of ways, looking at it from various angles, trying to define the distinctive characteristics, and attempting possible solutions, researchers come to define for themselves the subtleties of the problem.
   - Preparation is generally systematic but may include previous experience and intuition.
2. Incubation: This involves a period of intense subconscious activity that is hard to define or describe.
3. Illumination: The idea may begin to emerge gradually or the researcher may leap to a hypothesis and a possible solution to the problem.
4. Verification:
   - Once a hypothesis is formed, the next stage is to systematically test to verify it.
   - In the sciences, the verification is often highly rigorous, involved and lengthy.
   - To be judged as sound or verified, a hypothesis must survive the critical scrutiny of the research community.

2.5 Characteristics of Research

A popular view of research is "to find out something new or unknown". However, this description is not always accurate. For example, a person may find out about the location of a new restaurant. Does this "finding" qualify as research?

Research is concerned not with "finding out what is where" but with looking for explanations, relationships, comparisons, predictions, generalizations and theories, that is, the "why" questions. The difference between research and non-research activity is in the process by which answers are derived: the process must meet certain requirements to be called research. These are discussed below (DePoy and Gitlin 1994; Phillips and Pugh 1994; Cryer 2000).

2.5.1 Logical

Research needs to follow a certain logical sequence, which clarifies the logical thinking and action processes by which the information was derived. "Logical" in this context means that the thought and action processes in research are clear and conform to accepted norms. Logic is a science that involves defined ways of thinking and relating ideas to develop an understanding of phenomena and their relationships. The systematic nature of research requires that the investigator proceeds logically and articulates each thought and action throughout the research inquiry.

2.5.2 Understandable

The research process, outcomes and conclusions need to make sense and be precise, intelligible and credible to the reader or research consumer.

2.5.3 Valid, Rigorous and Verifiable

Validity entails that whatever is concluded on the basis of the outcomes is correct and can be verified by others. Therefore, it is necessary to ensure that the procedures followed are relevant and justified. Consequently, the researcher needs to clearly identify the strategies used in the study so that others can reasonably follow the path of analysis and arrive at similar outcomes and conclusions. It is the aim of research to obtain valid generalizations because this is the most efficient way of applying understanding in a wide variety of appropriate situations. However, the claims made by the researcher should be supported by the research strategy and be accurate and credible within the stated boundaries of the study.

2.5.4 Controlled and Critical

Research needs to be conducted under "controlled" conditions, that is, when exploring causality in relation to two variables the study should be set up in a way that minimizes the effects of other factors affecting the relationship.

This can be achieved to a large extent in the physical sciences. However, in the social sciences it is extremely difficult, as research is carried out on issues that are often related to and influenced by other factors. Therefore, in the social sciences controlling external factors is difficult; instead, researchers are expected to quantify their impact.

The critical aspect of research is the most important element in distinguishing a research approach from others and researchers from practitioners and lay people (Phillips and Pugh 1994). Critical scrutiny of the procedures used and the methods employed is essential to a research inquiry. The process of investigation must be foolproof and free from any drawbacks. The process adopted and the procedures used must be able to withstand critical examinations. This can be achieved through the researchers continually asking if they have the facts right. Can they improve on the data quality? Can the results be interpreted differently?

2.5.5 Useful

Research generates, verifies or tests theory and knowledge for use. In other words, the knowledge derived from a study should inform and lead to a better understanding of the issues involved. Usefulness is a subjective criterion in that it is based on one's judgement about the value of the knowledge produced by a study. However, the value of a study and the usefulness of knowledge become more widely accepted as the new knowledge increasingly stimulates further research, promotes the testing or verification of new or existing theory and practice and ultimately can lead to an improvement in the quality of life for the society at large.

2.5.6 Produces Outputs

Research needs to produce tangible outcomes. These include

- A new or improved product. Examples include a book, a synthetic fabric or a synthetic food. There is a hazy borderline between a new product and an improvement on an existing one. For example, a design for a five-bedroom house could be regarded as new in itself or as a development of a design for a two-bedroom house.
- A new theory or a reinterpretation of an existing theory. Examples include Darwin's theory of evolution and Einstein's theory of relativity.

The research problems of research students often involve reinterpretations of existing theories, rather than the development of new theories; for example, how far an existing theory is valid in a new context or how far it needs to be reappraised in the light of new evidence.

- A new or improved research tool or technique. Examples include a measuring device, a computer package to undertake certain tasks, a piece of equipment to identify disease, or a set of questionnaires to identify problem areas in certain sections of the community.
- A new or improved model or perspective. Examples include the perspective of thinking about time as a fourth dimension, which can be travelled through, like the other dimensions of length, breadth and height.
- An in-depth study. Examples include the study of something that has never been studied before, such as the moons of Jupiter following the enormous amount of data collected by the Galileo probe, or the Van Gogh painting that was thought to be lost and has recently been rediscovered.
- An exploration of a topic, area or field. This is a particularly useful starting point where the main features of the work are not known at the outset.
- A critical analysis. Examples include an analysis or reanalysis of a novel or of the effects of a government on the economy.
- A fact or conclusion, or a collection of facts or conclusions. This is a particularly common outcome of research in all fields. Examples include the determination of a scientific constant or factors that favour the occurrence of floods within a geographical area.

References

Baban, S.M.J., ed. 2006. *Writing Up Research*. A workshop developed for the University of the West Indies, Trinidad and Tobago. St Augustine: University of the West Indies.

Cryer, P. 2000. *The Research Student Guide to Success*. 2nd ed. Buckingham, UK: Open University Press.

Denzin, N.K., and Y.S. Lincoln. 1994. Introduction: Entering the field of qualitative research. In *Handbook of Qualitative Research*, ed. N.K. Denzin and Y.S. Lincoln, 1–17. Thousand Oaks, CA: Sage.

DePoy, E., and L.N. Gitlin. 1994. *Introduction to Research: Multiple Strategies for Health and Human Services*. St Louis, MO: Mosby.

Flick, U. 1998. *An Introduction to Qualitative Research*. London: Sage.

Guba, E.G., and Y.S. Lincoln. 1994. Competing paradigms in qualitative research. In *Handbook of Qualitative Research*, ed. N.K. Denzin and Y.S. Lincoln, 105–17. Thousand Oaks, CA: Sage.

Grinnell, R. Jr., ed. 1993. *Social Work, Research and Evaluation*. 4th ed. Itasca, IL: Peacock.

Phillips, E.M., and D.S. Pugh. 1994. *How to Get a PhD*. 2nd ed. Buckingham, UK: Open University Press.

Chapter 2 Activities

Activity 2

Based on the information provided on the Research Description Form:

- Explain your view of research in no more than ten words.
- Define the main characteristics of research.

This is an individual activity followed by comparing notes and seeking areas of agreement within small groups and between the groups in the class.

The facilitator will intervene when necessary and will also summarize and condense the outcomes.

Activity 3

- Explain why what you are doing or proposing to do is research.

This is a group activity. Each participant will, based on the outcomes from activity 1 (see chapter 1), attempt to explain why his or her activity, based on the completed Research Description Form, is research. This will be followed by a class discussion.

The facilitator will intervene when necessary and will also summarize and condense the outcomes.

3

Types of Research

▸ PATRICIA MOHAMMED

3.1	Introduction
3.2	The Application of the Research Study
3.2.1	Pure Research
3.2.2	Applied Research
3.3	The Objectives in Undertaking the Research
3.3.1	Descriptive Research
3.3.2	Exploratory Research
3.3.3	Correlational Research
3.3.4	Explanatory Research
3.4	The Type of Information Sought
3.4.1	Alternative Terms for the Main Research Paradigms
3.4.1.1	Quantitative Research
3.4.1.2	Qualitative Research
References	
Chapter 3 Activities	

3.1 Introduction

The purpose of this chapter is to examine various types of research that may be undertaken, examining each for its conceptual and methodological specificity, while also establishing continuities and commonalities between and among all types of research. We should be guided by the ideas presented in section 2 of this book that research may take many forms and involve different methods of arriving at the knowledge we seek to create. Generally, research is understood to follow a relatively structured path that guides the researcher. The boundaries of this structure are set by the specific focus of the topic of research, the discipline and methods that are normally observed for this subject and discipline and the kind of analysis and format for delivery of research findings that are expected. The formal structure or organization of research may not flow in a linear process, however, and may vary depending on the subject matter itself and the availability of data or informants and the manner of working of the individual researcher. The following steps, however, are usually part of most basic and applied formal research. It may be useful to remind ourselves of these at this time:

- Formulation of the topic
- Hypothesis
- Conceptual definitions
- Operational definitions
- Data gathering
- Data analysis
- Conclusion and revision or revisiting of hypothesis

As the reader proceeds with this section, it is useful to situate the particular piece of research that you are engaged in carrying out at present against the categories and insights provided. In this chapter we look at the two basic typologies into which all research is grouped: pure and applied research. Then we break this first stage division down into another categorization of research by objectives. These are descriptive, exploratory, correlational and explanatory, a categorization that is developed in Collis and Hussey's very useful research guide for graduate as well as undergraduate students (2003). We further qualify research typologies by type of research data sought and discuss these under two main yet overlapping paradigms: positivist and phenomenological.

3.2 ▸ The Application of the Research Study

3.2.1 Pure Research

The term *pure research* tends to refer to research that is undertaken for the purpose of seeking new knowledge, where the findings do not appear to have an immediate, self-evident or obvious link to concrete issues or problems that affect human society. You will also find that pure research is referred to as *basic* research or *fundamental* research. The latter two formulations suggest research that is of a less specific nature in that the research may be conducted to improve our understanding of general issues, without emphasis on its immediate applications. It is often driven by the researcher's curiosity or might begin with a hunch and be conducted without any practical end in mind, although such research may have unexpected results pointing to practical applications. The terms "basic" or "fundamental" indicate that, through theory generation, basic research provides the foundation for further, sometimes applied, research. It is regarded as the most academic form of research, since the principal aim is to make a contribution to knowledge, usually for the general good, rather than to find a solution for a specific problem experienced in one institution or society.

For example, a research organization might be involved in carrying out research on the value that religion serves in shaping the moral conduct of the individual in society and in which no specific religion is being privileged over the other. Such research may have in the first instance no direct application but might simply be carried out to establish that there may or may not be a relationship between levels of formalized religious practice in a society and the moral turpitude of its people. Or similarly a researcher might be interested in which aspects of genomes explain the complexity of an organism.

3.2.2 Applied Research

Applied research is research that is designed to apply its findings to solving an existing or perceived problem either in the present or in the future. It is important to point out that both pure and applied research may be done in all disciplines and fields and is not a shorthand for scientific versus nonscientific research. Applied research can be carried out by academic or industrial institutions. Often, an academic institution such as a university will have a specific applied research programme funded by an industrial partner or a department within a ministry of government that has a specific mandate to intervene in this area. Common areas of applied research include electronics, informatics, computer science, social policies on health, safety, the welfare of citizens and so on.

The distinction between basic and applied research can be difficult at times. The researchers may choose to present their project in one or the other category depending on the requirements of the funding sources or even the results of the research process, findings and data analysis. The question of genetic codes is a good example. Unravelling it for the sake of knowledge alone would be basic research – but what, for example, if such knowledge had the benefit of making it possible to alter the code so as to make a plant commercially viable and either relieve poverty or produce a plant from which valuable medicinal ingredients may be extracted? It is difficult to draw a precise dividing line between the two types of research and one should not attempt to do so. It is thought that the *difference* between *basic* and *applied* research lies in the time span between research and reasonably foreseeable practical applications.

3.3 The Objectives in Undertaking the Research

The kind of research undertaken is usually influenced by the *purpose* or *objective* of the research, that is, the reasons you have chosen or are directed to conduct such research. The purpose of the research, nonetheless, cannot be separated from other intermediating factors which define the type of research you may eventually end up actually doing. Among these might be

- The availability of data in a specific area, your access or lack of access to it, and how you may collect it
- The logic of your research, that is, whether you want to move from the specific to the general or vice versa
- The outcomes expected, that is, whether you are trying to solve a particular problem, make a general contribution to knowledge, or identify the factors or questions that require further research and thus which lead you to a different approach and type of research than the one you first started with

The objectives of research might be usefully viewed as four different categories of research outcomes that the researcher is attempting to achieve.

3.3.1 Descriptive Research

Descriptive research describes phenomena as they exist. Descriptive research tends to be used to identify and obtain information on the characteristics of a particular problem or issue, the findings of which might be used to inform another kind of research agenda. Descriptive research questions may be framed to elicit information on feelings, attitudes, recurrence of particular behaviours (not restricted to human behaviour), and to characteristics of pertinent issues. For example, a company might wish to know what qualifications and characteristics are necessary for the kind of recruits needed for expansion of a new department. Often, the kinds of data collected in descriptive research are quantitative, with statistical techniques employed to analyse and present information. At other times, it may be necessary to present qualitative data to summarize the moods or itemize the responses of the subjects researched as for instance if a number of case studies are used rather than a representative sample survey or if open ended questions and interviews resist full quantification.

3.3.2 Exploratory Research

A researcher or group of researchers engages in exploratory research into a research problem or issue where there are very few or no earlier studies to which they might refer for previous insights or information. The general aim of this research is to look for patterns or ideas that might help the researcher to develop firm *hypotheses*, rather than to test or confirm an existing hypothesis. It might be useful to explain here immediately, if you have not already encountered the term *hypothesis*, that this refers to an idea or proposition that can be tested for association or causality. To test a hypothesis, one must have empirical evidence for assessing and analysing the problem. *Empirical evidence*, as you will find out in section 2 of this book, is data based on observation or experience.

The main purpose of exploratory research then is to gain insights into and familiarity with the subject area, and prepare you for a more rigorous and calculated approach in investigating the phenomenon at a later stage.

The techniques in exploratory research include the range from which both quantitative and qualitative data may be obtained. Among these you might list case studies, observation and historical analysis. It is also important to include in exploratory research literature reviews where such literature might exist on phenomena tangential or related to the subject area that you want to further understand since they might also point you to the gaps that have persisted in this knowledge area and why they have done so.

Exploratory research tends to be seen as very open, impressionistic, allowing the researcher to cast the net wider to gather a range of data. In this sense, the objective of exploratory research is not generally or necessarily that of providing conclusive answers but to point more strategically to how the research may best be conducted.

3.3.3 Correlational Research

Correlational research is referred to as making sense of observations. The purpose of correlational research is to discover relationships between variables or to identify the causes of effects of important phenomena. Correlational research produces a correlation measure, which is a measure of the association or covariation of two or more dependent variables. This kind of research is generally conducted through the use of correlational statistics (r). The square of a correlation coefficient yields the explained variance (r-squared). A correlational relationship between two variables is occasionally the result of an outside source, so we have to be careful and remember that correlation does not necessarily tell us about cause and effect. If a strong relationship is found between two variables, causality can be tested by using an experimental approach.

In carrying out correlational research the following procedure is helpful:

- Defining the problem – identify specific variables that may be important determinants of the characteristics or behaviour patterns being studied. For example:
    - *Question:* Why are children aggressive?
    - *Hypothesis:* aggression is a learned behaviour as a result of modelling.
    - *Test:* look for associations between aggressive behaviour and family abuse.
- Reviewing existing literature in identifying variables.
- Selecting research participants – only those who can be measured by the variables being investigated.
- Collecting data: must be in quantifiable form.
- Analysing data: correlate scores of measured variable (x) that represent the phenomenon of interest with scores of a measured variable (y) thought to be related to that phenomenon.

Some types of correlational studies are

1. Observational research, for example, class attendance and grades;
2. Survey research, for example, living together and divorce rates; and
3. Archival research, for example, violence and economics.

The correlational method permits the researcher to analyse the relationships among a large number of variables in a single study. The correlation coefficient provides a measure of degree and direction of relationship. Correlations do not have to be positive to be important. The limitations, however, are that correlations do not establish cause and effect relationships between variables, and that correlations break down complex relationships into simpler components, perhaps too simply to really be of explanatory value. To explore the characteristics and uses of correlational research further you may wish to look at the relevant websites on this category of research listed in the references.

3.3.4 Explanatory Research

Explanatory research (which may sometimes also be referred to as analytical research) is a continuation of descriptive research. Here the researcher moves further than merely describing the characteristics found in studying data sources, to analysing and providing a *why* or *how* explanation. Since explanatory research attempts to provide analytical explanations more explicitly than the previous types of research, it identifies and, if possible, tries to control variables in the research activities, particularly those associated with the data-gathering process. Controlling variables allows the researcher to make informed analytical statements regarding causal links between characteristics being examined. A variable in this case may be applicable to both physical sciences and humanities or social sciences research. It is an attribute of an entity that can change or take on different values which may lend themselves to observation or measurement. For example, in focus group research, group interaction affects responses, as individuals can be influenced by the collective view of a group. Hence, responses obtained from an individual within a focus group may vary from those gathered in a one-to-one interview with that individual.

3.4 The Type of Information Sought

There are two main research paradigms or philosophies. The two paradigms are neither clear-cut nor without overlap and are labelled *positivist* and *phenomenological*. The latter is also referred to by some as *interpretivist*, to distinguish this paradigm from the methodology known as phenomenology. The good researcher should, however, be careful to understand these as not two main and dichotomized paradigms, but to regard them as the two extremes of a continuum in which real research and researchers work, in many instances combining elements of both. What is more useful to remember is that each of these has strengths or weaknesses in allowing data collection of particular kinds, and strengths and weaknesses that facilitate particular kinds of analyses. The topic and subject area of the research, the data available for collection and analysis and the purpose of the research may all guide where each researcher works on this continuum.

Individual researchers have different capacities and potential for producing knowledge and, as such, the choice of research paradigm may depend on the modes in which they work more efficiently. For instance, a researcher who is unable to make sense of quantitative or numerical data or apply statistical tests may veer towards a paradigm that involves examining and reflecting on perceptions or making quantitative sense of qualitative phenomenon. In the past few decades, while the differences between the two paradigms continue, there has been a greater rapprochement between researchers in considering the mutual benefits of each in the goals of good research.

3.4.1 Alternative Terms for the Main Research Paradigms

Positivist Paradigm	**Phenomenological Paradigm**
Quantitative	Qualitative
Objectivist	Subjectivist
Scientific	Humanist
Experimental	Interpretivist

Let us examine each in turn while attempting to deduce the nature of this continuum between the two paradigms. The material developed in the following two sections have benefited from and are further elaborated upon in Darlington and Scott (2002), Glaser and Strauss (1967) and Yin and Campbell (2003).

3.4.1.1 Quantitative Research

- The *ontological assumption* (how reality is constructed whether external to the researcher or socially constructed and understood only by examining the perceptions of human actors) of quantitative research or the positivist paradigm is that reality is objective and singular, and apart from the researcher.
- The *epistemological assumption* (what we accept as valid knowledge) is that the researcher is independent from the subject being researched. Quantitative research or positivist research believes that only phenomena that are observable and measurable can be validly regarded as knowledge. It thus tries to maintain an objective stance.
- The *axiological assumption* (that is, assumptions concerned with the role of values) for positivists is that research is value free and unbiased. Positivists believe that they are completely detached from the objects they are studying, that these objects or phenomena predated their existence, and that the phenomena and objects will remain unaffected by their research activities. It is useful to note here that these assumptions might apply more to research carried out in the natural sciences and less so in the social sciences, but that this does not always hold true for research in the natural sciences (for example, research on animals for cosmetics, medical research and so on).
- The *rhetorical assumption* is concerned with the language of research. The quantitative approach to research and data presentation is that it is a formal language, based on a set of definitions that have meanings within the discipline, that the research will be presented in an impersonal voice, usually in universities, one that is acceptable to supervisors and examiners. For instance the use of the first person "I" is generally eschewed in favour of the passive voice. Rather than "I caged a dozen male and female white mice for . . .", the researcher is encouraged to write "Six male and six female white mice were enclosed in one cage for . . .".
- The *methodological assumption* is concerned with the process by which the research is actually undertaken. Your choice of paradigm already predisposes you to the type of methodology you will adopt. The quantitative

approach employs a deductive process based on cause and effect, uses a static design with categories isolated before the study, and assumes a context-free situation so that generalizations may be made to allow predictions, explanations and understanding. Building on the values of positivism argued by Karl Popper in *The Logic of Scientific Discovery* (1959), one of the strongest recommendations for quantitative and positivist research is that the data and findings are judged for accuracy through reliability and validity, by replication of the same sets of circumstances and with the same materials.

3.4.1.2 Qualitative Research

- The *ontological assumption* of qualitative research is that reality is subjective and multiple.
- The *epistemological assumption* is that the researcher invariably interacts with that being researched, that is, either the subject matter or the subjects of research.
- The *axiological assumption* is that research is value laden and biased and that it is difficult if not impossible to do away with all bias or values.
- The *rhetorical assumption* in qualitative research allows for the evolution or development of a voice and language that reflect the interests and positions also of your subjects under research. First-person statements are allowed and welcomed although qualitative research at the same time guards itself against self-indulgence or opinions of the researcher that are not derived from some inductive method of analysing data.
- The *methodological assumption* involves the use of the inductive process based on an emerging research design where categories are identified during research. The research is always context bound, but, at the same time, there is room for proposing theories for understanding the phenomena further. In addition, the accuracy and reliability of the data, research and method are ensured through verification of data sources and method.

These are nonetheless purified renditions of both paradigms and there have been criticisms of each that serve to strengthen the value of the other, thus making a better case for a continuum between these two paradigms.

References

Collis, J., and R. Hussey. 2003. *Business Research: A Practical Guide for Undergraduate and Postgraduate Students*. 2nd ed. Oxford: Palgrave Macmillan.

Darlington, Y., and D. Scott. 2002. *Qualitative Research in Practice: Stories from the Field*. Milton Keynes: Open University Press.

Glaser, B.G., and A.L. Strauss. 1967. *The Discovery of Grounded Theory: The Strategies for Qualitative Research*. Chicago: Aldine.

Popper, K.R. 1959. *The Logic of Scientific Discovery*. London: Routledge.

Yin, R.K., and D.T. Campbell. 2003. *Case Study Research: Design and Methods*. London: Sage.

Chapter 3 Activities

Activity 4

Request a few (not more than three) volunteers from different disciplines who are present to categorize their research into pure and applied research and discuss whether their research might straddle both.

Activity 5

Workshop leader exercise – Based on the description forms submitted by participants, the workshop leader should select specific topics and elicit discussion from those selected on where they would place their research based on the typologies of research developed under section 3.3.

Activity 6

To ensure that workshop participants are reasonably acquainted with the material in this chapter, each participant should take two to three minutes to jot down points related to the following:

(a) With reference to the positivist and phenomenological paradigms identified above, what assumptions inform each participant's research project and how does this direct the data-gathering process?
(b) Does their research fit snugly into either quantitative or qualitative research typologies or does it reside on the continuum of quantitative to qualitative?

At least four participants from different disciplines should share their notes with the group, thus allowing the leader to engage the group in a rounded discussion on types of research.

4

Originality and Thinking of Research

▸ SERWAN M.J. BABAN

4.1	The Concept of Originality
4.2	Research: A Way of Thinking
4.2.1	Questioning and Research
4.2.2	Research as Thought and Action Processes
4.2.2.1	Deductive Reasoning
4.2.2.2	Inductive Reasoning
4.2.2.3	Inductive versus Deductive Reasoning
References	
Chapter 4 Activities	

4.1 The Concept of Originality

In order for a work to be categorized as research it needs to contain some kind or level of originality. This is typically expressed in regulations or guidance for postgraduate degrees in very general terms, such as "an original project", "an original contribution" or "containing evidence of original thinking". The same is true for journal and refereed conference papers. But what is originality?

A PhD, for example, is awarded for "an original contribution to knowledge" and in the statements that most universities have to guide examiners on the grading of theses, there is usually some reference to "unaided work", "significant contribution" and "originality". Refereed journals indicate that they will publish work that is "original" or provide a forum for papers describing the results of original research. What is *original*? How original is *your* work?

The following are several definitions of originality. Francis (1976) has provided the following definitions:

1. Setting down a major piece of new information in writing for the first time.
2. Continuing a previously original piece of work.
3. Carrying out original work designed by the supervisor.
4. Providing a single original technique, observation or result in an otherwise unoriginal but competent piece of research.
5. Having many original ideas, methods and interpretations all performed by others under the direction of the postgraduate.
6. Showing originality in testing somebody else's idea.

Phillips (1992) has provided the following definitions:

1. Carrying out empirical work that hasn't been done before.
2. Making a synthesis that hasn't been made before.
3. Using already known material but with a new interpretation.
4. Trying out something in this country that has previously only been done in other countries.
5. Taking a particular technique and applying it in a new area.
6. Bringing new evidence to bear on an old issue.
7. Being cross-disciplinary and using different methodologies.
8. Looking at areas that people in the discipline haven't looked at before.
9. Adding to knowledge in a way that hasn't previously been done.

As the definitions indicate, while conducting research on any topic, it is feasible to be original in terms of subject/theme/focus/issues/methodology/ approach or presentation. The conclusion of this is that research is often original by nature in one way or another, and that it is not copied from someone else's research. However, if the researcher is in doubt, he or she should verify it as early as possible with those who will judge the originality of the research. Experience shows that more in-depth and extensive discussions are required between students and their supervisors of what constitutes originality. While students and staff use the same vocabulary to describe a range of different concepts they tend not to discuss with each other the definitions to which they are working.

4.2 Research: A Way of Thinking

4.2.1 Questioning and Research

According to Kumar (1999) research is more than a set of skills; research is a way of thinking and a mindset: examining critically the various approaches and practices to deal with issues and manage problems, understanding and formulating guiding principles that govern a particular procedure, and developing and testing new approaches. Doing research is about the mindset to query, examine and probe with the view to understand and improve the effectiveness of utilized approaches to manage an issue, application or a problem. In general, this tends to be discipline dependent. For example, in the field of health and well-being, some questions may include the following:

- What are the most frequent illnesses among patients?
- What are the causes of these ailments and complaints?
- Why do some people have a particular condition whereas others do not?
- What are the health needs of the community?
- Why do some people use the service while others do not?
- How effective is the service and how can the service be improved?

In business studies, questions to ask may include the following:

- What is the best strategy to market a particular product?
- What is the effect of a particular advertising campaign on the sale of this product?
- How much are consumers prepared to spend on this item?
- What do consumers like or dislike about this product?
- What type of packaging do consumers prefer for this product?
- What training do the salespersons need to promote the sale of this product?
- What are the attributes of a good salesperson?

Some questions a manager may ask include the following:

- How many people are being served by the organization?
- What are the socioeconomic or demographic characteristics of clients?
- Why do some people use the service while others do not?
- What are the most common needs of clients who come to this organization?
- What are the strengths and weaknesses of the service?
- How effective is the service and how can the service be improved?

4.2.2 Research as Thought and Action Processes

According to DePoy and Gitlin (1994) an important component of research refers to the reasoning, actions taken during the conduct of research and methods of logic used to arrive at a conclusion based on information assumed to be true. Inductive and deductive reasoning are two methods used in such a context to arrive at a conclusion.

4.2.2.1 Deductive Reasoning

Deduction is in some sense the direct application of knowledge in the production of new knowledge. This method aims to indicate, through pure logic and the use of a hierarchy of statements, the conclusion in its entirety based on a few premises. In short, deductive reasoning arrives at a specific conclusion based on generalizations. Deductive reasoning works from the more general to the more specific. Therefore, at times it has been referred to as a "top-down" approach. The reasoning often begins with developing a "general theory" followed by a "specific hypothesis" that can be tested through "observations", which can result in either confirming or rejecting the theory.

Experimentally based research tends to use deductive reasoning and begin with the acknowledgment of a general principle then apply that principle to explain a specific case or phenomenon. For example, in detective work, profiling researchers use available information by application of personal experiences as opposed to theoretically driven inductive profiling based on all available instances of a crime. Profiles constructed by the police, clinical psychologists and criminologists tend to obtain inferences about, for example, the behaviours of juvenile delinquents based solely on work experience, intuition and the motivation of the offender.

4.2.2.2   Inductive Reasoning

Inductive reasoning is essentially the opposite of deductive reasoning. It involves trying to create general principles by starting with many specific instances. Therefore, it is an empirically based approach where conclusions are derived from scientific analysis. Inductive reasoning functions through moving from specific observations to broader generalizations and theories. It can be viewed as a "bottom up" approach. It begins with specific observations and measures then attempts to detect patterns and associations, develop some speculative hypotheses that can be explored, and finally discover some general conclusions or theories. Therefore, the inductive method involves a process in which general rules evolve or develop from events or observations of phenomena. An important step in the inductive profiling method is to formalize operational definitions (hypotheses) for testing. This step is followed by coding the data for statistical analysis in which the results are supported with theories. For example, inductive profiling derives general principles about the behaviour of juvenile delinquents by empirically examining and testing particular facts or instances of a large number of cases.

4.2.2.3   Inductive versus Deductive Reasoning

Although in a project a researcher uses both types of reasoning, the overall research process can be characterized as following the structure of one or the other type of reasoning. An inductive reasoning approach has no prior acceptance of truth and is used to reveal theory, rules and processes, whereas deductive reasoning is based on acceptance of truth and is used to test the application of theory and rules to specific areas of concern and predict their outcomes.

Both approaches can be used to describe, explain and predict phenomena, although traditionally only deductive reasoning has been valued as contributing to explanation and cause and effect relationships. However, these methods tend to project different sensibilities when used. Inductive reasoning is more open and exploratory, and therefore arguments based on experience or observations are best expressed within this approach. Furthermore, this approach has a holistic perspective, examines relationships among unrelated pieces of data and overall attempts to develop concepts based on repetition of patterns. On the other hand, deductive reasoning is more restricted and is concerned with testing or confirming hypotheses; therefore, arguments based on laws, rules or other widely accepted principles are best expressed deductively. Furthermore, this approach has an atomistic perspective: it examines associations among discrete phenomena and overall attempts to test concepts based on application to discrete phenomena.

References

DePoy, E., and L.N. Gitlin. 1994. *Introduction to Research: Multiple Strategies for Health and Human Services.* St Louis, MO: Mosby.
Francis, J.R.D. 1976. Supervision and examination of higher degree students. *Bulletin of the University of London* 31: 3–6.
Kumar, R. 1999. *Research Methodology: A Step-by-Step Guide for Beginners.* London: Sage.
Phillips, E.M. 1992. The PhD: Assessing quality at different stages of its development. In *Starting Research Supervision and Training,* ed. O. Zuber-Skerritt. London: Jessica Kingsley.

Chapter 4 Activities

Activity 7

Explain why your research is original.

Activity 8

Write down the questions that your research project seeks to address. Begin each one with a questioning word, such as "how", "who", "what", "when" or "why".

Activity 9

Explain the following in no more than twenty words:

- The main concepts in my research are . . .
- The main issues in my research are . . .
- The main contexts in my research are . . .

Activity 10

Discuss and evaluate the information in sections 4.2.2.1 to 4.2.2.3 as a group activity.

5

Strategies for Identifying Issues for Research

▸ Patricia Mohammed

5.1   Introduction
5.2   Strategies for Identifying Research Topics
References
Chapter 5 Activities

5.1   Introduction

"The belief that 'science makes knowledge, practice uses it', has been claimed to be one of the assumptions of positivism, yet 'scientific' methods of investigation have great difficulty coping with the dynamic and complex social world of human services" (Rein and White 1981, 36). There is a prevalent if unwarranted dichotomy between the world of research and the world of practice. This is paralleled in many ways by the notions of objectivity and subjectivity.

Practitioners, who deal every day with a multiplicity of issues in their professions or jobs, are constantly making observations based on deductions from their practice that researchers would consider "hypotheses". They might say, "I think that the reasons why . . . " or "I wonder if we understand enough about . . . " or "I have a hunch that . . . ". These observations are often viewed as subjective assessments, even though the practitioner, for instance a small-town general medical doctor, may have experienced the problem over a long period of time and with many patients and might be led to make this deduction on the basis of such detail. For instance if he works in a district where a particular industrial plant that emits substances has been in operation for a number of years, he might observe a trend in the kind of complaints that his clients seek attention for.

Unfortunately, these observations, hunches or questions may not reach those who live and work in areas where objective "research" is carried out. Worse yet, it may not be in the interests of various industries to have such research carried out. There is no guarantee that, having identified a research topic, one has the freedom to carry out this kind of research. It might mean having to find alternative ways to structure the topic of research so that you can bring attention to a problem worth researching.

5.2 Strategies for Identifying Research Topics

Those who carry out research generally are interested in the value of their research to advancing human knowledge and to problem solving, even if this may happen at a secondary level. How do we therefore actually go about the task of selecting the issues and specific topics for research in any field? What is the relationship between the researcher and the community of practitioners and how, if at all, must this gap be bridged? Here are some suggested strategies for beginning to think about how you might identify a research topic. Some of these are based on ideas developed by Mikkelsen (1995) and Darlington and Scott (2002).

Strategy One – You might try to locate the research issue in the subject matter being taught in courses you are taking by identifying, for example, the areas or topics that appeal to your own scholarly instincts or interests, or by examining, in the literature in your course readings or from a range of sources, how others have looked at a problem and how you might approach it differently based on your knowledge or intuitive feeling about the findings or analysis produced by others. If you want to give yourself the chance to examine hunches further you can do a preliminary course work project or essay on the research area and thus isolate with greater precision how you would want to approach or define the research topic. For example, if "multiculturalism" is viewed by the scholars of a particular society or state as unsettling, even though it has allowed migrant groups to reside as labour regimes, how might you view this issue of multiculturalism differently from the position of the outsider or someone who views the process of migration and cultural exchange as vital to the growth of human "culture" itself.

Strategy Two – Are there any studies carried out in the past that are worth replicating even with the same populations or substances to see if they reveal similar results? Or there might have been a study carried out in another society and replication in your own setting might reveal comparative findings that are valuable for advancing knowledge in the area.

Strategy Three – If you have had previous work experience, what questions or problem areas have been raised during or after this work period that you might want to answer or respond to through research. For example, if you have worked with small farmers who deal with a perennial problem of flooding and crop losses due to drainage, how might you tackle such an issue either on a micro or macro scale to benefit agriculture?

Strategy Four – What personal or other experiences may group themselves into a set of research issues that need systematic examination rather than clichéd responses by press and public? For example, topics such as violence in the household and sexual abuse in the workplace became valid topics for research based on the voiced experiences that emerged over time from the abused and from the medical and other staff who had dealt with cases of abuse.

Strategy Five – What new technological, scientific, economic, social or political developments are taking place at present that we might need to anticipate in order to understand their potential for growth or for retardation of a society or an industry? For example, what have been the effects of sophisticated computer technologies that allow for pirating and downloading music on the livelihoods of those who themselves create music? Or, has there been any research carried out on the voting patterns of a younger generation who may have now taken the "right" to vote as a given and do not therefore exercise this right?

Strategy Six – What recurrent issues keep surfacing in the society that have not yet been perceived as problematic for a society or a group of persons? In other words a researcher might be futuristic in his or her approach in anticipating problems or issues or proposing, through research, solutions for existing phenomena that others have not yet considered problematic.

References

Darlington, Y., and D. Scott. 2002. *Qualitative Research in Practice: Stories from the Field*. Milton Keynes: Open University Press.

Mikkelsen, B. 1995. *Methods for Development Work and Research: A Guide for Practitioners*. London: Sage.

Rein, M., and S.H. White. 1981. Knowledge for practice. *Social Service Review* 55: 1–41.

Chapter 5 Activities

Activity 11

Explain which one of the strategies described in this chapter you have utilized to identify and develop the research topic you are now pursuing, and state as clearly as possible how you arrived at this topic.

Activity 12

Are there any strategies or processes by which you arrived at identifying your research topic that we have not included in this chapter? Please share these with a colleague.

The Research Process

▸ SERWAN M.J. BABAN

6.1	Introduction
6.2	Approaches to the Research Process
6.2.1	The Exploratory Approach
6.2.2	The Established Approach
6.2.3	The Hypothesis-Based Approach
6.3	The Research Process
6.3.1	Topic Recognition and Definition
6.3.2	Literature Review
6.3.3	Conceptualization and Research Design
6.3.3.1	Quantitative Studies
6.3.3.2	Qualitative Studies
6.3.3.3	Research Design
6.3.4	Confidentiality and Ethical Issues
6.3.4.1	Ethical Approval
6.3.5	Data Collection
6.3.5.1	Primary Data Collection
6.3.5.2	Secondary Data Collection
6.3.5.3	Evaluation and Validity of Resources
6.3.6	Data Analysis
6.3.7	Validity and Reliability of Outcomes
6.3.8	Dissemination/Publication
References	
Chapter 6 Activities	

6.1 Introduction

Researchers make sense of the "world" by asking questions, seeking answers and validating the answers. Therefore, the construction of reality depends on the nature of the questions and, consequently, the objectivity of researchers is a critical component in scientific investigation and the accurate understanding of the world.

Scientific investigation follows a step-by-step procedure and generally involves identifying, locating/mapping, assessing, analysing, and then developing and expressing ideas leading to successful research outcomes. Furthermore, as the process advances, it is often necessary to reflect, revise, edit and add additional material. As a result, in some cases, due to reasons such as the topic having a broad focus or the unavailability of information resources to support the project, the researcher might need to change the research focus or direction and adjust the research plan in response to findings in the literature and available experience.

Selecting a research topic needs to be supported by a clearly articulated rationale for the undertaking. Appropriate consideration of the topic should prompt a hypothesis to be tested or a thesis to be developed or interrogated. The research must then be located in relation to other work in the area and its scope and limitations clearly understood and defined. After an assessment of current thinking on the subject the researcher should review the literature and frame the chosen topic in the relevant theoretical orientation. The process also includes data collection issues, recording all observations and methods for analysing the information/data collected and specified in the research design. Finally the research needs to be documented, setting out the findings, discussing implications and drawing inferences. This undertaking is often underestimated; therefore, to avoid disappointment adequate time and energy must be reserved for this task (Baban 2006).

This chapter aims to assist with developing and implementing a successful research process.

6.2 Approaches to the Research Process

When selecting a research pathway it is important to develop clear and achievable research objectives and deliverables with the available resources and within the time frame. It is also helpful to decide which of the following three alternative approaches is the most relevant pathway for the research.

6.2.1 The Exploratory Approach

The exploratory approach is the most appropriate when the research is focused on a critical and timely issue which is information poor. Consequently, researchers can only start with a broad and provisional concept of the topic of interest and of its context. These preliminary notions will improve steadily with time due to a gradual process of gathering information about the research topic. In the absence of established approaches and tested concepts, a way forward is to start with what is available and conduct a holistic examination of the research topics, through gathering as much information as possible, and deferring the task of discarding unnecessary data until a better picture emerges about what is relevant and essential for the work.

Any topic can be examined from several different viewpoints, either from the angles of various established sciences or just from miscellaneous practical points of view. The researcher, once able, should specify the chosen viewpoint of the study and explain how he or she "understands" the topic. This does not mean clearly defining the essence of the study as this isn't possible at this stage; instead, the researcher is expected to ponder and explain how he or she perceives the topic. For example, in the case of a project in social sciences: should the topic be defined on a micro level as a result of the researcher's instincts, drives and experiences, or alternatively on a macro level as an expression of developments in society?

Defining a viewpoint will assist with data collection as after this it is only necessary to gather data directly related to the research issue. However, in some cases the definition can only become possible through analysis. In such cases it is recommended to start by studying one single item, case or site which illustrates the research problem, and then continue by studying a gradually growing number of items/cases/sites until it becomes apparent that the study of new items/cases/sites no longer reveals new interesting information. Analysis in exploratory research is essentially focused on *abstraction* and *generalization*. Abstraction means translating the observations, measurements and the like into concepts; generalization means arranging the material so that it disengages from single persons, occurrences, and the like, and focuses on those structures that are common to all or most of the cases. For example, the purpose of exploratory research is to extract a structure from the source material which in the best case can be formed as a rule that governs all the observations and is not known earlier (in keeping with the definition of exploratory study).

Finding the unknown structure may need some creative innovation, as the researcher needs to formulate a tentative pattern for the assumed structure in the observations and then estimate how well the data corresponds to the model. In this approach, solving the research "mystery" does not always require answering the exact questions that were asked at the outset of the project. On occasion, the most interesting questions are generated at the end of the research, when the researcher has become an expert on the topic and data-based evidence is showing clear trends and patterns, such as linking events, people and locations.

6.2.2 The Established Approach

The existence of an established approach helps in selecting the logical structure of the entire research project and in planning it. The approach helps with data collection and recording of observations and analysis; therefore, many of the problems of exploratory research can be avoided if the researcher can start with an established model that can be used as a "working hypothesis". This can either consist of cases or of concepts. During the analysis, the researcher needs to determine whether the collected material conforms to the adopted model or the model should be modified, or perhaps to seek a more suitable one. In this approach, often research proceeds by enlarging an earlier model. For example, when mapping land use or cover, the researcher starts from what is known, that is, the available map and expertise, then proceeds by enlarging the mapped area and connecting the new information to the known facts. Sometimes all that is required are a few modifications to the existing model. This is often the case when the study is focused on forecasting or new product development and the environment of intended application is slightly different from the one of the earlier study. In some other cases the research may proceed through the successive stages of the assessment of the original situation by defining the need for development and enhancement, investigation of associations and possibilities to change things, creation of a proposal for improvement and finally an appraisal of the final conditions. This sequence may need to be repeated several times before achieving satisfactory results.

6.2.3 The Hypothesis-Based Approach

On occasion, the research topic is well understood and defined and the researcher may wish to investigate it under specific conditions and environments. In such a case, the research can involve the formulation and testing of a hypothesis, that is, a preliminary answer to the question being examined. As a hypothesis cannot be proved directly, a null hypothesis is established to give the researcher an indirect method of testing a theory. This research path requires careful planning through

- Posing well-formulated and significant questions.
- Devising testable hypotheses to resolve the questions.
- Developing logical consequences of the assumptions.
- Testing the assumptions and methodologies for relevance and reliability; analysing and interpreting the results.
- Evaluating the integrity of the assumptions, the reliability of the techniques and determining the domains in which the assumptions and the techniques hold true.

This approach is well suited for studies with a focus on establishing factual knowledge about the topic of study, and the criterion that is used in accepting or rejecting a hypothesis.

6.3 The Research Process

The procedure for the research process can be categorized as outlined below.

6.3.1 Topic Recognition and Definition

Selecting a research area of interest and defining the specific goals and objectives of the project are important steps in the research process. Clearly stated goals keep a research project focused. The process of selecting a research topic, goal and definition needs to be guided by the following:

1. Selecting a general area of interest guided by answering the following questions:
    - Why does this area interest you?
    - What do you already know about your topic?
    - How would your qualifications and experience assist with this topic?

- Is it worth doing (not trivial)?
- Does it relate to a body of relevant knowledge and literature in the given discipline or branch of the discipline?
- Does it make any original contribution to knowledge and/or theory?

2. Attempting to develop a narrow and a clear focus for the research. A way forward is by selecting a broad topic, then identifying one or more subtopics of interest. Alternatively, you may select a topic, then list possible questions, such as "who", "what", "where", "when", "why" and "how". As the process continues, the research issues are narrowed and the goals become more clearly defined. Dealing with the following questions will also assist with the process:

- What are the main issues to be examined and why?
- Is it rooted in some question to be answered, some problem to be solved, some issue to be addressed?
- What are the main deliverables?
- Is it achievable? (Data sources must exist, and be accessible and usable, or capable of being created.) Is the time frame sufficient to complete the project?

3. Developing a list of subjects or keywords that can be useful for locating literature, material, relevant organizations and learned bodies.

6.3.2 Literature Review

The literature review is critical because it eliminates the need to reinvent the wheel for every new research question. More importantly, it gives researchers the opportunity to build on each other's work. Therefore, it is essential that existing sources of evidence, especially systematic reviews, are considered carefully prior to undertaking research. Typically, a researcher formulates an opinion during the literature review process. The process of reviewing other scholars' work often clarifies the theoretical issues associated with the research question.

6.3.3 Conceptualization and Research Design

Defining a research problem provides a format and a pathway for further investigation and points to possible methods of investigation. In general, there are two types of studies, quantitative and qualitative.

6.3.3.1 Quantitative Studies

These studies employ deductive logic, where the researcher starts with a hypothesis, and then collects data to confirm or refute the hypothesis. In terms of analysis, basic and advanced statistical techniques are used. Often computer-based programmes are available to perform the necessary tasks and therefore the process tends to be fast and inexpensive. Here, frequently the researcher is guided by a preplanned analysis process, without having to make subjective decisions about the data.

6.3.3.2 Qualitative Studies

These studies are based on inductive logic, where the researcher first designs a study and then develops a hypothesis or theory to explain the outcomes. The objective of qualitative research is to develop a hypothesis and provide broad, general theories that can be examined in future research. In terms of analysis, it often involves face to face interviews and therefore the process tends to be labour intensive and costly. Deriving information from qualitative data is a subjective process and depends heavily on a researcher's ability to exclude personal biases (Spector 1981).

6.3.3.3 Research Design

The research design provides the cement and the configuration that shows how all the major parts of the research project are linked and collectively are addressing the central research questions. Consequently, developing a design requires careful thinking and it must rest on some fundamental considerations, including

- Selecting an issue to be addressed.
- Rationale for the undertaking.
- Selecting a theoretical paradigm or perspective through which you may approach the research.
- A strategy (including objectives, timescales and milestones, and methodology).

- An estimate of resources and time required.
- Choosing an experimental design (methods for observations and measurements, that is, instruments; procedures and analysis, for example, statistical test to be used; timeline for completion).

Furthermore, development of the design should demonstrate that an assessment has been made of the key factors that will influence the success of the project in terms of achieving its objectives, including collection of an adequate amount of data or information, its proper statistical analysis, and budget and time constraints.

In terms of structure, proposals can be varied. The following represents a typical structure:

- Title
- Abstract or summary
- Background or rationale of the project
- Aims and objectives
- Experimental design and methods
- Ethical considerations
- Benefits of the study
- Resources and costs

6.3.4 Confidentiality and Ethical Issues

6.3.4.1 Ethical Approval

A significant number of research projects need to be reviewed by research ethics committees and the researcher must obtain approval before conducting the research (see chapter 8). Furthermore the researcher should be aware of data protection and confidentiality issues, which emphasize that

- The appropriate use and protection of participant data is paramount in the research setting.
- All those involved in research must be aware of their legal and ethical duties, particularly in terms of ensuring confidentiality of personal information.
- When collecting and storing data on human participants, identities should be disguised by use of codes; all details should be made anonymous; the use of information that could identify an individual person

should be avoided and access to such information should be on a strict need-to-know basis.
- To deal honestly and honourably with data collected and "allow the data to teach the researcher"; never to ignore or suppress relevant evidence because it conflicts with the researchers' theory; never reading documents or texts out of their context; giving up the initial hypotheses if the evidence can't support them.
- To fully acknowledge the work of others through full referencing.

In terms of conduct, researchers are responsible for

- The day-to-day conduct of research, ensuring that the research follows the agreed protocol (or proposal).
- Making sure that participants receive appropriate care while involved in research.
- Protecting the integrity and confidentiality of records and data generated by the research.
- Reporting any failures in these respects or suspected misconduct through the appropriate systems.
- Retaining data collected in the course of research for an appropriate period to allow further analysis by the original or other research teams subject to consent, as well as supporting the monitoring of good research practice by relevant authorities.

6.3.5 Data Collection

6.3.5.1 Primary Data Collection

There are a wide variety of techniques for data collection. Often, however, the selection of a technique involves a series of trade-offs. For example, there is often a trade-off between cost and the quality of information obtained. Time constraints sometimes force a trade-off with the overall research design. Therefore, budget and time constraints must always be considered as part of the design process.

Methods of data collection in qualitative research include telephone surveys, mail surveys, e-mail and Internet surveys, focus groups and structured interviews, for example, oral history interviews. As indicated previously, here, the relationship between the researcher and the topic could become conflicting as researchers may be influenced by their beliefs and hopes or by existing or new theories that they wish to prove by governing ideologies that they accept or resist.

Methods of data collection in quantitative research focus on what to measure, in terms of the characteristics of the subjects, and the *independent* and *dependent* variables defining the research question. The research question defines the main variables to be measured. For example, if the researcher is interested in "weight loss", the dependent variable (or outcome variable) is automatically some measure of weight loss. The next task is to identify a method to measure this dependent variable with as much precision as possible. The researcher then pinpoints all the factors that could affect the dependent variable. These are the independent variables: diet, exercise, lifestyle and so on. It will also be useful to measure mechanism variables as this will help with explaining how the treatment works. Researchers should be able to select and employ the most appropriate method for their research project. There are three basic methods of research to choose from. Each method has its advantages and disadvantages.

1. The survey method. This is most commonly used for gathering information in the social sciences. It can be a face-to-face interview or telephone or mail survey. A personal interview is one of the best methods of obtaining detailed information. It allows for extensive questioning by the interviewer and gives respondents the ability to elaborate their answers. Telephone interviews are similar to face-to-face interviews. They are more efficient in terms of time and cost; however, they are limited in the amount of in-depth questioning that can be accomplished, and the amount of time that can be allocated to the interview. A mail survey is generally the most cost-effective interview method. The researcher can obtain opinions, but trying to probe opinions meaningfully is very difficult.
2. The observation method. This method allows the research to monitor the respondents' actions without interacting directly with them. For example, psychologists often use one-way mirrors to study behaviour. Social scientists often study societal and group behaviours by simply observing them. The expansion of observation research has been assisted by bar code scanners at cash registers where, for example, purchasing habits of consumers can now be automatically monitored and summarized.

3. The experiment method. In this method the investigator changes one or more variables over the course of the research. When all other variables are held constant (except the one being manipulated), changes in the dependent variable can be explained by the change in the independent variable. It is usually very difficult to control all the variables in the environment. Therefore, experiments are generally restricted to laboratory models where the investigator has more control over all the variables.

6.3.5.2 Secondary Data Collection

To find coverage of all the relevant research literature on a particular subject, the researcher needs to examine and carry out the following:

- Indexing publications: these list basic descriptions of articles and other literature relevant to a specific field, usually grouped by subject and/or author. They provide enough information to indicate usefulness or otherwise for a particular project. Many indexes are now available as computerized databases.
- Abstracting journals: these provide similar information to indexes. In addition they provide a summary of the article (the abstract). The abstracts are usually listed numerically, under subject groupings. Many abstracts are now available as computerized databases.
- Electronic databases: many print indexes and abstracts are now available in electronic format, making them faster and easier to scan for information. Some databases now provide the full text of the article.
- The Internet: the Internet provides access to a range of information types, stored in networked computers around the world. Experience indicates that searching the Internet is unpredictable as available material tends to be of mixed quality and a great deal of time sifting, sorting, and selecting can be spent before finding information that is truly useful.
- Research consultation: if the necessary information cannot be found, then library staff can be consulted. Some libraries have subject librarians to advise on the best approach to take.

6.3.5.3 Evaluation and Validity of Resources

Evaluation begins at the start of the literature review process and continues throughout by making judgements on the authority, accuracy, objectivity, currency, and coverage of literature for the topic being examined. Critical thinking is therefore a necessary skill to develop while examining the information found on the research topic. Most research publications are subjected to an external editing or peer review process that helps verify the authority and accuracy of the information presented. Reputable newspapers and magazines also check their facts. Additional issues needing to be examined include objectivity, currency of information, and how thoroughly the topic is covered. It should be noted that the majority of Internet resources lack peer review evaluations or even simple fact checking, which means that the researcher must thoroughly evaluate anything found before deciding to use it.

In terms of validating data collected by outside data collection services, researchers often validate the data collection process by contacting a percentage of the respondents to verify that they were actually interviewed.

6.3.6 Data Analysis

In qualitative research, data processing and analysis may involve the following: analysis, case study, life history, cross-examination of sources, decoding and deconstructing documents or texts, computer-assisted analysis and applying statistical significance tests.

In quantitative research, data processing and analysis usually involve the following:

- Determining the level of measurement (nominal or category, ordinal, interval or quantitative). This choice will determine the type of statistics that can be used.
- Checking the data assumptions. Analysis techniques should adhere to the data assumptions, for example, linearity, normal distribution.
- Adhering to the principle of statistical analysis. Data should be analysed in terms of structure and nonstructure, explained variance and nonexplained variance, predicted regression line and residuals. The statistical analysis will often involve
    - Cleaning and editing the data sets (ensuring that the data is correct and makes sense, and editing inappropriate data sets).
    - Understanding the data sets (producing descriptive statistics, for

example, means, standard deviations, minima and maxima for each variable).
- Producing graphics, for example, histograms or box plots that show distribution; developing graphics or tables to show relationships (for example, scatter plots, interval data or cross tabulations).
- Calculating coefficients that measure the strength and the structure of a relationship (for example, strength measured by Pearson's R for interval data, and structure measured by the regression coefficient).
- Calculating coefficients that describe the percentage of variance explained (for example, R^2 in a regression analysis).

With research based on the experimental method, the main challenge is to determine the magnitude and confidence intervals of the treatment effect. Computer software has made the necessary statistical analysis of collected data an easy task. However, the danger is that the researcher might be unaware of the assumptions and limitations in the use and interpretation of outcomes. Therefore, before proceeding with these analyses, the researcher needs to understand the theoretical and conceptual foundations of the analytical methods used. Each method has its own assumptions and limitations.

Ideally, when the results and analysis show differences between samples, locations and respondents, they are due to real differences in the variable being measured. However, the researcher needs to be aware that a combination of systematic and random errors can reduce the accuracy of a measurement. *Systematic error* is introduced through a constant bias in a measurement. It can usually be traced to a fault in the sampling procedure or in the design of a questionnaire. *Random error* does not occur in any consistent pattern, and it is not controllable by the researcher.

6.3.7   Validity and Reliability of Outcomes

Validity refers to the accuracy of a measurement and it can be established through several methods, all of which are subjective and depend heavily on the understanding, opinions and biases of the researcher. The methods are face validity, content validity and criterion-related validity.

In *face validity* each question is examined and modified until the researcher is satisfied that it is an accurate measure of the desired construct.

Content validity attempts to establish if a reasonable treatment of a topic has been provided through expert opinions and literature searches. *Criterion-related validity* is used to test established dependent and independent relationships between two or more variables through developing a mathematical model. It can be *predictive*, that is, testing the ability of an independent variable (or group of variables) to predict a future value of the dependent variable. It can also be *concurrent*, that is, examining the relationship between two or more variables at the same point in time.

Reliability is a measurement that produces consistent results over time. A measurement that lacks reliability will necessarily be invalid. There are three basic methods to test reliability: (1) a *test and retest* measure is carried out by administering the same instrument to the same group of people at different times. The degree to which the findings are in agreement is a measure of the reliability of the instrument. (2) The *equivalent form approach* consists of creating two different instruments designed to measure identical constructs. The degree of correlation between the instruments is a measure equivalent to reliability. (3) *Internal consistency* is a method used when an instrument includes a series of questions designed to examine the same construct. The questions can be arbitrarily split into two groups. The correlation between the two subsets of questions is a measure of reliability (Carmines and Zeller 1979).

6.3.8 Dissemination/Publication

This is the most critical stage of the research process and requires sufficient time for writing, revising, reflecting and proofreading. It is also important to consider the nature of the audience and to remember that the purpose is to communicate information, make valid and substantiated arguments and, therefore, the document should be prepared and structured specifically with the readers in mind.

The process often starts by reviewing the organizational plan, drafting and deciding between relevant types of organization (chronological or thematic organization, or a mix of both), followed by selecting, developing and including relevant and informative illustrations. This is followed in the case of dissertations by consultation with supervisor(s), revision, documentation (including discipline-appropriate modes of referencing and bibliography), and proofreading (Baban 2006).

Sometimes the format for the report will be predefined for the researcher, for a dissertation, while at other times the researcher will have complete autonomy regarding the structure of the report. At a minimum, the report should contain an abstract, problem statement, methods section, results section, discussion of the results, and a list of references.

References

Baban, S.M.J., ed. 2006. *Writing Up Research*. A workshop developed for the University of the West Indies, Trinidad and Tobago. St Augustine: University of the West Indies.

Carmines, E., and R. Zeller. 1979. *Reliability and Validity Assessment*. Beverly Hills, CA: Sage.

Spector, P. 1981. *Research Design*. Beverly Hills, CA: Sage.

Chapter 6 Activities

Activity 13

In small groups, outline a plan for arriving at a design for your individual research topics.

1. In relation to the topic selected:
   - State the rationale for conducting research.
   - Frame a central research question and suggest additional questions.
   - Consider a hypothesis with which you might begin (which can be tested).
   - Articulate the problem to be solved.
2. Locate the topic in relation to existing work:
   - Consider originality.
   - Assess contribution to the field – new knowledge and/or new theoretical perspectives.
3. Discuss your findings with a peer.

Activity 14

Reflecting on the Research Process

On a separate sheet please reflect on the challenges and successes you faced during the research process. Make reference to each of the categories below, but focus on those issues that are most relevant to you.

1. **Planning**: Reflect on the process of focusing your research. What challenges did you encounter in developing a question, hypothesis, or thesis?
2. **Gathering**: Describe any problems or successes you had as you

searched. Did any particular search strategies work well or disappoint you? Which databases and search engines worked well? What were the major barriers to your search for balanced and credible resources?
3. **Organizing**: How did you ensure that your information comprehensively addressed the question, hypothesis or thesis? How and why did you modify your original question, hypothesis or thesis? What strategies did you use to reorganize the information? Did these strategies lead you to connections, patterns and so on?
4. **Documenting**: Did any issues arise as you documented your sources?

Discuss your findings with a peer.

7

Developing and Articulating Persuasive Research Arguments

▸ Serwan M.J. Baban

7.1	Introduction
7.2	What Is an Argument?
7.3	Elements of Argument
7.3.1	Claims and Evidence
7.3.2	Warrants
7.3.3	Qualifications
7.4	Developing Convincing Arguments
7.4.1	Using Connectives and Indicators
7.4.2	Critical Reading
7.4.3	Audience
7.4.4	Counterargument
References	
Chapter 7 Activities	

7.1   Introduction

This chapter introduces the requirements for making effective research arguments while presenting research. It provides examples based on everyday communications, linking them to the researcher's background and research areas. In addition, it outlines the essential elements of an argument and the process for developing effective research arguments.

7.2 What Is an Argument?

In academia, an argument is usually the main idea, a thesis statement or a collection of statements of which one is a proposition or claim (or conclusion) based on one or more grounds that are backed up by evidence. The supporting statements of an argument are called premises (Gage 1991; Booth, Colomb and Williams 1995; Anson and Schwegler 2000; Baban 2006). Therefore, an argument can be used to support, assert, and claim or to convince an audience of the merit of a theory, an approach, a course of action, a position or a point of view of merit.

Arguments are essential for furthering our understanding as differences of opinion are how human knowledge develops, and academic scholars tend to invest their time engaged in debate regarding what may be considered as "true", "real" or "right" in their fields. For example, is poverty linked to geography? Why does flood management need to be focused on highly developed hydrological catchments?

While dealing with these issues, it is expected that the researcher will develop an academic argument, that is, go beyond presenting or regurgitating information gathered or developed by others, hence the need to follow the process of critical thinking through selecting a point of view and providing evidence to shape the material and offer a personal interpretation of the material. In other words, the researcher will declare a position on a topic then defend it by using a well-reasoned argument (Baban 2006). Arriving at a convincing argument requires a deep understanding of the issues involved, including current and ongoing debates, then revisiting the research question in hand and developing an answer based on the outcome from the research and the literature. The claim is the main point, thesis or hypothesis for which an argument needs to be developed in an academic context. The evidence will be the reasons that justify the claim or conclusion.

7.3 Elements of Argument

7.3.1 Claims and Evidence

A claim is an alternative expression for a statement or a thesis that is basically an interpretation or point of view and thus needs support (Booth, Colomb and Williams 1995; Lunsford and Ruszkiewicz 1999). A claim, for its part, is made because of a reason. Reasons explain why a claim may be true. But merely providing reasons is not enough. Reasons must be supported by evidence such as statistics and the conclusions obtained from relevant literature. In terms of evidence, every discipline has slightly different requirements for acceptable evidence; therefore, researchers need to be familiar with and utilize the type of argument and evidence used within their chosen field. For example, the claim that good agricultural soils should be excluded from development in the Caribbean region is a useful claim, because it is exposed to reasonable debate and needs to be supported. Questions raised could include: Why make such a claim? On what basis is it made? A reason is because it assists with achieving food security. At this point the researcher has developed a claim, and the reason for the claim. But the reason needs to be supported; hence the need for evidence suggesting that growing agricultural products is essential for meeting the population's nutritional needs, thereby achieving food security. What evidence does the argument provide? It refers to several statistically based facts and scholarly papers (Baban 2006).

When either claim or evidence is presented without the other, it would often seem as either pointless data or ungrounded opinion. Therefore, claims and evidence must always be presented together and stated explicitly. The claim will need to state what the researcher wants his or her readers to believe, while the evidence will be the reasons they should believe it. Making basic claims and providing obvious evidence are often enough to convince readers or an audience in ordinary conversations (Lunsford and Ruszkiewicz 1999). Examples are:

Claim: It must have rained recently and soil erosion must be a problem in this area.

Evidence: Because the river is full, running fast and contains masses of sediments.

However, experience indicates that when significant claims are made, that is, a claim that requires asking or challenging people to change or modify their viewpoint about something important, most people correctly resist this process and start questioning the claim. In such a case the researcher will need to strengthen and consolidate his or her argument with two more elements, namely warrants and qualifications.

7.3.2 Warrants

A *warrant* is the principle that connects the claim to the reason in an argument. A warrant explains how the reason is relevant to the claim. Therefore, the warrant of an argument is its general principle, an assumption or premise that links the claim and its supporting evidence in a coherent manner. The researcher's warrant answers questions about whether it is relevant to the claim and whether the claim can be inferred from the evidence (Booth, Colomb and Williams 1995).

In casual conversations, a warrant is not required. In the example of the statement that "it must have rained recently and soil erosion must be a problem in this area", few would ask in response, "why should the fact that the river is full, running fast and contains masses of sediments make me believe your claim that it rained recently and soil erosion is a problem in this area?" Almost everyone just takes for granted the warrant, the general principle that links the evidence of a full, fast and sediment-laden river to claims about rain and soil erosion. Whenever the evidence of a full, fast and sediment-laden river is seen, it can be concluded that it probably rained recently and soil is eroding rapidly in this catchment. Therefore, it is possible to deduce the claim from the evidence. However, for critical kinds of claims, questions about warrants are inevitable. For example, if a person was weighed and the health worker indicated, based on the outcome, that the person should be examined by a doctor (*claim*), because the weight reading is 150 kilograms (*evidence*), almost everyone would ask why weighing 150 kilograms indicates the need for an examination by a doctor. This process means that we are simply asking for a warrant, a principle that justifies connecting particular evidence – 150 kilograms on the scale – to a particular claim – that we should see a doctor. The response could be that when a person with this type of gender, age, frame and body shape weighs more than 100 kilograms, it could be a reasonable indicator for obesity. Researchers tend to ask their readers to adjust their viewpoint about occurrences, events and issues that are not apparent. Therefore, they need to convince their audience that their evidence is in fact relevant to their claim. This process will often press researchers to expand by providing the additional supporting structure made available by an explicit warrant.

7.3.3 Qualifications

Qualifications limit the certainty of the conclusions, identify the conditions in which the claim holds, address potential objections, acknowledge the obstacles that interrupt the movement between the evidence and claims, and make the researcher appear judicious, cautious and thoughtful (Booth, Colomb and Williams 1995). Whenever a claim is made, it is only exact under certain conditions; therefore, it is essential to qualify the argument appropriately. Complex research arguments need good qualifications as evidently the claims are only true under specific sets of physical, environmental and social circumstances, which need to be identified clearly. Most audiences will want to learn why a claim is being made, not to challenge the researcher, but to understand the argument better, to participate in the dialogue. When the researcher acknowledges their interest, the researcher presents him- or herself as a considerate writer (Lunsford and Ruszkiewicz 1999). Therefore, a researcher who makes a claim, provides good reasons and adds qualifications is acknowledging the readers' desire to work with him or her in developing and testing new ideas. In this light, the best kind of argument is not verbal intimidation but an act of cooperation and respect.

7.4 Developing Convincing Arguments

An important step in the process of developing argumentation is understanding the concept. Arguments in academic writing are usually complex and take time to develop. An argument will need to extend beyond a basic statement such as, "poverty can have a significant impact on development". Such a statement might capture initial impressions; however, the researcher needs to look deeper and express specifically what caused the "linkages between poverty and development". Therefore, it is expected that the outcome should provide proof that the researcher understands the material and demonstrate the researcher's ability to use or apply the material beyond what he or she has read or heard. A good argument first and foremost needs to be convincing. The audience should believe the claim, or at least find the conclusion reasonable. This entails several things:

- That the premises are acceptable, reasonable or likely to be true.
- That the evidence or reasons are relevant to the claim.

- That the reasons provide sufficient grounds to accept the claim.

More specifically, developing effective arguments requires awareness and the utilization of the following basic characteristics:

- Understanding the issues, developing and articulating a position or a viewpoint.
- Identifying and including supporting evidence to sustain the position taken.
- Understanding, evaluating and acknowledging counterarguments or counterevidence.
- Using the right language and discourse markers.

Developing an effective research argument has the same characteristics as a lively intellectual discussion, for example, with a senior scientist asking questions and examining issues from various perspectives to find a way through a complicated problem. Observe the following discussion between a postgraduate student and his supervisor regarding an upcoming conference.

Supervisor: How is your preparation going for the conference? [The supervisor is raising an issue.]

Postgraduate student: I think I'll be ready and do well. [The student is making a *claim*.]

Supervisor: Why do you think so? [The supervisor is asking for *evidence* to support the *claim*.]

Postgraduate student: I have finished all my courses and now I can focus on research. [The student is offering *evidence*.]

Supervisor: Why will that make a difference? [The supervisor does not see why finishing the taught courses counts as *relevant evidence*.]

Postgraduate student: I do better when I have more time to focus on research. [The student offers a *principle* about courses and motivation that *connects the claim to the evidence*.]

Supervisor: But what about your discomfort with presentations? [The supervisor points to evidence that might *counterbalance* the evidence provided.]

Postgraduate student: I know I have had difficulties with presentations in the past, but I have been teaching the undergraduates and practising presentations over the last semester and now I am much more confident with presentations. [The student acknowledges the contrary evidence, but rebuts it by *offering more evidence*.]

Supervisor: But you have not been to any conferences. [The supervisor raises another reservation.]

Postgraduate student: I know. It won't be easy. [The student concedes a point he cannot rebut.]

Supervisor: Do you think you might win the best presenter award? [The supervisor asks about the limits of the claim.]

Postgraduate student: I can't promise, but I think I'll do well, providing I don't get nervous on the day. [The student *limits the scope of the claim* and then stipulates a *condition that qualifies* his confidence.]

This conversation contains all the necessary elements to develop an effective research argument. The elements are the same. The only difference is that when developing an argument in writing, the researcher will have to ask all relevant and critical questions on the readers' behalf and then proceed to answer them.

As the researcher develops a research argument he or she should imagine a conversation with the audience. The researcher is making claims, while the audience is asking questions and demanding that the researcher attempt to answer them.

The answer constitutes the argument. It should offer the following elements:

1. A claim
2. Evidence or grounds that support your claim
3. A warrant, a general principle that explains why you think your evidence is relevant to your claim
4. Qualification – this will limit the certainty of your conclusions and stipulate the conditions in which your claim holds

7.4.1 Using Connectives and Indicators

In addition to the elements of making a claim and presenting evidence to support that claim, developing a successful argument will also require utilizing the right connectives, indicator words or discourse markers. These will indicate why a particular piece of information has been included, and its relevance to the overall claim communicated through the linkages between the ideas, the literature and the statements being made.

For example, in terms of using supporting premises, there is a need to use words such as:

because (of) ..., given that ..., the reason is that ..., not only ... but also ..., whether or not ..., due to ..., since ..., in order to ..., in order that ..., rather than ..., if ... then ....

In terms of conclusions, there is a need to use words like:

so ..., therefore ..., thus ..., then ..., it follows that ....

In terms of discourse markers, there is a range of different words that can indicate the logical connections between ideas, attitude to the research and the relationship between the evidence and what is being claimed. These are called logical connectives (and, but, or, either/or, if/then, therefore) and discourse markers.

7.4.2 Critical Reading

Critical reading is an important part of understanding and evaluating an argument. Although some of the material presented might be very persuasive, a critical frame of mind while evaluating the argument is necessary. This can be achieved through asking questions such as the following: "What is the researcher trying to prove?" "What is the researcher assuming that the audience will agree with?" "Do the authors adequately defend their argument?" "What kind of proof is being used?" "Is there something missing that should be added?" "Will adding the missing information diminish the argument?"

7.4.3 Audience

Arguments are frequently developed for a specific audience. Therefore, the researcher needs to understand which arguments work in different situations. While developing an argument it is a good practice to imagine the audience in an academic setting as intelligent persons, but who do not necessarily agree with the researchers. The researchers are not just expressing their opinion in an argument ("it's true because they said so"). In most cases the audience is knowledgeable on the topic being handled, hence the need for a strong and a properly constructed proof.

7.4.4 Counterargument

An effective way to strengthen an argument is to anticipate and address counterarguments or objections. The researchers should not assume that because the audience knows the material they will understand what part of it you are using, what you think about it, and why. By considering what someone who disagrees with the position developed might have to say about the argument, the researcher shows that he or she has thought things through, and disposed of some of the reasons the audience might have for not accepting the argument.

It is possible to generate counterarguments by asking what someone who disagrees might say about each of the points made or about the developed position as a whole. Once some counterarguments are identified, the researcher needs to consider how to respond to them. Will he or she concede that the opponent has a point but explain why the audience should nonetheless accept the argument? Will the researcher reject the counterargument and explain why it is mistaken? Either way, the researcher will want to leave the audience with a sense that his or her argument is stronger than opposing arguments. The researcher needs to make sure that the reply is consistent with the original argument. If considering a counterargument changes his or her position, he or she will need to go back and revise the original argument accordingly.

When summarizing opposing arguments, the researcher needs to be considerate and present each argument fairly and objectively, rather than trying to make it appear to be thoughtless. It is usually better to consider one or two serious counterarguments in some depth, rather than to give a long but superficial list of many different counterarguments and replies. The objective is to show that all sides of the issue have been seriously considered, and that the researcher is not simply attacking alternative concepts and explanations.

References

Anson, C.M., and R.A. Schwegler. 2000. *The Longman Handbook for Writers and Readers*. 2nd ed. New York: Longman.

Baban, S.M.J., ed. 2006. *Writing Up Research*. A workshop developed for the University of the West Indies, Trinidad and Tobago. St Augustine: University of the West Indies.

Booth, W.C., G.H.G. Colomb and J.M. Williams. 1995. *The Craft of Research*. Chicago: University of Chicago Press.

Gage, J.T. 1991. *The Shape of Reason: Argumentative Writing in College*. New York: Macmillan.

Lunsford, A., and J. Ruszkiewicz. 1999. *Everything's an Argument*. Boston: St Martin's Press.

Chapter 7 Activities

Activity 15

Construct a research argument based on your submitted research form. Then clearly state the claim, evidence, warrant and qualification.

Activity 16

Working in groups of two, play the roles of researchers 1 and 2 using the following questions, then identify the weaker components of your research argument and suggest ways for strengthening them.

Researcher 1	Researcher 2
What is your point?	I claim that …
What evidence do you have?	I offer as evidence …
Why do you think that your evidence supports your claim?	I offer this general principle …
But how about these reservations?	I can answer them. First, …
Are you entirely sure?	Only if … and as long as …
No reservations here at all?	I must concede that …
Then just how strong is your claim?	I limit it to …

8

Research and Ethics

▸ DAVID LLOYD

8.1	Introduction
8.2	Legal Requirements
8.3	Animal Research
8.4	Social Research
8.4.1	Informed Consent
8.4.2	Should We Pay Respondents?
8.4.3	Making Research Inclusive
8.4.4	How People May Be Excluded from Your Sample
8.4.5	Dealing with Privacy and Security of Personal Records
8.4.6	Ethics of Indigenous Research

References

Chapter 8 Activities

8.1 Introduction

Ethics is a part of all our lives and is a challenge to every profession; whether it is medical, military, journalistic or judicial all actions are subject to ethical considerations. Usually, with scientific research ethics falls into one of the following two headings. These are, first, the morality of topics and findings under investigation, where we ponder the question of whether science is good or bad, especially in the arenas of science where human or animal subjects are involved. The second heading is the rigour of method and process, which addresses the nature of the design, the experimental procedures and the reporting of the research effort.

As researchers, we find ourselves in situations where we must answer ethical questions that arise in the context of our research, whether we are working with animals, people or even economic data. When many beginning (and experienced) researchers think of having to submit their proposals for ethics approval, a cold shiver runs down their spine. "Why do these people want to look over my shoulder? I have so much else to do, why are they wasting my time with more paper work? What right do strangers have in judging my work? After all I am a moral person, why am I being treated as if I am not?" However, this is not what the ethics approval process is for. It is not to challenge your personal values, nor is it to explain why you should be moral. Carried out correctly, ethics clearance is a process to help you reflect on ethical questions that you face, in your capacity as a researcher, and to provide you with the tools and checklist you need to ensure your research conforms to the ethical values of the community. Ethical approval is a requirement for

- Conducting research on humans and animals
- Ensuring lawful conduct of research
- Ensuring scientific merit of proposals and competency of researchers
- Protecting the rights, safety, dignity, privacy and well-being of all research participants

If things go wrong, a well-run ethical clearance process shows that you have submitted your programme for scrutiny by a panel of experts who have supported your approach. I have known many researchers thankful for this defence when journalists and reporters arrive on their doorstep.

> In speaking of good and bad, we must distinguish carefully between moral and nonmoral values. Only the former lies within the realm of ethics. Nonmoral values involve preferences among colors, foods, clothes, music, sports teams, climate and the like. Moral values including loyalty, honesty, humility, arrogance, and the like involve attitudes toward people and other living things. (Seebauer and Barry 2001, 72)

Sometimes it is easy. Most of us realize that we should not cut corners, cannot forge results, ignore information contrary to our thesis, trim the data to remove outliers that may contradict our thesis, manipulate outcomes by asking leading questions, use data that belongs to others without attribution or make unfounded accusations. Sometimes it is hard. How do we determine if the value of our research is worth the disruption we may cause to lives? Also there are actions which many would see as ethical that are in fact illegal, and things which, while legal, would generally be seen as unethical.

8.2   Legal Requirements

This is a specialist area and will differ from country to country and even between administrative divisions within a country. They will relate to the welfare of the subjects (human and animal), occupational health and safety, the protection of subjects' rights and the management of personal records and data collected for social research. Some jurisdictions require all projects to obtain either human or animal ethics clearance and provide strict guidelines as to considerations these committees must make in granting permission to proceed with research. The National Health and Medical Research Council in Australia (NHMRC), for example, provides guidelines for the conduct of human research (NHMRC 2008). You will need to understand your legal obligations and how these will change if you cross borders.

8.3   Animal Research

The issue of the ethics of conducting research on animals is fraught with emotion. Many people have very firm views about whether it is right or wrong to use animals in scientific research. Animal research ranges from observational (nonmanipulative) studies (for example, bird watching) to studies involving multiple deaths (or worse) of laboratory animals (for example, pharmaceutical research). At one end of the spectrum there are comparatively few concerns, unless the researcher's presence may be detrimental to natural behaviour, such as the disturbance to nesting birds. At the other end the battle lines are drawn.

In Australia the NHMRC first issued a brief set of guidelines on animal experimentation in 1969 to ensure the ethical and humane care and use of animals used for scientific purposes. In 1979 these were expanded into a Code of Practice, and the seventh edition was published in 2004 providing guidelines for the humane conduct of scientific and teaching activities, and for the acquisition of animals and their care, including their environmental needs (http://www.nhmrc.gov.au/publications/synopses/ea16syn.htm).

The NHMRC code encompasses all aspects of the care and use of, or interaction with, animals, including their use in research, teaching, field trials, product testing, diagnosis, the production of biological products and environmental studies. The code provides general principles and responsibilities for the care and use of animals, specifies the responsibilities of investigators and institutions, and details the terms of reference, membership and operation of animal ethics committees (AECs) to

- Ensure that the use of animals is justified, taking into consideration the scientific or educational benefits and the potential effects on the welfare of the animals.
- Ensure that the welfare of animals is always considered.
- Promote the development and use of techniques that replace the use of animals in scientific and teaching activities.
- Minimize the number of animals used in projects.
- Refine methods and procedures to avoid pain or distress in animals used in scientific and teaching activities.

Extract from the *Australian Code of Practice for the Care and Use of Animals for Scientific Purposes*, 7th edition (NHMRC 2004)

General principles for the care and use of animals for scientific purposes (section 1 of the Code)

The Code emphasises the responsibilities of all those involved in the care and use of animals. This embraces a duty of care that demands a genuine commitment to the welfare of the animals, a respect for the contribution the animals make to research and teaching and a desire to promote the animals' well-being.

Encapsulated in the Code is the need in scientific and teaching activities to consider:

- The Replacement of animals with other methods (see 1.8 of the COP)
- The Reduction in the number of animals used (see 1.9–1.13 of the COP); and
- The Refinement of techniques used to reduce the adverse impact on animals (see 1.14-1.28 of the COP)

Box continues

Justification

1.1 Scientific and teaching activities using animals may be performed only when they are essential:
- to obtain and establish significant information relevant to the understanding of humans and/or animals;
- for the maintenance and improvement of human and/or animal health and welfare;
- for the improvement of animal management or production;
- to obtain and establish significant information relevant to the understanding, maintenance or improvement of the natural environment; or
- for the achievement of educational objectives.

1.2 Projects using animals may be performed only after a decision has been made that they are justified, weighing the predicted scientific or educational value of the projects against the potential effects on the welfare of the animals.

1.3 Investigators and teachers must submit written proposals to an AEC for all animal projects which must take into account the expected value of the knowledge to be gained, the justification for the project, and all ethical and animal welfare aspects taking into consideration the 3Rs.

Responsibilities

1.4 Investigators and teachers who use animals for scientific purposes have personal responsibility for all matters relating to the welfare of these animals. They have an obligation to treat the animals with respect and to consider their welfare as an essential factor when planning or conducting projects.

1.5 Institutions using animals for scientific purposes must ensure, through an AEC, that all animal use conforms to the standards of the Code.

1.6 Scientific and teaching activities must not commence until written approval has been obtained from the AEC.

1.7 The acquisition, care and use of animals for all scientific purposes in Australia must be in accordance with the Code and with Commonwealth, and State or Territory legislation.

Box continues

Replacement

1.8 Techniques that totally or partially replace the use of animals for scientific purposes must be sought and used wherever possible.

Reduction

1.9 Each project must use no more than the minimum number of animals necessary to ensure scientific and statistical validity.

1.10 The principle of reducing the number of animals used should not be implemented at the expense of greater suffering of individual animals.

1.11 Scientific and teaching activities involving the use of animals must not be repeated unless essential for the purpose or design of the project.

1.12 Teaching activities must involve no more than the minimum number of animals required to reach the educational objectives.

1.13 Overproduction of animals bred for scientific purposes should be avoided so that the need to kill healthy animals is minimised.

Refinement

1.14 Animals must be suitable for the scientific purpose taking into account their biological characteristics including behaviour, genetic attributes and nutritional, microbiological and general health status.

1.15 The design and management of animal accommodation should meet species-specific needs. Special consideration is required where this is precluded by the requirements of the project.

1.16 Animals should be transported, housed, fed, watered, handled and used under conditions that meet species-specific needs. The welfare of the animals must be a primary consideration in the provision of care, which should be based on behavioural and biological needs.

1.17 Wildlife should not be taken from natural habitats unless animals bred in captivity are not available or are not suitable for the specific scientific purpose.

1.18 Investigators and teachers who use animals for scientific purposes must employ the best available scientific and educational techniques and be competent in the procedures they perform or must be under the direct supervision of a person competent in the procedure.

Box continues

Refinement

1.19 Projects should be designed to avoid both pain and distress in animals. If this is not possible, pain or distress must be minimised.

1.20 Pain and distress cannot be evaluated easily in animals and therefore investigators and teachers must assume that animals experience these in a manner similar to humans unless there is evidence to the contrary. Decisions regarding the animals' welfare must be based on this assumption.

1.21 An animal with signs of pain or distress not predicted in the proposal, must have the pain or distress alleviated promptly. Alleviation of such pain or distress must take precedence over completing a project. If this is not possible the animal must be euthanased without delay.

1.22 Scientific and teaching activities that may cause pain or distress of a kind or degree for which anaesthesia would normally be used in medical or veterinary practice, must be carried out using anaesthesia appropriate to the species and the procedure.

1.23 Pain management appropriate to the species, the procedure and the circumstances must be provided.

1.24 The use of local or general anaesthetic, analgesic or tranquillising agents must be appropriate to the species, and should at least parallel their use in current medical or veterinary practice.

1.25 Where it is established that the purpose of the project precludes the use of anaesthetic or analgesic agents to alleviate pain, the planned end-point of the project must be as early as feasible to avoid or minimise pain or distress in the animals.

1.26 Neuromuscular blocking agents must not be used without appropriate general anaesthesia, except in animals where sensory awareness has been eliminated. If such agents are used, continuous or frequent monitoring of paralysed animals is essential to ensure that the depth of anaesthesia is adequate to prevent pain or distress.

1.27 "Death as an end-point" (see definition) must be avoided wherever possible.

1.28 Scientific and teaching activities involving the use of animals must be of minimum duration compatible with the objectives of the project.

8.4 Social Research

When designing social research it is important to consider, if roles were reversed, if you or your family would be happy to be subjects in the research project. Safety, both physical and emotional, of the research participant is your main concern. Ethics committees carefully consider the risk and benefit of the research before making an assessment and usually monitor more high-risk research as it proceeds.

8.4.1 Informed Consent

Not surprisingly the researcher must obtain informed consent from each research participant, which should be freely given. This should be in writing (oral consents are sometimes acceptable but should be recorded) after the participant has been informed of the reasons for the study, how data is stored and secured, and their rights to not participate or opt out during the process. Participants should never feel obliged or compelled to take part in research. It is important to gain informed consent so that research participants are clear what they have agreed to, the limits of their participation and any potential risks.

The amount of information that will be needed to ensure that someone is adequately informed will vary between different research projects. It is inappropriate to overwhelm potential participants with unnecessary information but it is also unethical to withhold information that would be likely to affect an individual's willingness to participate. It is equally important that the information is given in a clear, easy to understand way; plain English should be used and the use of jargon avoided. Finally, participants must be competent to give consent. If they are not competent, due to mental status, disease, or emergency, a designated surrogate may provide consent if it is in the participant's best interest to participate. In certain emergency cases, consent may be waived due to the lack of a competent participant and a surrogate but this is rare.

8.4.2 Should We Pay Respondents?

This is a vexing question for many researchers from an ethical and economic point of view. In broad-scale cross-sectional surveys we can have a situation arise where some groups may be offered sitting fees while others not. Incentives would not normally be paid for participation, primarily because of large sample sizes and the large cost involved. There is also a danger of creating an "incentives culture" if payment is expected for participation in all research, although the authors are aware of the increasing difficulties in recruiting respondents. Many indigenous groups see the payment of a sitting fee as recognition of their specialist knowledge and perspectives.

8.4.3   Making Research Inclusive

This is both a methodological and an ethical issue. You may decide not to sample a hard to reach population (for example, one that is hundreds of kilometres away) if they have, for the purposes of your study, similar demographic features to a population that is easier to access (for example, one in your own town). It depends on the scale and the context of your study. It becomes an ethical issue if all members of a population or sample do not have an equal opportunity to participate in the research. Reasons for non-inclusion may include

- Communication barriers
- Cultural barriers
- Financial barriers
- Geographical barriers

Including potentially excluded groups is important because, on ethical grounds, as many people as possible should be given the opportunity to exercise their right to voice their views. Being more inclusive also increases the validity of the data, because it reduces sampling bias and means that data emanating from groups that may have a common view or experience is not excluded (see chapter 11 for further details). When designing research it is important to consider which groups may be potentially excluded and at what point during the research process. It is then possible to work out strategies for maximizing inclusiveness.

8.4.4   How People May Be Excluded from Your Sample

At each stage of the research process it is possible to inadvertently exclude groups. When developing the sampling frame people without a permanent residential address or telephone number may not appear on administrative databases (see chapter 11 for further details). When recruiting participants, people who are unable to read or understand the "invitation to participate" letter may just ignore it and, in addition, they will not understand the opt-out letter. Finally, the data collection process can exclude different groups of people:

- Postal surveys – a postal survey is likely to exclude people with reading difficulties (for example, dyslexia), people with learning difficulties, people with visual impairments, and people whose first language is not English.
- Telephone surveys – a telephone survey is likely to exclude people with speech impairments, people with hearing problems, people who do not own a telephone (a small minority of the population but the proportion without a telephone increases with age), and people whose first language is not English.
- Face to face surveys/in-depth interviews/focus groups – unless provision is made, this type of research will potentially exclude people with speech impairments, people with hearing problems, people whose first language is not English, and women from some ethnic communities.

8.4.5   Dealing with Privacy and Security of Personal Records

There has been a fair amount of conformity in respect to privacy provisions relating to personal records. Anyone processing personal data must comply with the following eight principles of good practice in relation to personal data. Data must be

1. Fairly and lawfully processed
2. Obtained for specified purposes
3. Adequate, relevant and not excessive for the specified purposes
4. Accurate
5. Not kept longer than necessary
6. Processed in accordance with the data subject's rights
7. Secure
8. Not transferred to countries without adequate protection

8.4.6 Ethics of Indigenous Research

In terms of researcher per capita, indigenous communities are often described as "the most researched group in the world". Their experience in dealing with researchers continues to be that of being exploited, with little or no value being accrued by individual indigenous knowledge holders or their communities. While many issues of consultation, ownership, control and community involvement are of fundamental importance to all minority groups, some are specific when working across cultures (Gaines 1991; Lane 1997; Lloyd and Norrie 2004; Lloyd, Nimwegen and Boyd 2005; Jackobson 1999). Specific research groups will already have developed their own guidelines, or principles, for ethical research to protect and respect the rights of indigenous communities and to ensure a high standard of research design. These will attempt to

1. Promote research that meets the needs and aspirations of indigenous communities, particularly those participating in the research.
2. Encourage research in which indigenous individuals, families, groups or communities determine, define and have input into the research project.
3. Take account of cultural and personal sensitivities and their right of refusal to participate as a valid part of the ethics of the research.
4. Promote the recognition and use of indigenous/traditional knowledge, community expertise and resources.
5. Ensure that relevant community members receive the results of research in an accessible and acceptable manner.
6. Facilitate research that is collaborative and offers useful outcomes for participating communities.
7. Take account of individual and community wishes with respect to publication, the identification of individuals and the use of photographs and indigenous technical knowledge.

You must ensure you have support for your proposed project from relevant participants in the project. A simple letter usually will not suffice; you must secure informed consent (discussed above under legal requirements) in a culturally appropriate way from the participants or the community you hope to work with. You must make sure you consult with "the right people", the people able to talk for indigenous individuals, families, groups, communities, as well as seek approval from the appropriate "umbrella" organizations, such as land councils, treaty organizations, clan groups and the like, where such organizations exist. Your proposal should indicate how the research will benefit the community (for example, identify specific outcomes such as potential for the employment and or training of local people in the research activities and appropriate payment according to awards if appropriate). As with all other groups you should explain their right to opt out of the research at any time. Also, indicate if there will be a reference group and how they will be represented. Do not underestimate the time needed for adequate consultation to occur. Having obtained consent from the community, individuals and your ethics committee then two other areas require ethical consideration. These are the conduct of the research and the ownership of data.

There is a responsibility to ensure that the community or participants are not misused or exploited, or subjected to repetitive and burdensome demands. Make sure there are adequate research funds to cover costs caused by the research within communities as many may be economically disadvantaged. Consider training and employing (if appropriate) indigenous people to assist with the project and acknowledge their guidance in the research, remembering the need to ensure anonymity and confidentiality of participants. Before you start, develop a communication strategy to inform the community about what you are doing, why, how the information will be used and, importantly, what you have discovered. Most importantly ensure all research staff know and adhere to cultural and customary rules and laws of the indigenous communities you are working in (Lloyd and Norrie 2004). Ownership and publication of data is another major issue which must be addressed at the planning phase. Otherwise an expensive data collection phase may remain unpublished as disputes arise over rights to use data. Before starting your research, it is essential to clarify

1. Who owns, and who has the right to use, raw data obtained through the research project and how it is to be secured and stored. What permissions are needed if other researchers wish to use data or information gathered during the research for any purpose other than that for which consent was gained? This may also be needed to protect the interests of the principal researcher as sometimes communities may give the data

to another researcher, impinging on the intellectual rights of the research instigator.
2. Who has the right, and under what circumstances, to publish research and information either independently or jointly or to use the research results commercially or otherwise. This is an issue during the project and once the project is completed. Are embargoes needed or distribution of results to be limited?
3. The rights of single or multiple funding bodies/sponsors, to use information and results across projects should be carefully defined and explained to all parties.

The web document compiled by Sing (2003), Librarian Aboriginal and Torres Strait Islander Learning and Engagement Centre Library – South Queensland, provides an excellent annotated bibliography of issues. For indigenous health research the World Health Organisation (WHO 2000) provides detailed guidelines for conducting health research with indigenous communities.

References

Gaines, J.M. 1991. *Contested Culture: The Image, the Voice, and the Law*. Chapel Hill: University of North Carolina Press.

Jackobson, A. 1999. Wunggomalli model: A consultative model and data base for cultural heritage management in the Great Barrier Reef Marine Park. *Australian Aboriginal Studies* 1: 51–58.

Lane, M.B. 1997. Aboriginal participation in environmental planning. *Australian Geographic Studies* 35 (3): 308–23.

Lloyd, D.J., and F. Norrie. 2004. Identifying training needs to improve indigenous community representatives' input into environmental resource management consultative processes: A case study of the Bundjalung Nation. *Australian Journal of Environmental Education* 20 (1): 101–14.

Lloyd, D.J., P. Nimwegen, and W. Boyd. 2005. Letting Indigenous people talk about their country: A case study of cross-cultural (mis)communication in an environmental management planning process. *Australian Journal of Geographical Research* 43 (4): 406–16.

NHMRC (National Health and Medical Research Council). 2004. *Australian Code of Practice for the Care and Use of Animals for Scientific Purposes*. 7th ed.

http://www.nhmrc.gov.au/publications/synopses/ea16syn.htm (last visited March 2008).

NHMRC (National Health and Medical Research Council). 2008. *Guidelines for the Conduct of Human Research*. www.nhmrc.gov.au (last visited March 2008).

Seebauer, E. and R. Barry. 2001. *Fundamentals of Ethics for Scientists and Engineers*. New York: Oxford University Press.

Sing, A. 2003. http://education.qld.gov.au/information/service/libraries/atsi/docs/library42.doc (last visited March 2008).

WHO (World Health Organisation). 2000. *Indigenous Health Research*. http://www.who.int/ethics/indigenous_peoples/en/index.html (last visited March 2008).

Chapter 8 Activities

Activity 17

As a group, choose two of the following case studies to discuss. First write down your own ideas about the ethical and the legal issues raised by these scenarios and what you would personally do if in a similar situation. Then have each member read his or her responses before discussing as a group. Note differences of opinion and interpretation various group members will have of these scenarios. (The following cases are modified from *On Being a Scientist: Responsible Conduct in Research*, http://www.nap.edu/readingroom/books/obas/contents/appendix.html# Career.)

Case 1:   Where Do Your Priorities Lie?

Bird flu is about to strike and you discover the key gene sequence responsible for making the strain so virulent. Knowing this, a cure could quickly be produced. Each day is important as the virus spreads rapidly, increasing exponentially, and 20 per cent of those who are exposed will die. What will you do? Share the knowledge immediately on the World Wide Web? Wait to publish in a reputable journal? Or start a bidding war with pharmaceutical companies who might want to use this information to develop a cure?

Case 2:   Doctored Data

You are working as part of a team doing significant work into human birth defects under the guidance of a chief scientist with a global reputation for his discoveries. You notice that your work showing contrary findings to that being promoted by the lab is being excluded from the data set. Talking to your colleagues you find that other important information is left out and the team is reporting false data. You find the courage to mention this to the chief scientist, who becomes agitated and warns you about the confidentiality agreement you have signed. What should you do?

Case 3:   Protecting Your Own Work

You recently sent a paper you have spent months writing that summarizes your research into the impacts of rising sea temperature on coral reef communities to the key coral reef ecology journal. The journal's editorial committee sends your paper for review to other experts in the field for comment. Your paper is rejected, with the committee citing referee claims of major errors and poor interpretation of the data. The following year, you find an article containing data very similar to your own, and using phrases and interpretations that appeared in your unsuccessful paper. What should you do?

Case 4:   To Tell or Not to Tell?

In talking to your good friend, who is also a graduate student in your faculty undertaking related social research, it is revealed that he has not conducted all the surveys he claimed as it was too time consuming. You discover that a substantial part of his data was fabricated to support his original research question. You have also quoted him liberally in your related thesis. What should you do?

Case 5:   Whose Data Is It?

A scientist is awarded a contract to undertake research for a government agency, on the link between exposure to certain chemicals and cancer. The scientist has agreed that all data belongs to the contracting agency. In doing the research the scientist discovers an important link and recognizes this would enable him to publish in a prestigious journal. The paper is written and submitted even though the agency claims he has been paid a fee for service and the data belongs to them. They wish to review it before they publish the results in their in-house journal, acknowledging the scientist's authorship (although this would not be read by much of the scientific community). Is the scientist justified in proceeding to use the data for the more prestigious scientific publication? What if the agency withholds permission for the use of the material for publication? What if the scientist believed the agency was trying to suppress the results to avoid a law suit?

Activity 18

Discuss with others the following scenario.

You are a graduate student working for a leading medical researcher. Your job is to use a sophisticated gene mapping technique to study patients with type II diabetes. After several weeks of analysing data, you realize you have discovered a totally new link to a gene sequence that produces a protein that can readily be blocked – one that provides a cheap method for managing the disease without daily injections. Your boss congratulates you for your fine work, writes a major report on it, and wins a Nobel prize.

Is what the supervisor did legal?
Is what the supervisor did ethical?
What should you do?

Activity 19

Ask yourself and your friends and family, "How many animals' lives or pain is the alleviation of one person's suffering worth?" You may be surprised by the responses you get even from people you thought you knew well. Responses will also be determined by the species being used – a dog will get more public sympathy than a salamander. Responses will also be determined by the type of suffering being experienced; for example, a person suffering from cancer will get far more sympathy than someone suffering a "bad hair day" from untested shampoo. The debate will also rage about whether we can even compare suffering across species. These all involve value judgements about the difference between the "ethics of outcomes" versus the "ethics of process".

Activity 20

Discuss with others the following scenario.

Mrs Jones, a 41-year-old psychiatric patient under your care, has been asked to participate in a clinical trial testing a new drug designed to help improve her condition. You were present when the clinical investigator obtained a signed informed consent a few days earlier. However, when you visit Mrs Jones today and ask her if she is ready for her injection, she looks at you blankly and seems to have no idea what you are talking about.

How will you proceed and why?

Compare your actions and justifications with a peer.

Activity 21

Read the following examples. In each case a payment has been requested before the subject will participate. Consider whether you believe a payment should be made and your justification. Is there a moral dimension and what is it?

- How do the case studies compare?
- Discuss your findings with a peer

1. As part of a survey of all community stakeholders on the impacts of a change of opening hours for a regional medical clinic, you approach the head of a regional indigenous land council, Miriam J, for her views on the impact on the local indigenous community. She agrees to see you but asks for a $200 sitting fee for the 30 minute discussion. No other groups have received payment.
2. Jerry M is a traditional knowledge holder for a remote indigenous community living within a tropical rainforest. You want to find out how his community uses local plants for traditional medicines. You want him to take you for a walk into the forest around the camp and talk about the plants found there but he is reluctant without payment. Your salary for this survey does not include provision for paying respondents.
3. You are doing a qualitative "families and children" study which will involve three sessions of over an hour per session plus the maintenance of a detailed diary for four weeks. Angella S is on welfare and is an alcohol abuser. You have a budget to pay fees but are suspicious as to how the money will be used.

Activity 22

The following is a selection of groups commonly overlooked in research. Suggest strategies for designing your methodology to include them in your sample. Discuss your ideas with others.

- People with mental health problems
- People who are deaf or have a speech impairment
- People who have difficulty reading
- People whose first language is not English
- People living in socially excluded communities, for example, areas where interviewers are unwilling to travel
- People believed to pose a possible threat to interviewer safety
- People with drug and alcohol problems
- People without a permanent residential address
- People without a telephone

Section 2

Accomplishing Research

Developing the Research Proposal

▸ BILL BOYD

9.1	Introduction
9.2	Formulating a Research Problem and Conceptualizing the Research
9.3	Moving towards an Appropriate Research Design
9.4	Anticipating Outcomes, Writing Your Results
9.5	Rounding up: Approaches to Research
9.6	Conclusions
References	
Chapter 9 Activities	

9.1 Introduction

In this chapter, I consider the processes behind the formulation of a research problem and the development of a research proposal. The research proposal is a document that allows the researcher to do three things. First, it provides a formal way to organize the researcher's thoughts, using a frame that takes his or her ideas from initial conception through to the practicalities of conducting the research that will provide an investigation of and, if things go well, the answers to the initial questions posed. Second, it provides the researcher with a public statement of his or her intentions and methods. This allows colleagues and supervisors to review the plan and to provide constructive input to the design of the proposed research. This also often provides the basis for applications for necessary permits (see chapter 8), including human ethics or animal experimentation clearances or permits to conduct research under legislation such as national parks or fisheries acts. Finally, the proposal provides the basis for seeking funding. Grant bodies need to be convinced not only that the research is worth doing and will provide benefit to society or advancement of knowledge, but that the proposed work is realistic and that the researcher is the person to successfully tackle the problem (see chapter 12).

By considering the content of a proposal, we have a useful way to examine underlying principles behind designing a research project. So what should be in a research proposal? One way to think of this is to consider how we might introduce a student to the research proposal. In the course I teach, we offer students the opportunity to conduct a mini-research project in their third year. Within the first few weeks, each student must write a research proposal. The headings in that proposal provide a useful template for all proposals: title of project, literature review, problem definition, aims, objectives, methods, timing, special features and references. This sequence progresses the student's thoughts from an initial idea, through an external review of what has already been done, to a statement of the problem. The latter statement should provide a brief summary of the problem and how the student envisages it may be addressed; it should also indicate why the problem is worth studying. From there, the proposal refines the approach, from the broad statement of outcome – a one sentence aim – through the steps required to be completed to achieve that aim – the objectives. The proposal then defines the methods to be applied to gather, synthesize and interpret the information required to achieve the objectives, and the chronological structure under which these methods will be applied. The special features heading allows a student to consider needs or constraints that might limit the researcher's ability to complete the project in a suitable time. The references section is a list of the published material that supports the student's proposal. The important point about this structure is not that it sets a research project in concrete – many research projects evolve as they are conducted – but that it organizes thinking and planning.

An example of a format for a research proposal used in the training of students was developed by Gardiner and Hughes (2000). The format fits the basic requirements that apply at whatever level we are writing research proposals, although the headings or the emphasis on specific content may vary depending on the requirements of the proposal and the instructions under which we are writing them. A proposal used for a human ethics project, for example, is likely to focus more strongly on the methods, especially from the perspective of their impact on the subjects of the research (Boyd et al. 2008; see chapter 8). A proposal for innovative research seeking funding from a source supporting innovative research may, on the other hand, need to focus more on the ideas and potential impacts of the outcomes than on the methods themselves (see chapter 12).

The Australian Research Council (ARC) is one of Australia's most important public research funders. Their applications are governed by a body of rules that require researchers to write their proposal to very specific requirements. Let us briefly consider the headings in their application section E, that is, the research description section:

E1. Project Title
E2. Background and Aims
E3. Significance and Innovation
E4. Approach and Methodology
E5. National Benefit
E6. Communication of Results
E7. Role of Personnel
E8. References

Some of these are already familiar, and echo our requirements of undergraduate students. What is the aim and background of the proposed research? What are the proposed methods? In the ARC's case, it is also important to consider who will conduct the research; this is, to a large extent, a methodological question, in that the ARC needs to be convinced that the researchers have the ability, experience and skills to complete the research satisfactorily. In addition, the ARC has a national research agenda, and so is interested in national benefits; other organizations may have regional interests or their own organizational interests, so you may be required to identify these. Whatever the case, these are statements that help justify the relevance and importance of the proposed research (see chapter 12).

In this chapter, I will dissect these ideas a little further. This allows us to consider the essence of research, and, while producing a research proposal may be viewed simply as a technical aspect of writing, the process demands that we think a little more carefully about what research is and how we relate to it as individuals within a community of scholars (Glassick, Huber and Maerof 1997; see chapters 1 and 2).

In practical terms, we need to consider the relationships between proposal title and research topic, and between research questions and rationale. Are approach and methodology the same or different? Are they interconnected? What is the importance of context and thus the role and purpose of, for example, the literature review and other prior knowledge? What will be the sources upon which the proposed research will be based? How will the researcher define these and make key decisions regarding their appropriateness? What influences him or her in making such decisions?

Once the aims, backgrounds, approaches, methods and sources have been identified and justified, how do we break down the proposed topic and issue within the research question to make a manageable research project? And have we got prior expectations regarding outcomes? This latter issue is increasingly important in a time of growing commercialization of research where external bodies are often seeking – and funding – outcomes rather than the research process per se. There is a role for identifying expected major findings or conclusions, but how practical is it to place emphasis on these at an early stage of the research? Does, indeed, such consideration threaten or enhance the research process? This chapter will not answer all these questions, but will provide the problem-focused basis (Chappell 2001) on which they can be addressed, a basis founded on a sound research proposal.

9.2   Formulating a Research Problem and Conceptualizing the Research

Constructing and writing a research proposal should be regarded as the core preliminary activity for a researcher. It is the process of arriving at a clear and direct statement of the research problem. The problem is often articulated as the aim of the research. It may vary from seeking answers to a relatively straightforward question to developing deep understandings of complex analytical problems. Examples of the former can be found in survey-type research, the what-is-where or who-does-what type of questions often posed in the early stages of a study or in the early phases of a new field of research, to provide base data and a sense of the patterns of information available within the study (Neuman 2003). Research conducted outside academe often, although not necessarily, stops at this stage (for example, market research or data collection associated with local government planning or legislative requirements [Zikmund 2003]). However, academic research seeks deeper understanding of the world, whether it is, for example, how an ecosystem functions or what the underlying forces and influences were during a particular historic event (Williams 2000). Such deeper understanding demands closer analytical techniques, and thus the aim of a research project, the research problem, demands an already deeper understanding of the discipline and of higher-order analytical techniques that may be applied (Ashley and Boyd 2006).

Whatever the case, all research is motivated by questions arising from prior work or observations of the world, and defines an issue that needs to be analysed at some level. The research problem, therefore, needs to contain some fundamental properties (Cresswell 1994; Maykut and Morehouse 1994; Jones et al. 2000; Flyvbjerg 2001; Robson 2002). It must: (1) articulate a real and justifiable issue, grounded, in all likelihood, in prior research experience, and thus worth doing; (2) clearly relate to a body of relevant prior knowledge within the given discipline; (3) be formulated with a full understanding of the appropriate analytical tools; and (4) make some potentially original contribution to knowledge and/or theory (see chapters 1 and 2).

Identifying the real and justifiable issue and appropriate analytical tools thus defines what level of analysis is anticipated. In the growing world of research relevance, that is, where academic research is seen as both a scholarly endeavour and a practical activity, providing potential tangible commercial, social, economic or environmental outcomes. The research problem may also be linked to expected outcome and outputs. An important starting point, however, is the identification of a viable topic and of a core question around which the research will develop. The research proposal, therefore, must be rooted in some question to be answered, some problem to be solved, some issue to be addressed.

A theme I keep returning to in my own reflections on research is the importance of the researcher reflecting on and understanding the nature of scholarship, especially within his or her own discipline (Kolb 1984; Schön 1987; Cloke et al. 1994). With such understanding, the researcher will have greater control over his or her research design, and increased success in writing proposals that result in projects running and funded. Examples of the types of understanding required may be found through academe (Williams 2000). Scientific research, for example, is often understood, at a popular level, in simple ways – it requires highly trained, often lab-coated, experts to make measurements and observations of unambiguous objects. However, for a trained and experienced scientist, the complexity of measurement and observation is an everyday understanding. Such research often requires measurements in numbers on some kind of variable, so the mathematics of variability within a system needs to be fully understood, as does the mathematics of measurement and analysis of complex data sets in which multiple variables may interact; it is often that interaction that provides the real data on a system under investigation, so the scientist involved in measurement-based science requires a detailed tool kit, and a mastery of the underlying principles, to make what from the outside may seem simple observations (Jones et al. 2000). They also require these skills to make observations and derive conclusions that can be authenticated and verified independently, thus allowing the broader scientific community to have confidence in the new information being generated. The scientist under such conditions usually also requires access to instruments for measuring the variable or variables, and thus has to have a sound grounding in the technical aspects of his or her science, often with a sound understanding of the history of the development of that science. Furthermore, that scientist also has to understand how to apply the instruments and techniques to generate, under the correct and controlled conditions appropriate to his or her field, as many replicate measurements as possible or necessary to allow testing for statistical significance (Dowdy and Wearden 1991; Easley, Madden and Dunn 2000). This then forces the scientist to consider appropriate research design – we are returning to some earlier comments on the importance of defining approach and method within the research proposal.

Scientific investigations may broadly be clustered into two basic types, those in which (1) data on a key variable is collected on a clearly defined population, which has not been subjected to any experimental treatment; and (2) a specified experimental treatment is applied in a controlled way to individuals of a defined population and data collected in response to that treatment. For a scientist to make the appropriate choice prior to commencing research requires training, experience and, most importantly, active consideration of the problem in hand and a full understanding of the discipline.

9.3 Moving towards an Appropriate Research Design

Once a research problem has been identified, it is important to consider the research design. Design reflects the researcher's selection of a theoretical paradigm or perspective through which he or she may approach the proposed research, as well as, perhaps more commonly understood, identifying a strategy, and thus the experimental design, for collecting the information considered appropriate to tackling the problem. There are many constraints on the practicality or viability of a research project, stemming not only from the credibility of the research question being posed, but also from many practical aspects of the proposed research. Disciplinary constraints may shape the research process, distinguishing one design from another as appropriate to different topics; this often reflects the history of the discipline (James 1972), in which certain types of ideas or forms of interpretation have become accepted practice.

An example can be found in the world of the social sciences. It does not take long in any reading of the social sciences to discover that there is a huge range of approaches to research possible: a reader will come across terms such as qualitative, interpretive, multicultural, postcolonial, empirical, quantitative, participatory, action-oriented, multiculturally situated, evidence or source based, action learning, and so on (Denzin and Lincoln 1994; Cornwall and Jewkes 1995; Hay 2000; Aranda and Street 2001; Neuman 2003; see also chapters 2 and 6). What does this tell us? That people in the social sciences do not know what they are doing? Hardly. What it tells us is that the subject of social science research is hugely diverse, and that methodology, research questions and subjects are intimately linked. The purposes to which social science research are put are equally diverse. The implication? That the social scientist needs to be fully aware of the breadth of his or her discipline, and needs to have a sound understanding of its possibilities, questions, approaches, techniques, methods and so on (Martindale 1988; Fuery and Mansfield 1997). Does this sound familiar?

To consider the example, let us first think about the version of social science in which, in places, researchers hold great store in high level statistical sampling, in which the entire research problem is framed in terms of obtaining sufficiently large and appropriately structured or related samples, and in identifying the various forms of dependent and independent variables that may be tested using now established and widely accepted statistical tests (Dowdy and Wearden 1991; Cresswell 1994; see chapter 11). On the other hand, an increasing number of social scientists are using now-well-established methodologies that eschew statistical sampling and testing, but focus on what is known as qualitative information – ideas, opinions, experiences, values and so on – that can be gathered, recorded and, in due course, analysed in considerable depth, using techniques such as interviews (and there are many forms of interviewing techniques), case studies, and reflective practices (Brenner, Brown and Canter 1985; Bonoma 1985; Berg 1989; Patton 1991; Malterud 1993; Silverman 1993; Porteous 1996; Greenwood and Levin 1998; Murphy et al. 1998; Baskerville 1999; Shaw 1999). The adoption and acceptance of this latter package of methods has been a long process, and in some schools of thought, a researcher wishing to adopt them will still find resistance as they are regarded as uncontrolled and therefore unreliable methodology.

The point here is that the methodology being proposed may support or hinder the progression of the research. Where funding is attached to the project, there may be constraints in methodology. An archaeological sites survey, for example, run for scholarly purposes will be organized in a very different manner from one being run as part of a heritage impact assessment (Pearson and Sullivan 1995; Boyd et al. 1996). Articulating the methodology, therefore, will provide a test of the research problem. It will, furthermore, by providing a reality check, assist in developing the ideas of the research problem further.

In many cases, the idea of methodology is spoken of in very crude or general terms, in simplistic comparisons between the requirements of research in, for example, the humanities and the sciences, especially noting differences and similarities between qualitative and quantitative research. It is relatively easy to be seduced by the seeming differences between qualitative and quantitative research. Qualitative research, on the one hand, may be characterized by being owned as much by the subject of the research as by the researcher, so that the relation between observer and observed becomes a crucial consideration, and the research may be gendered, increasingly oriented toward social action, capable of multiple interpretations, concerned with how experience is created and how meaning is derived, or constructed rather, and value laden rather than value free (Maykut and Morehouse 1994). Quantitative research, on the other hand, focuses on external examination and seeming unambiguous observation of relationships between one thing (an independent variable) and another (a dependent or outcome variable) in a population, and thus its design may be either descriptive or experimental, establishing, respectively, associations between variables or causality (Ackoff 1962; see chapter 6). Qualitative research is often characterized by a sampling strategy in which samples of many subjects may be required (see chapter 11).

Despite these very different presenting characterizations the purpose of doing research is ultimately, however, to ask relevant questions about how the world works, to define appropriate methods to collect relevant data to address these questions, to apply sound and authorized methods to interrogate the data, and to come to the most parsimonious conclusion available, given the state of knowledge, questions asked and methods applied. Under these terms, the sciences and humanities are little different: the specific questions may differ because the disciplines within these broad areas address different aspects of the world, and the methods may differ in reflection of both the types of questions and the types of available data. The intellectual similarities, however, may be remarkably evident, and the two broad approaches may lend themselves to close alignment where each provides a relevant and appropriate approach to tackling a research issue (Tashakkori and Teddlie 1998; Taylor 2000).

With such consideration of potential research design and methodology, it is useful to return, briefly, to the theme of defining the research problem, and to reinforce the important point that the researcher needs to be fully aware of the discipline in which he or she is working. This also requires a need to understand the culture of that discipline, often as operating within the institution the researcher is studying in, and methodologies that are sanctioned within that culture (Geertz 1973, 2000). Such requirements place a burden of responsibility on the researcher seeking to define a new research problem, the responsibility of being knowledgeable within the discipline and being aware of his or her level of knowledge and experience within the discipline. It is very common, for example, for a student or early career researcher to wish to critique the discipline. This can be very easy, especially from a position of relative ignorance or lack of experience.

Almost every researcher will have stories of an early career attempt they have made at debunking the established views of their discipline or at least attempting to show that there are fundamental flaws in method or logic within the discipline. In a way, this is a normal phase for an apprentice who is being inducted into a profession that may best be characterized as a questioning profession. The same researchers will, in all likelihood, admit that their efforts either fell on deaf ears, were limited by inexperience or, worse, resulted in difficulties in their career. We all know of young researchers taking on the establishment and losing. Those who survive will also explain that, with their growing experience, they developed a deeper understanding of their discipline, being able to work within the uncertainties of methodology – measuring and recording this complex, dynamic and multifaceted world even with sophisticated tools, after all, demands that we simplify the information (called classification or data reduction) – or the generalizing tendencies of most analytical techniques.

Once the researcher is working within the methodological tradition of his or her discipline and institution, the next step is to design the research programme (Leedy 1993; Cresswell 1994). This is done at several levels, but is initially going to be broad based. Ultimately it will be expressed in terms of very detailed specifics – the number of samples to be collected, the exact chemical analyses to be conducted, the sampling strategy to ensure an even social spread of respondents, the number of days questionnaires will be administered, and so on. There are many handbooks available to guide this level of writing (see, for example, Jones et al. 2000; Neuman 2003). Often, however, it is tempting for a new researcher to focus on such day-to-day methods. That is, after all, what we get trained to do in a function sense, and can be controlled with ease, often becoming a routine or process-driven activity; it may even be applied by following a standard set of procedures, which the researcher can become very competent at carrying out. However, if this happens, the research runs the risk of being done because the methods allow one to do it. Because we can complete chemical assays for particular elements does not necessarily mean that these elements are relevant to the question being posed or that their measurement will provide useful data; it will provide data, but so would measuring something else. The point is that the design, while it may be constrained by method, is still required to be based on the nature and significance of the issues to be addressed.

The implication of such potential pitfalls is that any research design will need to articulate a rationale for the undertaking. Proper consideration of the topic will prompt a hypothesis to be tested or a thesis to be developed or interrogated. In some disciplines, hypothesis building has been formalized, with, for example, concepts of the null hypothesis – the idea that needs to be disproven – whereas in other disciplines, such formal statements are less crucial. In research that can be addressed using statistical analyses, formal statements are required by the very technique, statements of what is to be disproven or what levels of certainty in correlations between data need to be achieved for something to be considered a sound proof. Originally, the research problem will have been located in relation to other prior, and usually, published work in the area, and thus its scope and limitations within the discipline may have been clearly defined.

As an aside, it should be noted that the relevance of prior published data is that it has been tested by peer review, and therefore can be taken as a sound and authorized basis for further research; the researcher, however, should be able to read that prior literature with a critical and discerning eye, and develop the skills for a critical evaluation of published work (Boyd and Laird 2006). With this in mind, as the research proposal is being developed, consideration needs to be given to defining what needs to be observed, how that observation should be conducted, the form that collected data should take, how data will be interrogated and so on. This is done in large part by returning to prior work. In all likelihood, similar questions have been asked previously, perhaps in a different context, and appropriate methods have been developed. It is most unlikely for most researchers to come up with something completely novel more than once in their careers, and the vast majority of researchers will build on established questions, approaches and methods. Indeed it is critical for the growth of a discipline that there is some continuity in the questions being asked and some conformity in methodological approach; this allows researchers to contribute to a much larger, internally coherent and coordinated understanding of the world as a community than would be possible for an individual.

To recap, a research problem is always contextualized within the researcher's discipline and institutional setting. As a small component of a large, now global, scholarly project, the individual researcher's work should be considered as a contribution to a growing body of knowledge and understanding of the world. While a very small number of researchers may come up with a brand new idea or approach, and thus perhaps define new intellectual directions, the vast majority of researchers will be working within an established approach. It is very important, therefore, that the research problem be developed within an assessment of current thinking on the problem, an assessment usually gained by a review of the literature, often usefully moderated by practical experience and prior research. This allows the proposal to be framed within the most relevant theoretical and practical context.

With these bases, the proposal then needs to provide a realistic foundation for research grounded on information. This applies as much for theoretical as for applied research; it may be easier to understand practical observations as information, but one must not forget that a theorist builds conceptual analyses on component parts, theoretical building blocks, arguments and observation (Collins 1998). Once the relevant required information is identified, the proposal can consider the strategies for collecting accurate data and (something that is often overlooked) appropriate quantities of information; the data- or information-gathering methods, whether they are observational techniques, classification methods, statistics or experimental design, must be carefully defined. Finally, data collection alone, in most cases, is inadequate for developing deep understanding, and the data needs to be interrogated. The proposal, therefore, needs to consider the methods that will be used for analysing the information or data collected; this applies as much for researchers using statistical packages such as SPSS to identify correlations between measurement, as for those seeking to extract deep cultural or value meaning out of in-depth interview transcripts using, for example, N6, the updated name for the beautifully named NUD*IST software (Fielding and Lee 1991).

9.4   Anticipating Outcomes, Writing Your Results

Assuming that things go as planned, the researcher must expect that all observations will be carefully recorded and analysed, and that some form of answer to the original question will be available (and there will always be an answer). It will then be time to write up the research, to set out your findings, to discuss their implications, and to draw relevant inferences; in other words, to provide an answer to your original question. The proposal needs to consider how this will be done, and, in particular, be clear on the form of reporting.

Researchers, at least in noncommercial enterprises such as universities and public research agencies, have an obligation to the public who, after all, fund your research through their taxes. We need to consider questions such as how and where will you publish the work, or who will be your audience. These questions need to be addressed in the research proposal, and, just as above for methods, the answers may influence the design of the research. If, for example, the researcher has a very strong public-good ethos, and considers that his or her primary responsibility is to produce socially useful and maybe even activist research outcomes, that research is likely to be published in both the specialist scholarly and popular domains. These two domains demand very different writing and publishing styles (Boyd and Taffs 2004; Boyd and Laird 2006): will the analyses lend themselves to this difference? If so, how? What will the publishing strategy be? After, for example, the research is completed or during the progress of the work?

As an aside, it is important to note that anticipating publication is predicated on a bold assumption, that everything goes as planned. This is, in reality, a big assumption. Even the best-planned research design may, and perhaps should, be susceptible to change, and change can happen almost as soon as the first data are collected. The open mind of a truly enquiring researcher will be receptive to new ideas or questions, or responsive to doubts that the original question may not be valid, or that the proposed methodology may not be exactly correct. This is formally accepted in some disciplines as grounded research, and indeed all academic research is grounded in the experience of the research. While it may be easy to ignore the demands for a change or shift in design as the research progresses, and sometimes where research is following established protocols it may be very hard to depart from predetermined structures, this can result in a substandard outcome or, worse, irrelevant or incorrect answers.

The research proposal can be viewed as a solid frame for the proposed research, although more often it simply gets the process started, giving some shape to the start of the research. It can be hard for an inexperienced researcher to change the course of a research project once it has started, and some indeed consider that a departure from the proposal is some form of admission of inadequacy. It is, however, the exact opposite, and becomes easier with experience. The proposal is simply an opening gambit, albeit as strong and valid a one as possible, that sets the parameters for the project.

Let us return to the issue of writing up. By discussing writing and reporting in the proposal, the researcher, again, is forced to consider the cultural norms within his or her discipline or institution (Chanock 2007; Ellis, Taylor and Drury 2007). Writing in the sciences, health or medical fields, for example, is largely a process of reportage (Lindsay 1984; Alley 1996). That is, the data has been collected, samples have been subjected to analysis, analyses completed, and information processed to provide the answer to the original question. The task of the scientist is now simply to report the outcomes of the research.

In the humanities and parts of the social sciences, on the other hand, writing is an analytical technique used quite deliberately to interrogate evidence and ideas. Many scholarly history research books or analyses of cultural processes, for example, use language to explore the topic; social philosophers, historians and humanities scholars often write detailed and creative prose in their search for meaning within their scholarly subjects (Chamberlayne, Bornat and Wengraf 2000; Clandinin and Connelly 2000; Healey and Roberts 2004).

In some cases, notably in the new humanities and other areas broadly equating with postmodern scholarship, this may extend to playing with language, using metaphors and analogues to conceptualize intellectually difficult concepts, or even modifying words and grammar to force meaning previously not conceived from the text (see chapter 3). These techniques can seem quite obscure, especially to non-humanities scholars. They can backfire, of course, so they require skilful and experienced execution, just as the analyses of a skilled laboratory-based scientist will reflect many years of training and understanding in what can be equally (to the outsider) obscure intellectual endeavour. Once again we return to the importance of the proposal: the proposal contains both a practical requirement of articulating the writing and reporting required, and an intellectual requirement for the researcher to fully understand the disciplinary cultural role of writing and reporting (Hay 1996; Allen 1997; Marshall 2000).

Whatever the specific use of writing and reporting, the researcher has to do justice to the substantial work planned, and so must anticipate setting adequate time and effort aside for appropriate documentation, the development of cogent argument, and the clear reporting of information and scholarly outcomes. All this has to be done – is this familiar? – within the context of the discipline, which will also require that the researcher understands the culture of publication. In most sciences, for example, this involves publishing relatively short accounts in what is known as a paper – a short, often three-thousand- to five-thousand-word, self-contained account of the work – in a scholarly journal. That journal will be published by a reputable scholarly association or publishing company, and managed by an editor and editorial team, and will have specific house rules about style, content and the like.

Importantly, publication will go through a process of peer review, which is also often known as refereeing (see chapters 14, 15, 16 and 17). The research proposal, within such a discipline, should reflect the expectation that publication will be in a peer-reviewed and, increasingly, international journal. This does not preclude publication in other outlets, such as industry journals or magazines or more popular publications, where there is a good case for community- or industry-focused dissemination of the data. However, for a scholar, especially, such a plan should be discussed in the proposal, drawing attention to the specific needs of the research, such as its industry or social agenda focus.

In some disciplines, and notably often the newer ones – academic nursing or tourism studies for example – or disciplines that have an urgency about them, such as some areas of medical science, business or political studies, the relevant academic community may adopt a strong culture of publication through conference proceedings. Conference publication is present within all disciplines, but in many, conference publication is considered to be secondary to the peer review process. This stems from the role of conferences within individual disciplines: in some they are used for preliminary presentation and discussion of new data or ideas, whereas in others they are the primary locus for presenting final results. Yet other disciplines, such as the historical disciplines and some social sciences, publish by monograph; that is, the entire work is contained in a single, often single-authored, book, either a stand-alone volume or one of a series of monographs.

There is, of course, a gradation of publication outlets; all university departments expect their students to present at in-house seminars, often not for publication but to assist them in organizing their research inputs and outcomes, and start to learn about public presentation (Roberts 2004). It is expected that graduate research will be presented in an academic style appropriate to the discipline so as to facilitate successful evaluation and wide dissemination of the work. That, again, demands of the researcher a full understanding of the culture and practice of his or her discipline. Writing style, from form of language through to the structure of the written piece, varies between and within disciplines, often being specifically prescribed by the publishers, and so the researcher has to be both fully familiar with the expectations within the discipline and open to diversity.

There are many styles of writing, each appropriate to its own context, and the researcher's task is to get the right balance between different styles of writing; for example, which of the three modes of historical writing (narration, description and analysis) should an historian adopt under what circumstances? How does the researcher make decisions about the relevant structure of his or her writing – should it be a chronological and or thematic account, or a mix of both? – or make use of adequate and relevant illustration? And that old chestnut, referencing . . . what style is appropriate?

To help a researcher answer all of these, and many other aspects of writing, there is a solid body of literature, both general scholarly and discipline-specific, that provides guidelines to writing, assisting the researcher through the process of planning, drafting, reviewing, finalizing a manuscript, and submitting it for publication in a way that will allow his or her peers to accept that work as a bona fide statement of the outcomes of the research (start with, for example: Lindsay 1984; Alley 1996; Hay 1996; Allen 1997; Chamberlayne, Bornat and Wengraf 2000; Clandinin and Connelly 2000; Marshall 2000; Healey and Roberts 2004). It is contingent upon the researcher to be fully familiar with that body of literature, and, in the context of considering the research proposal, able to demonstrate an understanding of the demands of writing on the research design, demands that need to be articulated through the design.

9.5   Rounding up: Approaches to Research

Enough has been said above to make it clear that the researcher needs to be well versed in his or her discipline. While there is a common goal of academic or scholarly research – to ask relevant questions about how the world works, to define appropriate methods to collect relevant data to address these questions, to apply sound and authorized methods to interrogate the data, and to come to the most parsimonious conclusion available, given the state of knowledge, questions asked and methods applied – it is equally clear that the diversity of questions, intellectual traditions, methods and reasoning across the disciplines results in seemingly very different approaches being taken to interrogate the world. At a very simple level, for example, what would the relevance of a Linnaean plant classification scheme be to a classical architect attempting to understand the formal aesthetics of a historic period? Not only will the methods for data collection be incompatible, but the conceptual basis of the nature of knowledge required to answer the botanist's and architect's questions will be fundamentally different.

It may be easy, therefore, to ask, To what extent does the research process vary across disciplines? This is a question that often taxes the newer researcher, especially where groups of research students from different disciplines gather. It is a question that can rapidly become a my-discipline's-better/more relevant/more rigorous-than-yours discussion. The more important point is for researchers to recognize that whatever the interdisciplinary differences, the key is that process within a discipline is followed correctly and with internal logic. This, in turn, demands that the researcher become fully familiar with his or her own discipline, understanding that their discipline is not the only valid approach in understanding the world, but is one, internally logical approach to understanding some aspect of the world.

How does a new researcher do this? Part of the solution is immersion in the discipline – reading and studying the objective material of the discipline, and gaining as much practical experience as possible. That can lead to some understanding and level of competence, but if doing the work becomes routine and unthinking, an insightful or deeper understanding of the discipline can be lost or obscured. This is where common misunderstandings about the nature of the discipline may arise. Think of popular ideas of what science is; for example, many people believe that scientific fact must be unambiguous or completely objective, despite the large corpus of literature in the sciences that examines issues of (un)certainty and (in)accuracy. A way to overcome this gap in understanding is for students to move beyond the material being studied in their discipline, and to examine the underlying philosophies of their discipline. Such material is taught more in some disciplines than others; it used to be commonplace for science courses to have some form of "History of Scientific [or Geographical, Geological and so on] Thought" content, but seems to be less popular within the university system at present.

Some disciplines, on the other hand, spend considerable time within their undergraduate courses discussing the intellectual foundations of the discipline; this is notable in the social sciences and, especially, the humanities. Many of the social sciences deal with this matter through detailed methods courses. The social sciences have undergone significant changes over the last half century, developing an impressive range of observational and analytical tools, all of which are grounded in a wide range of conceptions of what knowledge is and how it is constructed (two of the pillars of philosophy). In effect, the social sciences, and latterly the new humanities, are still inventing themselves, and so these detailed debates and discussions of philosophy and methodology are integral parts of a growing discipline. Science, in its broadest sense, has had several centuries to become fully familiar with its foundations, and as a consequence seems to require relatively less self-reflection and consideration of the origins and assumptions of established techniques and methodologies and, indeed, of underlying concepts.

In contrast to the social sciences' *sensu lato*, in which the researcher may be able to work within one of many theoretical contexts – racialized discourses, feminist or queer theory, Marxist models, postmodern perspectives, structuralist and post-structuralist models, to name but a few – scientists generally do not have to consider selecting a theoretical paradigm or perspective within which to work; much science is framed in a positivist and/or reductionist paradigm, which by definition for most scientists is unproblematic (see chapters 3 and 4). While it is entirely possible to work within these frames, it does the researcher no harm to examine them a bit further and, just perhaps, come up with a critical perspective that may allow a questioning of approach and method.

Interestingly, it is common in the humanities to question the very process of research, interrogating the researcher as well as the researched, and the researcher-topic relationship. This reflects a sound scholarly tradition that questions the degree to which a researcher, by being aware of conceptions of the self and others, may be influenced by his or her beliefs, existing or new theories, or ideologies. Such an approach introduces an explicit role for ethics and politics in research, a role that is readily ignored, but should be considered within any proposal; in cases, as alluded to above, where the proposed research requires some form of permission – ethics clearance, statutory permits and so on – it is commonplace for the researcher, scientist or not, to address such issues.

9.6 Conclusions

The research proposal, on the face of it, is a simple document. It allows the researcher to set out a train of reasoning that justifies a research question, placing it in its scholarly, intellectual and/or practical context, and thus assisting in planning the execution of the project. It would be relatively easy to describe the writing of a research proposal in technical terms, the headings that need to be filled in, the style of referencing required, and so on. However, it takes very little looking beyond the technical aspects of writing to recognize that the research proposal places significant demands on the researcher. Importantly, it requires the researcher to be able to demonstrate his or her immersion within the discipline, not only as a technically competent practitioner of method, but as a scholar who understands his or her discipline's structures, rules, culture and context. With that understanding, the research proposal can become a powerful document, setting the foundations for a successful research project.

References

Ackoff, R.L. 1962. *Scientific Method: Optimizing Applied Research Decisions*. New York: John Wiley and Sons.
Allen, M. 1997. *Smart Thinking: Skills for Critical Understanding and Writing*. Melbourne: Oxford University Press.
Alley, M. 1996. *The Craft of Scientific Writing*. New York: Springer-Verlag.
Aranda, S., and A. Street. 2001. From individual to group: Use of narratives in participatory research process. *Journal of Advanced Nursing* 33: 791–97.
Ashley, P., and W.E. Boyd. 2006. Quantitative and qualitative approaches to research in environmental management. *Australian Journal of Environmental Management* 13 (2): 70–78.

Baskerville, R.L. 1999. Investigating information systems with action research. *Communications of the Association for Information Systems* 2 (Article 19).

Berg, B. 1989. *Qualitative Research Methods for the Social Sciences*. Boston: Allyn and Bacon.

Bonoma, T.V. 1985. Case research in marketing: Opportunities, problems, and a process. *Journal of Marketing Research* 22: 199–208.

Boyd, B., and W. Laird. 2006. *Analysing Global Environmental Issues: A Skills Manual*. 2nd ed. Sydney: Pearsons.

Boyd, W.E., M.M. Cotter, W. O'Connor, and D. Sattler. 1996. Cognitive ownership of heritage places: Social construction and the cultural heritage management. *Tempus* 6: 123–40.

Boyd, W.E., R.L. Healey, S.W. Hardwick and M. Haigh, with contributions from P. Klein, B. Doran, J. Trafford and J. Bradbeer. 2008. "None of us sets out to hurt people": An essay on The Ethical Geographer and geography curricula in higher education. *Journal of Geography in Higher Education* 32: 37–50.

Boyd, W.E., and K. Taffs. 2004. *Mapping the Environment: A Professional Development Manual*. Frenchs Forest: Pearsons.

Brenner, M., J. Brown, and D. Canter, eds. 1985. *The Research Interview: Uses and Approaches*. London: Academic Press.

Chamberlayne, P., J. Bornat, and T. Wengraf, eds. 2000. *The Turn to Biographical Method in Social Science*. London: Routledge.

Chanock, K. 2007. What academic language and learning advisers bring to the scholarship of teaching and learning: Problems and possibilities for dialogue with the disciplines. *Higher Education Research and Development* 26: 269–80.

Chappell, A. 2001. Challenging the teaching convention in geography using problem-based learning: The role of reflective practice in supporting change. *Planet* 2: 18–22.

Clandinin, D.J., and F.M. Connelly. 2000. *Narrative Inquiry: Experience and Story in Qualitative Research*. San Francisco: Jossey-Bass.

Cloke, P., M. Doel, D. Matless, M. Phillips and N. Thrift. 1994. *Writing the Rural: Five Cultural Geographies*. London: Chapman and Hall.

Collins, R. 1998. *The Sociology of Philosophies: A Global Theory of Intellectual Change*. Cambridge, MA: Belknap Press of Harvard University Press.

Cornwall, A., and R. Jewkes. 1995. The use of qualitative methods: What is participatory research? *Social Science and Medicine* 41: 1667–76.

Cresswell, J.W. 1994. *Research Design: Qualitative and Quantitative Approaches*. Thousand Oaks, CA: Sage.

Denzin, N.K., and Y.S. Lincoln, eds. 1994. *Handbook of Qualitative Research*. Thousand Oaks, CA: Sage.

Dowdy, S., and S. Wearden. 1991. *Statistics for Research*. 2nd ed. New York: John Wiley and Sons.
Easley, R.W., C.S. Madden and M.G. Dunn. 2000. Conducting marketing science: The role of replication in the research process. *Journal of Business Research* 48: 83–92.
Ellis, R.A., C.E. Taylor and H. Drury. 2007. Learning science through writing: Associations with prior conceptions of writing and perceptions of a writing program. *Higher Education Research and Development* 26: 297–311.
Fielding, N.G., and R.M. Lee, eds. 1991. *Using Computers in Qualitative Research*. London: Sage.
Flyvbjerg, B. 2001. *Making Social Science Matter: Why Social Inquiry Fails and How it Can Succeed Again*. Cambridge: Cambridge University Press.
Fuery, P., and N. Mansfield. 1997. *Cultural Studies and the New Humanities: Concepts and Controversies*. Melbourne: Oxford University Press.
Gardiner, V., and K. Hughes. 2000. *Improving Students' Problem-Solving and Thinking Skills*. Cheltenham, UK: Geography Discipline Network.
Geertz, C. 1973. *The Interpretation of Cultures*. New York: Basic Books.
———. 2000. *Available Light: Anthropological Reflections on Philosophical Topics*. Princeton, NJ: Princeton University Press.
Glassick, C.E., M.T. Huber, and G.I. Maerof. 1997. *Scholarship Assessed: Evaluation of the Professoriate*. San Francisco, CA: Jossey-Bass.
Greenwood, D.J., and M. Levin. 1998. *Introduction to Action Research: Social Research for Social Change*. Thousand Oaks, CA: Sage.
Hay, I. 1996. *Communicating in Geography and the Environmental Sciences*. Melbourne: Oxford University Press.
———, ed. 2000. *Qualitative Research Methods in Human Geography*. South Melbourne: Oxford University Press.
Healey, M., and J. Roberts, eds. 2004. *Engaging Students in Active Learning: Case Studies in Geography, Environmental and Related Disciplines*. Cheltenham, UK: Geography Discipline Network.
James, P.E. 1972. *All Possible Worlds: A History of Geographical Thought*. Indianapolis, IN: Odyssey Press.
Jones, A., R. Duck, J. Weyers and R. Reed. 2000. *Practical Skills in Environmental Science*. Essex: Prentice-Hall.
Kolb, D.A. 1984. *Experiential Learning: Experience as the Source of Learning and Development*. Englewood Cliffs, NJ: Prentice-Hall.
Leedy, P. 1993. *Practical Research: Planning and Design*. 5th ed. New York: Macmillan.
Lindsay, D. 1984. *A Guide to Scientific Writing*. Melbourne: Longman Cheshire.

Malterud, K. 1993. Shared understanding of the qualitative research process: Guidelines for the medical researcher. *Family Practice* 10: 201–6.

Marshall, S.J. 2000. *Writing Guide: Suggestions for the Effective Completion of Assignments.* Sydney: Macquarie University.

Martindale, D. 1988. *The Nature and Types of Sociological Theory.* 2nd ed. Long Grove, IL: Waveland Press.

Maykut, P., and R. Morehouse. 1994. *Beginning Qualitative Research: A Philosophic and Practical Guide.* London: Falmer Press.

Murphy, E., R. Dingwall, D. Greatbatch, S. Parker and P. Watson. 1998. Qualitative research methods in health technology assessment: A review of the literature. *Health Technology Assessment* 2 (16).

Neuman, W.L. 2003. *Social Research Methods: Qualitative and Quantitative Approaches.* 5th ed. Boston: Allyn and Bacon.

Patton, M.J. 1991. Qualitative research on college students: Philosophical and methodological comparisons with the quantitative approach. *Journal of College Student Development* 32: 389–96.

Pearson, M., and S. Sullivan. 1995. *Looking after Heritage Places: The Basics of Heritage Planning for Managers, Landowners and Administrators.* Melbourne: Melbourne University Press.

Porteous, J.D. 1996. *Environmental Aesthetics: Ideas, Politics and Planning.* London: Routledge.

Roberts, C. 2004. Developing students' communication skills. In *Engaging Students in Active Learning: Case Studies in Geography, Environmental and Related Disciplines,* ed. M. Healey and J. Roberts, 55–58. Cheltenham, UK: Geography Discipline Network.

Robson, C. 2002. *Real World Research.* 2nd ed. Oxford: Blackwell.

Schön, D. 1987. *Educating the Reflective Practitioner.* San Francisco, CA: Jossey-Bass.

Shaw, E. 1999. A guide to the qualitative research process: Evidence from a small firm survey. *Qualitative Market Research: An International Journal* 2: 59–70.

Silverman, D. 1993. *Interpreting Qualitative Data: Methods for Analysing Talk, Text and Interaction.* London: Sage.

Tashakkori, A., and C. Teddlie. 1998. *Mixed Methodology: Combining Qualitative and Quantitative Approaches.* Thousand Oaks, CA: Sage.

Taylor, G.R., ed. 2000. *Integrating Quantitative and Qualitative Methods in Research.* Lanham, MD: University Press of America.

Williams, M. 2000. *Science and Social Science: An Introduction.* London: Routledge.

Zikmund, W.G. 2003. *Exploring Marketing Research.* 8th ed. Mason, OH: South-Western Publishing.

Chapter 9 Activities

Activity 23

Who are you and where do you fit into your academic niche?

1. Write a short account of your own academic history. This could be a timeline or a dot point list. Try to identify the key events in your education as an academic and researcher.
2. Briefly describe the social you: what is your social background? Do you come from a large or small family? Are you native born or a migrant to the place you live in? First or fifth generation? Working class or middle class? School education? Sporty? Musical?
3. Can you recognize any particularly important events or people that influenced you and helped you define who you are now and helped you make the career choices that brought you to this point in time? How have these events or people affected your life?
4. What are your basic beliefs? Do you have a guiding set of principles or religious beliefs that influence your behaviour and help guide you through life? How might they influence the academic and scholarly decisions you make? Do you, for example, have a strong sense of social justice, and if so, does this influence the subjects you choose to study and research?

When you have completed this activity, you will have a short written autobiographical account that may help you understand your own scholarly and academic choices. The account will not necessarily provide a deterministic control over your choices, but will assist in informing you about yourself and the ways in which you are likely to interact with the research culture, research problems and the subjects of your research.

Activity 24

Identifying the research aim.

1. In your own field of academic interest, consider what are the major themes being investigated by researchers and published in the literature. You are likely to make quite a long list, so annotate it with two conditions: the topic or couple of topics you think are most urgent at present; and the topic or couple of topics you are most interested in.
2. Select one of the topics that you consider either to be an important one within your discipline or that you are particularly interested in. Why have you selected it? What do you think will be the influence on your interest of the topic if you have selected a topic of disciplinary importance in comparison to one of personal interest?
3. From your present understanding of the selected topic, what do you think the burning question is at present? Why?
4. Write a one-sentence statement of the outcome of a research problem that will address that burning question.

When you have completed this activity, you will know what your research problem is and be able to describe it in a single short sentence. This may take longer than you anticipate, especially distilling the ideas to a single short sentence; that is quite normal. Now you are ready to begin justifying your choice of research topic.

Activity 25

Justifying the project.

1. Using the topic and aim identified in activity 24, write a short (one page) statement justifying why the topic is worth investigating. Your statement should recognize both the relevance of the topic to the broader research agenda in your discipline, and the social or technical significance of any potential research outcomes.
2. Where did you get the information you needed to write this statement? Do you need further information to complete this statement? How might you obtain it?
3. What are the historic, conceptual or philosophical and technical

contexts of your proposed research? Have you been trained in the foundations of your discipline or educated yourself in these? Does this background (training or no training) influence your understanding of the topic and ways in which you may tackle the research? How?

By the end of this activity, you should have a short written problem statement or statement of problem background. Now you are ready to think through the steps you will need to adopt to address that problem.

Activity 26

Establishing the research objectives.

1. Now that you have a topic, the aim and a statement of the problem, how will you go about achieving an answer to the research problem you are tackling? Think of the steps you require to do this – four or five steps will do; they will be big picture statements such as "describe and define prior research in this area and identify significant problems and methodologies" (which will be tackled in the next activity by considering the role of a literature review), "develop and test the data-gathering system", "collect relevant data". These have to result in the output building blocks that you will use to address the aim, that is, the packages of information and analyses required to answer the question posed. Remember to include an objective that deals with writing up the work for publication.
2. Identify the relationships between the objectives. Do these objectives have to follow in succession or can you work on several at one time? What is the sequence you require to tackle each objective?
3. Make a timetable for completing each objective.

When you have completed this activity, you will have the start of a timeline for completion of this research. You are now ready to think about specific methods that you will apply to tackling the research problem.

Activity 27

Planning your methods.

1. List the methods you think are likely to be useful in tackling your research question.
2. Reviewing the list, describe whether you are using predominantly quantitative or qualitative methods. Are they lab or field based?
3. Identify, for each method, the type of data you will be collecting. Will it be numerical or verbal? How will you synthesize and present it in your report?
4. For the data to be collected under each method, what analyses will be required? Again, consider whether you need to subject the data to statistical or other mathematical analyses, or whether you may involve some form of qualitative evaluation. Will you require specialist software?
5. How big a sample will you require for each method you have identified? How long will such a sample take to be measured or recorded? At what cost?
6. You should now be aware that you have the outline of a detailed work plan. However, take a moment now to reflect on the list of methods you have selected. Why did you select them? Are these the methods you have been taught in the past? Are they the ones other researchers use? Are they directly relevant or are you choosing them because you have previously used them and have the skills to apply them? Are there other methods that you are less familiar with that might be more appropriate?
7. In the light of your reflection, refine and finalize your methods list.

When you have completed this activity, you will know what you are about to do to tackle the research problem. You are now in the position where you can plan out your day-to-day activities for the rest of the project.

Activity 28

The project timetable.

1. How long do you have to complete this project?

2. Make a list of the tasks you have to complete. First identify those that require others to be completed before you can start them. Next, identify any tasks that can be run concurrently.
3. How much time will each task take? The answer to this question will depend on how large a sample you have planned to examine. Will there be enough time? Do you think you will need to change your sampling strategy? Remember, there are only so many working hours in a day – even if you know how long it takes to do any particular method, always assume things will take longer than planned.

When you have completed this activity, you are very close to the end of the process of writing your research proposal. All you need to do now is collate the references you have used to support this proposal.

Activity 29

Writing up the proposal and reflecting on the process.

1. Once you have completed these activities, you will have a resource base from which to write up your proposal. Use this to compose the text of a proposal. To give you some idea of the length, aim for: (1) a single sentence title and single sentence aim; (2) a one page background and justification; (3) a one page statement of objectives, with each objective being made in one or two sentences only; (4) a one page statement of methods; (5) a half page timetable (you may use a dot point list or present a calendar or flow chart for this); and (6) a half to one page of references.
2. In reviewing the process of planning and writing this research proposal, you should consider several key questions. First, how much did your personal background and prior education or research experience influence your choices of problem and methods? In what way? Second, how much more did you feel that you needed to know before really being able to answer the questions posed throughout the activities? How might you go about finding out that missing knowledge?
3. In retrospect, how realistic do you think your research plan is? Where do you think it may fall down? Ask yourself what you might do at, say, the half way point, when you are reviewing your progress and discover

that you have only sampled half of the samples you planned to have completed by then? Is this a huge problem? How might you reorganize your plan? Can you change the question you are asking? How? Can you change your methodological strategy? How? Indeed, have you asked the correct question in the first place? If not, are you concerned about changing tack half way through? What does this tell you about yourself and your comfort with being adaptable and flexible in the research process? What might limit or enhance your capacity for change?

10

Formulating and Conceptualizing the Research Problem

▸ BILL BOYD

10.1	Introduction
10.2	Understanding Your Background as a Researcher
10.3	Defining the Stakeholders
10.4	Formulating a Research Problem: The Big Picture
10.5	Formulating a Research Problem: Some Practical Matters
10.6	Formulating a Research Problem: Practical Steps
10.7	Formulating the Research Design: An Introduction
10.8	Formulating the Research Design: Study Design
10.9	Formulating the Research Design: Data Collection
10.10	Conclusions

References

Chapter 10 Activities

10.1 Introduction

This chapter looks at the issue of the research problem and the design of the frame with which the researcher interrogates his or her research problem. Formulating both the problem itself and identifying the appropriate design or conceptual basis for conducting the research lie at the centre of every successful research project (Preece 1994). It may seem almost tautological to say that without a stated problem there would be no need to seek an answer, that is, there would be no need to conduct research. In that light, a research project that ignores the centrality of a clearly defined problem is not likely to get off the ground. It is more likely to become an exercise in collecting data, unsynthesized and uninterrogated, which may not be designed to solve any problem and would be unlikely to provide anything other than a superficial description of the issue. In the worst case, such so-called research will provide incorrect and often very misleading understandings of the world.

To address the issue of how a researcher can successfully set about formulating the research problem and then conceptualizing the method framing the research, this chapter will briefly review a number of key matters. It is necessary for the researcher to understand his or her own background as a researcher, and be aware of the stakeholders – the public, funding bodies, governing agencies, commercial interests and other scholars – who may have an interest in the proposed research. The research then has to consider such matters as the problem and its prior context, the theoretical context of that problem, and the existing literature. Once the broad picture has been established, matters such as study design, data collection tools and approaches, and the form and scale of measurement and recording need to be addressed (Leedy 1993; Jones et al. 2000).

A number of issues influence the choice of the problem to be tackled. These range from the personal interests of the researcher – both the personal professional and personal nonprofessional interests such as extracurricular activities – the needs of the researcher's unit within the academy, the goals of the academy as articulated by policy makers, and the goals of the nation or region in which the academy belongs. By and large, the desire to solve a human problem or to learn more about a human society and the environment so as to be better able to manage such a society or environment are all contributory factors to the kind of research problem with which the academy engages.

10.2 Understanding Your Background as a Researcher

Before embarking on research, the researcher needs to understand his or her background as well as the background of the end consumer of the research; the latter is dealt with below as one of the stakeholders in the research. At the individual level, background will consist first of the researcher's informal or personal experiences and, second, the researcher's formal education or training. These will provide influences on the researcher, affecting the choices he or she makes in selecting fields of interest, approaches to scholarship, questions asked and reasons for conducting research. They will, importantly, be evidenced through a researcher's career. It behoves a researcher, therefore, to consider some self-reflection (Schön 1987).

Scholarly self-reflection is an activity that is becoming increasingly accepted and fashionable among some groups of scholars, notably in the social sciences and humanities, where it is recognized that the persona of the researcher has a significant influence on the action of research (Chamberlayne, Bornat and Wengraf 2000). Cloke, for example, provides a very cogent, useful and applied model. Writing in a volume (Cloke et al. 1994) of reflections and analyses of five authors' careers and work, he indicates how he has used his own reflections on the interactions between relationships with peers and teachers, personal views and philosophies, and directions his academic and intellectual work has taken over several decades, to understand more fully why he has developed the academic path he has now followed for half a career, and why he has chosen specific research topics and approaches.

10.3   Defining the Stakeholders

Of course the choice of research, while partly a personal choice, certainly for public scholars, will be influenced by the external stakeholders who may have a say in the problems to be investigated by the researcher – the public, funding bodies, governing agencies, commercial interests, other scholars and so on. These all contribute to a target community, and so it is important to understand their needs, constraints, histories and expectations.

In a 1993 article entitled "Cultural Phenomena and the Research Enterprise", Hughes, Seidman and Williams make the point that culture (broadly defined; I would include society) intersects all the major stages of a research project (and here they talk of "problem formulation, population definition, concept and measurement development, research design, methodology, and data analysis" [p. 1]), importantly noting that it "influences and constrains what researchers deem *worthy of investigation* and how they interpret what they observe" (p. 1). These authors, however, were not merely interested in the intellectual conception of culture as an influence on research behaviour, but in the pragmatic implication that a researcher needs to (1) be fully aware of the sociocultural context of the research through every step of the research, and (2) actively make decisions that result in what they term "a culturally anchored methodology that balances the demands for rigor and sensitivity" (p. 1).

So how might we apply such action? The implication is that we need to understand not only our own personal position and history, but also our place within the academic, governance, bureaucratic and social system. We need to also be fully aware of all other participants in the system. As the researcher, you are the primary investigator within the knowledge industry; this is a privileged position, reaping considerable rewards on success but mantled with responsibilities to work in rigorous and ethical ways.

No research is conducted in a vacuum, and the researcher will rely on colleagues for support, opinion, advice, specialist input and so on. Knowing one's colleagues, and understanding the relationship you have with them, can greatly enhance the research you conduct, and indeed the research an individual chooses to undertake. An extension of the body of a researcher's immediate colleagues is the institution within which a researcher conducts his or her research, and it is therefore important to understand that institution.

At the simplest level, some universities or colleges are known as conservative or liberal places, and thus it may be that certain types of research are preferred by that institution (Williams 2000). Whatever the case, when a university grants a PhD to a candidate or sanctions its staff to conduct particular research, it is attesting to both the research competence and perceived relevance of the individual and its own reputation, especially in an institution that considers that its true measure or identity is based on the quality of research and scholarship emanating from both its faculty and graduate students. Finally, with regards to scholars and scholarly institutions, a researcher must be fully cognisant of his or her specialist field of interest. Scholarship is now a global enterprise, and a researcher has a vast network of people and resources to draw on, including a rapidly increasing body of knowledge generated by other researchers. This places a responsibility on the researcher to be aware of that work and to place his or her own endeavours into this global context; it also offers significant opportunities to identify valid, relevant and cutting edge research problems.

No society develops without a cadre of abstract and problem-solving thinkers, although that position within society can, at times, be fragile. The encouragement of research at its broadest level is one of the ways a society ensures that such a cadre exists and is replicated from one generation to the next. At some times in the social history of a society, however, the focus is on demanding practical matters, and institutions are viewed in ways that may influence the types of research allowed to be conducted. National governments often express this as statements of national priorities – issues of climate change or national security are examples over the last few years. This approach to the national role of research within a society will influence both the big questions people are expecting researchers to address and, importantly, the funding available to support research.

While it may be argued that every society needs ideas to drive and inspire it to greatness at the level of culture and technology, exactly what these ideas may be often becomes an external political reality. Furthermore, popular views of what universities are and what they should be providing society are fluid, and can influence research agendas. This is not to say that academic researchers need become slaves of social fashion; yes, it is important that researchers understand the social politics of the times, and are able to respond to the social needs of the society they live and work within, but there is also an opportunity for academic researchers to assist in fashioning these social views.

The formal structures within society play a crucial role in defining research. At a thoroughly pragmatic level, the opportunities afforded researchers by government and nongovernment funding bodies and, increasingly, commercial interests, need to be fully understood. Every research funding scheme has its own set of rules and expectations, and with careful targeting of applications, a researcher may be able to devise and structure his or her research to suit his or her own needs and align with local, regional and national needs (see chapter 9). There is a growing interest among universities in training and developing researchers with a strong understanding of the commercial aspects of their research.

10.4 Formulating a Research Problem: The Big Picture

The emergence of a research problem is always contextualized within the culture and social behaviour of the researcher. External bodies – governments, commercial interests and industry partners – may set research agendas and may even pose specific questions. Grant funding bodies may provide targeted funding for specific fields or problems. These opportunities can provide a limiting frame for researchers to work within while formulating their research problems. They may find themselves already working in a field that has become popular or viewed as crucial to the national interest, and therefore can merely apply their expertise more or less directly. This may result in one of two situations: first, where the funding body continues to fund the research a researcher wants to do anyway; and second, where the researcher has to adapt his or her work to the funding body's agenda. More likely, a researcher may have to start thinking a little laterally.

In contrast to a research problem emerging out of practical opportunities, much research is generated as a result of the continuing growing body of research outputs within the scholarly world. While students are often trained to conduct literature reviews, and are expected to derive new ideas for enquiry from such reviews, the reality is that researchers are conducting a constant literature review. It is from this that we know what ideas are current, what the theory and practice behind them are, and what new problems there are (Martindale 1988). It is also through the literature that we understand the changing methodology, technologies and analytical capacity of the global research community; consideration of these often provides the stimulus to ask questions previously not considered. If we think of Newton's development of calculus to interrogate problems previously unthinkable, and the consequential expansion of the field of calculus and its myriad applications in both theoretical and applied research, we have a very good example of the role evolving methodology may play in formulating new research.

Linked to establishing a research problem is the need for a researcher to establish the theoretical framework that will guide the research. It is necessary to undertake a review of the relevant theoretical options that may be employed in a particular research. The researcher needs to consider his or her position in the larger context of Western scholarship; at such a broad level, the research may be, for example, sociological, historical, and/or comparative. It may be, for example, ideologically driven from the point of view of class or gender, with different academics adopting approaches within the scholarly frames of Marxism and feminism; it may, on the other hand, be structure driven, with frames of enquiry and social investigation under headings such as structuralism, modernism, deconstruction, liberal humanism, new historicism, and post-colonialism (see chapter 6). The choice of theoretic frame will strongly influence the approach adopted in answering the research question.

In simple terms, therefore, the research problem arises out of the existence of a number of conditions that need to be examined or assessed – these may be defined by prior research or by strategic context – so that solutions may be arrived at. Importantly, the research problem needs to be focused and have the potential to yield deep understanding of the situation being examined.

It is valuable for a discipline to examine itself periodically, and therefore for individuals within that discipline to maintain a watching brief on what research is being conducted and how effective it is. There are examples of this throughout the research world. Every discipline has its review journals and most other academic journals will have a review section; it behooves the researcher to be aware of these and to follow the discussions in such journals. In short, a well-stated and properly contextualized research problem makes it easier to formulate research and subsidiary questions that will guide the approach to, and structure of, the research.

From where does such a well-stated research problem emerge? We have discussed already the importance of both the individual's understanding of his or her discipline – often through training, prior research experience and a familiarity with the relevant literature. We have also discussed the researcher's need to understand the context of his or her work, and it is often within that context one can find a source for a research problem. In broad terms, therefore, sources of research problems may include the researcher's personal and professional experience and background; the discipline's own review of its interests and directions; the current research interests of the university or institution within which the researcher is working; matters of regional or national strategic interest or development; and, increasingly, global concerns.

10.5 Formulating a Research Problem: Some Practical Matters

So far, we have looked at the big picture behind the search for a research problem, the intellectual, disciplinary, professional and national contexts.

However, there are a number of more immediate and day-to-day or personal considerations that will influence an individual researcher selecting a research problem. We have alluded to them in the previous chapter, in reference to what a research problem should probably not be, especially where it reflects a researcher's desire simply to ask the same question again using the same techniques because that is what he or she does. However, the personal characteristics of a researcher will be important, and indeed this is why we discussed the importance of self-reflection and being able to understand one's own history and context.

In considering the selection of a research problem, it is important to consider both some personal aspects and some management aspects. Let us start with the personal ones. The researcher really must have a personal interest in the proposed work. Researchers are usually in the enviable position where they are being paid to work on things they enjoy, and indeed many researchers would view their work almost as a hobby; certainly academics such as historians and environmental scientists would be indulging in their passion anyway.

It is important for a researcher to choose a topic that will be able to keep his or her interest going for a long time. Research projects can run for a long time, or become complex, and do demand a high level of intellectual engagement of the researcher. Unlike many other jobs, it is often not possible simply to turn off at the end of a day; the researcher can go home and stop actually doing the work, but rarely does a researcher turn his or her mind off. Without a sense of passion, there can be a risk of getting bored long before the researcher gets to the end of the process. Allied to this matter is personal competence or the ability that a researcher brings to a project; again, research is usually more than merely a technical competent activity, and relies on the skilled application of higher-level techniques and analytical thinking.

In practical terms, and this is embedded in the planning and selection of methodologies, the researcher needs to be able to judge whether the project is of manageable scope. Simply put, can it get done within a realistic time and energy frame? Or if the scope is too wide, is the researcher likely to get frustrated and lose the zeal to continue? This is a planning decision that probably gets easier with experience; many student projects start off as extremely ambitious plans, in which perfectly reasonable questions are being asked, and quite suitable methodologies and approaches are being proposed, but which will result in a monster of a project. While it may be up to supervisors and mentors to guide such projects towards a more modest form, there are often external realities that limit the scope and mortality of such projects, that is, external funding. In my own early career, at a stage where I was just entering the "very large grant" scene, for example, a colleague and I created a strategy for a long-term environmental monitoring and analysis project. In order to obtain what we thought was a suitably large and appropriately replicated data set over a long enough period, we created what to us was a reasonable plan; indeed we, in our youthful enthusiasm, were vocal about the inadequacies of every similar previous study. We ended up, unsurprisingly, not being funded, having asked for a grant several times larger than the normal or probably maximum awarded by the funding agency we approached. Linked to this practical consideration, and perhaps more often the reason for a project being rejected by funding agencies, is the extent to which the topic can be researched. By this, we mean, can the data we plan to collect actually be collected, or will there be enough to provide meaningful analysis, or will it be relevant to the questions posed? There may even be a more fundamental doubt about the actual ability for the data required to be collected in the first place. It makes no sense to choose a topic for which relevant data cannot be obtained.

Returning to an earlier theme, but in the context of practical considerations, it behooves the researcher to consider to what extent the topic will have the potential for original contribution to knowledge. Originality as defined in this context will vary from one discipline to the next. In some disciplines, this may mean the discovery of new facts or principles, in others the establishment of new relationships between independently existing principles (through, for example, a comparative analysis), and yet elsewhere as new interpretations of existing principles (see chapter 6). Each discipline will also have a sense of how much research is required before it is comfortable with the outcomes. Because an over-researched topic will hardly afford the opportunity to make original contribution to knowledge, it may be advisable to choose under-researched topics. Of course, in many research laboratories or institutions, it may be that many of the researchers are replicating studies, and that the intention is not to provide new and original data or interpretations, but to test, confirm or validate existing models of knowledge. The lesson for the researcher planning a new project? Be fully aware of your context.

Finally, we return to the context: can your institution, regardless of your own abilities, skills and expertise, support your needs? This is especially important for graduate students, who should make sure that their institution has the necessary supervisory staff and support systems and resources, such as libraries and laboratories, for their type of research. If a postgraduate researcher is working towards a dissertation, it is useful to ask whether the topic allows the researcher to demonstrate his or her independent intellectual competence; this is a requirement to demonstrate the successful completion of the apprenticeship of the postgraduate student (Preece 1994). Indeed, any postgraduate research training institution should have a review process prior to accepting a potential research student that ensures that the appropriate supervision and material support is available. However, this matter is not confined to postgraduate students, and all academic or research staff need to be aware of the resources, opportunities and limitations of their institution. This does not necessarily mean that they cannot conduct the research they wish to conduct. It may be possible in-house, but may, equally, require the researcher to seek further external infrastructure or staffing funds, or to develop collaborative links with experts and institutions with the necessary expertise and infrastructure.

10.6 Formulating a Research Problem: Practical Steps

Much of this discussion is covered in chapter 9, where we discuss the background to writing a research proposal, the practical end of formulating a research problem, and, in the end-of-chapter activities, run through some practical exercises to assist a researcher to develop a proposal. Here, we will summarize the key points. It takes a long time, often, to come to a clear view of what the problem actually is. The proposal requires a single sentence, and a short one at that, as a title that captures the essence of the problem; this is linked to a single sentence statement of aim. These can take some time to compose; I was advised, as a more junior academic, by a senior and very successful research colleague of mine, that he often found the writing of these two items, along with the often-requested one-hundred-word summary of the proposal, to be the hardest part of writing a proposal. He could knock off three thousand to five thousand words of background, prior research, big problem stuff, methods and so on, with ease, but bringing it back to a short sharp statement is very hard. This just needs practice; one way is to practise writing abstracts or summaries of papers. In short, the bodies who will be judging your proposal, to give you permission to either conduct the research, obtain ethics clearance, or be funded, need to be given a clear and immediate impression of what you want to do and why it is so important that you should be allowed and/or funded to do it (Boyd et al. 2008).

With your research aim clearly stated, you now need to progress to, first, writing a clear statement that justifies the research, indicating that you know where it sits within your discipline, and why there is an urgent or relevant need to conduct that particular research. This problem statement should convince an outside reader that this work is worth doing (and, hopefully, worth funding). A problem statement may take one of several formats, depending on for whom you are writing (Hay 2006). It should introduce the main focus of the research; the hypotheses to be used (stated as a formal hypothesis or in more descriptive terms, depending on the norms of the researcher's discipline); and the context of the research, especially in terms of the need for and importance of the outcomes or outputs (Preece 1994). The problem statement may also contain a statement of the theoretical approaches to be employed, and the framework for presenting the findings. The latter may be more important in some types of research, such as those in the social sciences where there may be a strong social activist, capacity building or development agenda (Williams 2000).

Before we continue with these proposal elements it is worth considering briefly the formulation of the hypothesis. Every discipline has its own views on hypothesis building; indeed, the differences of language between American English and English English places confusion at the heart of the matter with their different ways of using the terms "theory" and "hypothesis". The simple lesson is that each researcher needs to be aware of the disciplinary norms he or she should work within. Is he or she expected to generate a null hypothesis? If not, what type and form of hypothesis statement is expected? An interesting example of such a discussion comes from the world of business management research.

In 2007, the *Strategic Management Journal* published a special issue concerned with strategic process research; in doing so, the guest editors made some bold statement about what future research in their field should be – "more holistic, emphasize more team work, focus more on corporate managers and be more supportive of action research methodologies" (Chakravarthy and Doz 2007: 1). Such an agenda demands a realignment of research from prior and more reductionist approaches, and demands a rethink of the hypotheses established to govern future research. This followed a previous discussion in the same journal, one year earlier, in which Seth and Zinkhan (2006) made the following equally bold statement:

> The purpose of this paper is to expand the discussion of the state-of-the-science in strategy research. ... From a philosophy of science perspective, we argue that: (1) both inductive and deductive methods are valid ways of generating theory; (2) the falsificationist perspective provides an inadequate model for describing the process of theory testing; and (3) managers, researchers, public policy-makers, the popular press, and the public at large all have important roles to play in the knowledge development process. (p. 1)

Clearly there is an agenda discussion in the field of strategic management research, a discussion that will have important implications for future researchers working in this field. They are not alone, and every researcher should expect that such discussions will arise from time to time within his or her own discipline.

Next you need to formulate your project objectives, three or four short (one or two sentence) statements of the steps by which you intend to achieve your aim. The objectives of the research should be articulated with the problem statement; in other words, they reflect the problem aim and statement, and provide a frame by which these may be achieved.

Finally, the proposal needs to consider the nuts and bolts of how the research will be conducted, the methods and methodologies or data collection, collation, synthesis, initial analyses, higher-order interrogation and so on. What are the facilities, equipment or infrastructure needs? Who will conduct the various stages? What will the timeline be for implementing these methods? This may require statements of operational definitions, the major terms and phrases – every discipline has its own specialist terminology, and a proposal reader or funding agency may not be fully familiar with the specialist end of the discipline – so that both researchers and readers have a common understanding. At the stage of planning the methods and their application, there may be a reality hit, with the realization that things take longer than expected; that is the time for a variation of the plans before things get out of control.

A core activity within these practical steps of formulating the research problem is reflection on the context. A key activity in this regard is the writing of a literature review, so before we move one, here are some guiding comments on the literature review (Hay 2006). The literature review provides an account of what exists on the topic to be researched, and identifies the major thrust in existing research. Done well, it should draw attention to gaps in existing research and perhaps highlight misinterpretations of data in existing research. Importantly, it should affirm the viability of the research topic and assist in providing the rationale for the need for new research. Equally importantly, the literature review allows the researcher the opportunity to review previous conceptual and theoretical approaches to the topic and to advance his or her own conceptual or theoretical approaches. In practical terms, it also allows the researcher to review the methodologies previously used and compare them with those he or she is thinking about employing.

On a practical level, the literature review should be both descriptive and analytical. It should, of course, be up to date, and it should be specific to the topic to be researched. However, there are several types of literature review a researcher may adopt. In a general survey of the literature on the topic, the researcher attempts a comprehensive review of all available literature on the chosen topic, usually within a specified time period or language domain. The researcher may also limit the review to research-based literature and/or journal articles. A focused survey of the literature on the topic, on the other hand, can introduce a number of parameters or limitations for the selection of items of literature to be included. If the topic is restricted by time and space, the review will be selective in favour of the context of the research topic.

Whatever parameters are adopted, they must be consistent with the demands of the research topic. A systematic review is often and mainly employed in medical and health-related research projects, in which specific conditions must be fulfilled in order for experiments to be considered adequate evidence of the conclusion. In such cases, the review is restricted to specific experiments or studies that meet a predefined scientific protocol of the discipline, such as blind trials. For a full range of possibilities, the researcher may need to review published and unpublished studies – this is common in the health sciences, although not unique to these fields; many management fields also rely on what is known as the grey literature, unpublished, government, consulting or progress reports. These may contain policy or methodology statements otherwise not published publicly, data sets also not widely published, or the results of unsuccessful experiments that may contain pointers to alternative ways of interpreting the variables.

10.7 Formulating the Research Design: An Introduction

Once the project has been defined, and plans for implementation commenced, it is important to consider the design of a research project (Cresswell 1994). This, of course, is largely dependent on the quality of the research question that is being asked, which in turn determines the hypothesis to be tested and the specific aims and objectives to be addressed by the research project. The design of a research project is, therefore, largely dependent on the specific aims of the study, moderated, as indicated above, by the availability of appropriate resources.

The specific study design chosen by a researcher will be dependent on the researcher's philosophical context, his or her own inclinations and experience, and the norms of the discipline or part of the discipline with which the researcher identifies. There will be pragmatic influences, often imposed by external influences such as government policy requirement or funding agency agendas: is, for example, a research project focusing on public health issues interested in measuring exposures (for example, smoking) or outcomes (lung cancer) – both valid research matters, and each important in understanding a public health situation – or perhaps is the focus on the relationship between exposures and outcomes? We have dealt with the background to much of these influences above, but reinforce here the importance of understanding context, *sensu lato*, in determining and formulating research design.

10.8 Formulating the Research Design: Study Design

There is much written in the discipline-specific literature about study design, and a researcher should be aware of the relevant literature (for example, Cresswell 1994; Denzin and Lincoln 1994; Flyvbjerg 2001; Robson 2002; Neuman 2003). Study designs may be experimental or observational, depending on the aims and objectives of the study. Experimental designs include randomized controlled clinical trials and interventions in which case randomization overcomes selection bias (Preece 1994).

Observational study designs provide research projects that may be either descriptive or analytical, and may include: case reports, which report observations made on a single subject; case series reporting, a collection of case reports on a particular topic; experience of an individual or specific event; cross-sectional studies providing a snapshot of the existence or prevalence of, for example, a particular exposure or outcome; cohort studies in which groups are followed up over a period of time and the occurrence of an outcome (for example, disease) is compared between the groups, allowing for the calculation of incidence as well as establishing temporal relationships between exposure and outcome; and case-control studies that involve matching the cases of interest with appropriate controls with characteristics similar to the cases.

All these forms of case study research have their own advantages and disadvantages, and are suitable to certain types of study (see, for example, Bonoma 1985). Randomized controlled trials provide a useful example. In such trials, subjects are randomly allocated into treatment or exposure, with control groups not receiving that treatment; group differences at the start of the study are expected to be due to chance, and outcomes expected to be related to the differences in treatment. In considering the appropriate study design, however, it is necessary and important to recognize the existence of, for example, mixing of effects between the exposure, outcome and other factors that may be associated with the exposure, but which independently affect the risk.

The other factor is called the confounding factor, and may be dealt with in the study design in the analysis of the results. Such an experimental design places important demands on the analytical skills of the researcher, and not only does the researcher need to be skilled in the sampling, case selection, and clinical procedures, but also have a firm grasp of statistical or other modelling analysis techniques that allow reasonable conclusions to be derived from the data collected (Dowdy and Wearden 1991; Silverman 1993; Preece 1994). Examination of the previous literature will inform the researcher of the suitability and appropriateness of adopting any of these approaches, and practical training and experience will provide the skills base required of the researcher (Jones et al. 2000).

Overall, experimental study designs are used when there is a need to control the exposure of the sample being studied; from this exposure, measurable outcomes may be assessed, and hypotheses may be tested. However, the importance of understanding the methods cannot be understated.

10.9 Formulating the Research Design: Data Collection

As with the choice of experimental design, the choice of instrument for data collection is dependent largely on the type of investigation being considered, the number and nature of the variables of interest, and the available resources (Preece 1994; Leedy 1993). Here we will close with a look at two clusters of research instruments: the questionnaire and measurement scales.

In much social research, the questionnaire is a widely used data collection tool (Maykut and Morehouse 1994). It may, however, vary in form and complexity depending on research needs. Questionnaires may, for example, be self-administered or interviewer-administered depending on, among other factors, whether the information required is qualitative or quantitative, available resources and cost, length of time required to complete the questionnaire, sensitivity of the questions, and literacy of the respondents (Berg 1989).

Questions in the questionnaire may be open-ended, where the respondent's full answer is recorded, or closed, in which case the respondent is asked to choose an answer from a list provided. There are many guides as to suitable design of questions: they should be, for example, intelligible, unambiguous, appropriate so as to reflect knowledge, ethical and neither offensive nor loaded.

Previously conducted research may be used to guide the content and question items for the questionnaire. If this is not available, and even if it is, it is useful to solicit expert opinions from colleagues who have similar research experience. Additionally, it is always desirable to conduct appropriate focus group discussions with people similar to those to be included in the study and to trial a draft questionnaire. Having decided on the items to be included, the next step is to organize the questionnaire layout; while there is plenty of published advice available, the researcher may also be constrained by project standards or be guided by his or her own prior experience. How best to optimize the visual appeal of the questionnaire? What about variety of question types?

A major constraint on questionnaire design will be the time required to complete the questionnaire and how it may be administered (Brenner, Brown and Canter 1985). While it may be desirable to limit the time required, so as to minimize respondent fatigue and to optimize the accuracy of the information collected, the purpose of the questionnaire and the audience it is designed for, along with the type of data required, will all influence the size of the final document.

The order of questions will, likewise, depend on the purpose of the research and the design of the data collection. It is often the case that information questions (male/female, place of residence, and so on) are placed early in the questionnaire (although their importance should always be questioned, since very often these basic bits of information turn out not to be relevant, so why ask them?), while it may be preferable to position sensitive questions towards the end of the questionnaire, when the respondent might be more comfortable with the interviewer. Questions may follow a train of thought or logic of ideas, with questions on similar subjects being clustered together; alternatively, questions may be mixed in a situation where basically the same questions are being asked in different ways to test a respondent's real views.

Finally, consideration should be given to the administration of the survey tool and extraction of data; should questions be answered in coding (for example, 1 agree strongly to 5 disagree strongly) or on some other scale; should there be scope for the respondent's own words? How will these various types of responses be extracted from the completed questionnaires? And how will they be synthesized for analysis?

Once a draft questionnaire is completed it should be pretested. Prior to pretesting, it may be useful to seek the guidance of experienced field workers. Pretesting involves administration of the draft questionnaire to a representative sample; this may comprise approximately 10 per cent of the final sample size to be used, although very often a smaller sample will provide clear guidance about problems. This may be viewed as a dress rehearsal of the major data collection exercise, since the survey tool will be administered, and the data captured and analysed, according to the project plan. It should be borne in mind, however, that this is a critical exercise, completed to develop the tool; any data collected during the trial cannot be used in the research, other than as evaluative data in the questionnaire trial. In this sense, the pretest or pilot study allows for adjustments to the project process and logistics, and provide data to try in the design of tables and other mechanisms for data processing and presentation. This exercise also allows for the assessment of the types of variables and measurement scales, and gives an appreciation of the potential errors that may exist in the data collection processes.

Moving on to measurement scales, the researcher needs to be aware of the variables to be measured. Again, in choosing these, it is important to bear in mind the aims and objectives of the research project, and to reconcile the variables to be measured with the research question. Measurement of the defined variables should allow for a clear answer to the research question posed. The outcome or dependent variable is the measurement of principal interest in a research exercise. Conversely, the exposure or independent variable is one of many contributors to the outcome variable.

Variables may be quantitative or qualitative (Ashley and Boyd 2006). A quantitative or continuous variable – such as waist circumference or income or temperature – is usually measured numerically. A quantitative variable may be processed to produce a ratio (for example, rate or percentage) or interval (for example, income). A qualitative variable, on the other hand, is descriptive, although it is often coded as numeric responses (for example, Yes = 1, No = 2).

There are two kinds of qualitative variables: nominal, such as gender or ethnicity, and ordinal, such as level of agreement or disagreement with a response using numerical responses. A commonly used qualitative scale is the Likert scale, which records responses on a scale of 1 to 5. Such a scale reflects people's ability to differentiate over a five- or six-point scale comfortably; asking people to scale responses over even a ten-point scale, and certainly over a more refined scale, exceeds most people's skill at differentiation.

The contribution of any variable to answering a research question is largely determined on the reliability (precision or repeatability) and the accuracy of the measurement of that variable. The realization that measurements are not absolute values, but may be influenced by other variables, the precision of the measuring methods, the size of the sample, and so on, demands that the researcher fully understands the calibration and standards of any measuring instrument or equipment he or she is using, and fully understands the statistical constraints of measurements (Dowdy and Wearden 1991). This is especially important where the results of research are being reported to the public, who may be unaware of, and unable to understand, the uncertainties associated with the results, and therefore expect the results to be more certain than the researcher knows them to be. This can result in disillusionment among the public for research and researchers. The researcher, therefore, has a public duty to ensure careful description and publication of his or her results. This issue is further highlighted in the situation where data is being collected by one or more researchers or at multiple research sites.

There is an entire science of verification that can be applied to allow for comparison of separately collected data, providing checks for reliability and validity of the information being obtained, and allowing normalization if necessary (Preece 1994). During training, user reliability and validity must be evaluated in a standardized manner. In the case of interviewers, this is done by checking the level of agreement of the data collected by the interviewers, each having interviewed the same group of qualified respondents. In the case of instruments or measurements, these must be calibrated and standardized so as to produce an acceptable variation when used repeatedly by multiple users. As mentioned above, the pilot study provides the opportunity to evaluate the results obtained; it also allows for adjustments in the research question, the study design and data analysis. Once these are reviewed and checks made of the reliability and validity of measurements then it is reasonable to proceed with the research project. In the social sciences, methods of triangulation between unrelated data sources have been developed to provide for such checking (Maykut and Morehouse 1994).

10.10 Conclusions

The processes of formulating the research problem and conceptualizing the research design for a research project comprise a series of overlapping concerns. While it may be considered that a research project is largely a technical matter of identifying a problem to be addressed and then applying the technical skills we have acquired as trained and experienced researchers, this chapter has suggested that such an endeavour should be placed in a larger context. To that end, it is important for a researcher to consider his or her background as a researcher. The researcher must be aware of his or her own educational and social background, as well the disciplinary context within which he or she works. This provides a broad context for the proposed research, and may even provide questions to be considered.

Coming closer into the problem itself, the researcher now has to consider the institutions and individuals who may have an interest in or influence on the research, the stakeholders who will commission, support and fund the research, and the communities who will consume the results of the research. This draws attention to the range of possibilities for sources of research ideas and problems. Once these have emerged, we are now able to start thinking about the practicalities of developing a research problem and plan.

This chapter, of course, should be read in conjunction with others. Chapter 9, dealing in more detail with the research proposal, is of particular relevance. Once a sound research statement has been developed, identifying a valid problem and giving a statement of aim, justification, and objectives, it is time to think about the overall research design. This, again, places demands on the researcher to understand his or her social, disciplinary and scholarly context; this awareness continues into the stage at which the researcher is building the nuts and bolts of the study, that is, considering the specific study design for the day-to-day implementation of the research. This requires both experience and skill, plus various organizational habits. It also may result in a reassessment of the ideal plan, especially where the realities of funding, personnel, time and external demands may also place real constraints on how much data can be collected, collated and analysed, and, therefore, how large a research project can be completed.

The skills of a researcher in reviewing progress and being able to make operational decisions regarding changing direction, questions or scale become important at this stage. Two examples of data collection issues, the questionnaire and measurement and scaling, were presented. The descriptions should not be taken as full accounts of these large areas of research activity – there are entire textbooks published and courses taught on each topic, as indeed there are for all other methods the researcher may encounter – but as an indicator of the range of diversity of thinking and decision making researchers must be prepared for if their efforts at formulating and conceptualizing a valid and credible research problem are to yield positive and authoritative research outcomes.

References

Ashley, P., and W.E. Boyd. 2006. Quantitative and qualitative approaches to research in environmental management. *Australian Journal of Environmental Management* 13 (2): 70–78.

Berg, B. 1989. *Qualitative Research Methods for the Social Sciences*. Boston: Allyn and Bacon.

Bonoma, T.V. 1985. Case research in marketing: Opportunities, problems, and a process. *Journal of Marketing Research* 22: 199–208.

Boyd, W.E., R.L. Healey, S.W. Hardwick and M. Haigh, with contributions from P. Klein, B. Doran, J. Trafford and J. Bradbeer. 2008. "None of us sets out to hurt people": An essay on The Ethical Geographer and geography curricula in higher education. *Journal of Geography in Higher Education* 32: 37-50.

Brenner, M., J. Brown and D. Canter, eds. 1985. *The Research Interview: Uses and Approaches*. London: Academic Press.

Chakravarthy, B.S., and Y. Doz. 2007. Strategy process research: Focusing on corporate self-renewal. *Strategic Management Journal* 13: 5–14.

Chamberlayne, P., J. Bornat and T. Wengraf, eds. 2000. *The Turn to Biographical Method in Social Science*. London: Routledge.

Cloke, P., M. Doel, D. Matless, M. Phillips and N. Thrift. 1994. *Writing the Rural: Five Cultural Geographies*. London: Chapman and Hall.

Cresswell, J.W. 1994. *Research Design: Qualitative and Quantitative Approaches*. Thousand Oaks, CA: Sage.

Denzin, N.K., and Y.S. Lincoln, eds. 1994. *Handbook of Qualitative Research*. Thousand Oaks, CA: Sage.

Dowdy, S., and S. Wearden. 1991. *Statistics for Research*. 2nd ed. New York: John Wiley and Sons.

Flyvbjerg, B. 2001. *Making Social Science Matter: Why Social Inquiry Fails and How It Can Succeed Again*. Cambridge: Cambridge University Press.

Hay, I. 2006. *Communicating in Geography and the Environmental Sciences*. Melbourne: Oxford University Press.

Hughes, D., E. Seidman, and N. Williams. 1993. Cultural phenomena and the research enterprise: Toward a culturally anchored methodology. *American Journal of Community Psychology* 21: 687–703.

Jones, A., R. Duck, J. Weyers, and R. Reed. 2000. *Practical Skills in Environmental Science*. Essex: Prentice-Hall.

Leedy, P. 1993. *Practical Research: Planning and Design*. 5th ed. New York: Macmillan.

Martindale, D. 1988. *The Nature and Types of Sociological Theory*. 2nd ed. Long Grove, IL: Waveland Press.

Maykut, P., and R. Morehouse. 1994. *Beginning Qualitative Research: A Philosophic and Practical Guide*. London: Falmer Press.

Neuman, W.L. 2003. *Social Research Methods: Qualitative and Quantitative Approaches*. 5th ed. Boston: Allyn and Bacon.

Preece, R. 1994. *Starting Research: An Introduction to Academic Research and Dissertation Writing*. London: Pinter.

Robson, C. 2002. *Real World Research*. 2nd ed. Oxford: Blackwell.

Schön, D. 1987. *Educating the Reflective Practitioner*. San Francisco, CA: Jossey-Bass.

Seth, A., and G. Zinkhan. 2006. Strategy and the research process: A comment. *Strategic Management Journal* 12: 75–82.

Silverman, D. 1993. *Interpreting Qualitative Data: Methods for Analysing Talk, Text and Interaction*. London: Sage.

Williams, M. 2000. *Science and Social Science: An Introduction*. London: Routledge.

Chapter 10 Activities

Activity 30

Using a research question you can identify in your area of scholarly or academic expertise or interest, discuss the relevance of the research to the university, the nation or the region you are working in, and the world.

How does it relate to your own research or scholarly interests? Should a research topic meet all relevancy requirements at all levels to be regarded as viable?

What are the implications for the research if it does not? For your own research question, consider to what extent the relevance at local (yourself, your university), regional (nation or region) or global levels played a role in your selection of the research problem.

Activity 31

Develop a problem statement around the research problem identified in activity 30. You may find the activities in chapter 9 helpful in this regard. Remember that the statement has to be very tight, and provide an immediate sense of what is proposed, how it will be achieved and why it is important to conduct the research. Remember that the importance of the research needs to be expressed in terms of both the urgency of the problem to be tackled and the likelihood that a viable outcome will be provided.

Activity 32

- If you are working with a group of researchers, exchange their problem statements with yours, and read them through carefully. Do you get an immediate sense of the problems? Does the need for the research seem well justified? Does the proposal seem likely to yield a valid and useful outcome? Rephrase their problem statements in your own words.

- Write a short evaluation of their problem statement (aim for no more than one page), in which you provide a balanced critique, that is, do not just say how poor or impractical it is, if that is what you think, but consider ways in which either the statement or the problem itself could be improved. In other words, write a positively constructive review of the statement.

Activity 33

- Building on your research problem from the previous activities, outline the main elements of a research design. Start with identifying three objectives, and identify the principal technique or method you would use to gather the relevant data. This, of course, demands that you can describe the relevant data required to address the problem. In a short paragraph, describe each method: what sampling and analytical methods will each require, what costs will be attached to these, who will conduct them, and how long will each take to complete? This should be a short account (no more than two pages).
- Exchange your summary with others in the group, and compare notes. Repeat activity 32, but critiquing the others' summaries of methods this time.

Activity 34

Explain how you will design your study to ensure that the *independent* variable has the maximum opportunity to have its effect on the *dependent* variable, while the effects that are attributed to *extraneous* and *chance* variables are minimized. This should be done, initially, as an individual activity, followed by comparing notes and seeking areas of agreement within your group.

You may find that this activity requires some group discussion while you work out what your independent and dependent variables are. You may also discover that in some research the answers are not very clear-cut; if this applies to you, consider why.

11

Using Statistics to Effectively Capture and Analyse the Real World

▸ SERWAN M.J. BABAN *AND* BRUCE LAUCKNER

11.1	Introduction
11.2	Why Sample
11.3	The Sampling Frame
11.4	Sampling Methods and Representative Samples
11.4.1	Sampling Methods
11.4.1.1	The Purposive or Subjective Sampling Approach
11.4.1.2	The Probability Sampling Approach
11.4.1.3	Sampling and Mapping Spatial Data
11.5	A Strategy to Implement Sampling
11.5.1	Thinking It Through
11.6	Processing the Data
11.6.1	Stages in Data Processing
11.6.1.1	Examination of Data
11.6.1.2	Initial Analysis
11.6.1.3	More Detailed Scientific Analysis
11.6.1.4	Presentation and Write-up
Reference	
Chapter 11 Activities	

11.1 Introduction

How can we find out the following information?
1. The average house price in a country.
2. The number of people who watched the world heavyweight boxing contest on television.
3. The proportion of households with a microwave.
4. The time spent by people travelling to and from work.

The first thing that needs to be done is to define more clearly each of the above requirements. What is the average house price in a country? The average of the price of houses recently sold or the average price of all houses whether recently sold or not? If the former, when is recent? The last week? The last month? In the case of the number of people who watched the boxing, does this refer to the people in a country of study or worldwide? Let us therefore define the information required with less ambiguity:

1. The average price of houses sold in the United Kingdom during the last month.
2. The worldwide television audience for the world heavyweight boxing contest.
3. The proportion of households in Barbados with a microwave.
4. The time spent by people who live and work in the Greater Kingston area in Jamaica travelling to and from work each day.

The research data needed is now quite clearly defined and, theoretically, all answers can be attempted by finding all the target populations and collecting the required data.

1. The average price of houses sold in the United Kingdom during the last month. This would require a list of all the houses sold. This could be done by trying to find all the real estate agents or by making contact with the government department that deals with transfer of land titles (and then going to the buyers/sellers and finding out the price).
2. The worldwide television audience for the world heavyweight boxing contest. This would require house-to-house surveys in each country where the fight was shown (but remember to include people who were watching in hotel rooms, sports bars, and so on).

3. The proportion of households in Barbados with a microwave. This could be done by visiting all households and asking whether there is a microwave in the home.
4. The average time travelling to and from work in the Greater Kingston area in Jamaica. This can be ascertained by a house-to-house census in the target area.

Each of the above methods is extremely costly, sometimes prohibitively costly, and beyond the budget of most research projects. The methods require censuses of the target populations. But it is a mistake to think that a census is always the most reliable way of gathering information.

Take the case of the average height of sugarcane plants in a five hectare field, three months after planting. It might take several days to measure all the plants, at the end of which the cane has grown so the average worked out will not refer to any particular point in time. Even if resources (time, and so on) are available, the scale of the census required often means exhaustion and fatigue. Under these conditions errors abound and these errors tend to be biased. Cases in point are recent general population and farming censuses in the Caribbean where some of the results reported were quite doubtful. Therefore, to find out research information of the types above (and many more types of research information) it is better to take a sample. This will be cheaper, much more feasible and, if properly designed, may even be more reliable than attempting a full census.

Research in many different fields often requires us to obtain a sample to estimate a population value. This is usually a mean (average) or proportion but sometimes we are interested in other statistics, such as the variation (variability) of the data and also such information as percentiles.

Some further examples of sampling situations include the following:

- The price of food at a market.
- The total yield of a certain crop (for example, orange or coconut) in a given season.
- The attitudes of school children (for example, what subjects are interesting; what do you think of your teachers?)
- Market research to find consumer preferences for packaging of merchandise.
- Quality control of a manufacturing process.

- Public opinion polls.
- Family income and expenditure studies.
- The state of preparedness of a population for disasters such as hurricanes or earthquakes.
- The status of health of the population (for example, numbers who can access health care; numbers of hospital-treated patients who recover/do not recover).
- Estimates of consumption of utilities (water, transport, electricity, telephones and the like).
- The cost of maintenance of electricity supply plants (lines, poles and so on) over the next ten years.

In summary, a number of questions need to be answered: How should these samples be chosen? How large should they be? How much reliance can be placed on the sample measurements as estimates of the characteristics of thousands (sometimes millions) of other people in the target population?

11.2 Why Sample

Sampling is desirable, for several reasons:

- It is quicker.
- It is cheaper.
- It may be impossible to measure everything.
- Where the population is changing quite rapidly we may wish to measure it at one moment in time only.

As already mentioned, an example of the last reason is when we are measuring plant height. Another example is when we want to know weather information on a daily basis. In the United Kingdom, for example, there are hundreds of weather stations. Certain of these are chosen as sampling sites and current weather information is sent regularly to the Meteorological Office. No attempt is made to immediately receive and analyse the weather at every location.

11.3   The Sampling Frame

This is the setting in which the population to be sampled is found and represents the total number of items (the population) from which the sample is taken.

It is important to be completely clear about the nature of the sampling frame because this has a bearing on the reliability of the results of a sample taken from it. Examples of possible sampling frames include the following:

1. A telephone directory, from which addresses can be sampled. The sampling frame is people who possess telephones and are not unlisted. The sample may be biased for several reasons:

    - Less wealthy people (particularly those in remote communities) do not have land line telephones.
    - People with unlisted numbers may differ from those who are listed.
    - These days many people are abandoning their land line phones and using only mobile/cell phones which are not listed in telephone directories.

2. House occupants who are to be interviewed. This is biased against people who are difficult to find at home. There are also bias problems caused by people who refuse to answer your questions.

Spatial sampling frames, such as maps and satellite images, are of particular relevance to geo-based scientists as, often, the purpose of the study entails aspects of geographic location, such as the calculation of areal coverage, the recognition of a distribution pattern or the analysis of spatial variations. Spatial sampling frames differ from nonspatial frames in that geographic location influences the choice of individuals from the sampled population.

The precise characteristics of the sampling frame must be known if fair conclusions are to be drawn from the sample. Above all one must avoid *bias*.

11.4   Sampling Methods and Representative Samples

Selecting a sampling method needs to be guided by its ability to choose samples that are *representative* of the population. For example, suppose that a standard grid square method of selection is used to sample an urban area with mixed housing density, and areas A and B occupy equal land areas, but area A contains one thousand houses and area B contains one hundred houses. It is likely that the outcome will produce a sample that contains too few houses from area B and too many houses from area A. Assuming that the intended sampling rate was 5 per cent overall, this might mean choosing ten houses from area A and ten houses from area B, since they both occupy approximately the same area of land. As there are one thousand houses in area A, the representation rate in this area is 10/1,000, or approximately 1 per cent. For area B, however, the representation rate is 10/100, or approximately 10 per cent. As the intended sampling rate was 5 per cent, area A is *underrepresented*, whereas area B is *overrepresented*. This would have serious repercussions on the results of the survey. Therefore, we have to be very careful in choosing samples; in this case we could still follow the grid sampling method (if this is most convenient), but we need a stratified approach, discussed below.

When we carry out stratified sampling, we divide the population into strata where the characteristics of the population within each stratum are similar, but there may be differences as we move from one stratum to other strata. The choice of sampling method should be made so as to avoid, as far as possible, this and other types of bias.

11.4.1 Sampling Methods

Depending on the sampling frame, sampling methods can be divided into spatial (locational) or nonspatial (nonlocational). Selecting the most suitable method for a specific study depends on the nature of the situation, the purpose for which the sample is required as well as an understanding of the distinctions between sampling approaches and the handling necessary when sampling spatial data and mapping spatial phenomena. There are two main approaches for selecting samples, the purposive or subjective approach and the probability approach. Many surveys use the former approach as it is usually simpler, but statisticians will always prefer the latter (probability) approach. The advantage of the probability approach is that *sampling error* can be calculated. Sampling error is the degree to which a sample might differ from the population. When inferring to the population, results are reported plus or minus the sampling error. In nonprobability sampling, the degree to which the sample differs from the population remains unknown.

11.4.1.1 The Purposive or Subjective Sampling Approach

This approach is also referred to as the nonprobability approach. Here samples are chosen subjectively by the investigator; therefore, samples are selected from the population in some nonrandom manner. Purposive samples are not typical, but are likely to be unusual and biased. It is difficult to draw valid conclusions about a population if the measurements from it have been sampled purposively. For example, an environmentalist examining landslides may decide to examine thirty of these along a main road in a mountainous area as these are accessible, practical and achievable. Sampling methods under this approach include the following four methods:

1. Convenience sampling. This method is used in exploratory research where the researcher is interested in getting an inexpensive approximation of the truth. It is often used during preliminary research efforts to establish a general idea and a coarse estimate of the results, without incurring the cost or time required to select a random sample.
2. Judgement sampling. This is a modification of convenience sampling where the researcher selects the sample based on judgement. For example, a researcher may decide to draw the entire sample from one or two "representative" locations, even though the population includes many locations. When using this method, the researcher must be certain that the sample chosen is truly representative of the entire population.
3. Quota sampling. This method is the nonprobability equivalent of stratified sampling. Therefore, the researcher first identifies the strata and their proportions as they are represented in the population. Then convenience or judgement sampling is used to select the required number of samples from each stratum. For example, the researcher may decide to interview a certain number of people in each age group and will select people at a sampling location until the required numbers in each age group are interviewed.
4. Snowball sampling. This method is a special nonprobability method used when the desired sample characteristic is rare. It may be extremely difficult or cost prohibitive to locate respondents in these situations. Snowball sampling relies on referrals from initial subjects to generate additional subjects.

11.4.1.2   The Probability Sampling Approach

In this approach the preferences of the investigator are not allowed to influence the process of selecting samples. Every member of the population must have an independent and known chance of being selected as a sample. When this condition is met, the selected sample can be considered representative and unbiased. Statistical methods can then be used to draw valid references about the population from the characteristics of the sample. Sampling methods under this approach are discussed below.

Simple random sampling. This is the purest form of probability sampling; here the choice of individuals for inclusion in the sample is left entirely to chance. Picking names from a hat or choosing spots on a map where raindrops pitch are therefore random sampling. Here, the choice of any particular individual is in no way influenced by the researcher at any stage in the sampling process. Once one name or one spot on a map has been picked there is no way of knowing which name or spot will be picked next. A simple random sampling method should satisfy two important criteria:

- Every individual must have an equal chance of inclusion in the sample throughout the sampling procedure.
- The selection of any particular individual should not affect the chance of selection of any other individual.

To put these criteria in more formal probability terms: the probabilities of inclusion in the sample must be equal and independent of each other. So, if the aim is to pick a random sample of ten people from a population of one hundred, every person should have the same 10/100 or 0.1 probability of selection throughout the process.

Systematic sampling. A systematic sample is one that is selected in some regular way. It is also called an *Nth selection* technique. After the required sample size has been calculated, every *N*th record is selected from a list of population members. Consider again taking a sample of ten people from a population of one hundred. Taking every tenth household from the list of one hundred will produce a systematic sample. Intuitively, this would seem to produce an even, and therefore "fair", coverage of the population in the sense that sample members are selected evenly from throughout the list, avoiding the "bunching" that can often occur with random sampling. Certainly in a systematic sample no individual can be picked more than once. It may not be immediately obvious that this "evenness" does not necessarily produce a sample that is unbiased and representative of the population from which it is taken. However, it is not difficult to show that systematic sampling does not give every individual in a population the same chance of selection. Suppose a 10 per cent systematic sample is being taken from a list of one hundred names. If every tenth name is selected starting from number one, then the first, eleventh, twenty-first, thirty-first, and so on, name has a probability of 1.0 of selection. All the other names on the list (90 per cent of the names on the list) have lost all chance of representation in the sample. This can be overcome by having a random starting point between one and ten. Suppose this is four; then the fourth, fourteenth, twenty-fourth, and so on, names are taken. Thus, at least before we choose our random starting point every individual has an equal chance of being chosen. However, there is zero probability of two names next to each other on the list being chosen; therefore, the selection of an individual does affect the chance of selection of another individual.

Systematic sampling has certain practical advantages over random sampling. In particular, it is usually easier and quicker to implement. Both systematic and random samples should be able to estimate without bias the population characteristic of interest (for example, mean number, proportion with a characteristic and so on), but we can only reliably estimate the precision of this characteristic (that is, how accurate it is) if we have a truly random sample. The important point is to ensure that the sampling method does not introduce a consistent bias into the sample, as there is danger that a systematic method will pick out regularities in the base. For example, when sampling plants in the field, taking every, say, tenth plant might result in selecting only plants at the end of a row, or may lead to plants being selected according to some uniform fertility pattern.

Stratified sampling. Very frequently a simple random or systematic sample may not contain enough information about groups or strata with small populations and particular spatial dimensions. A stratum is a subset of the population that shares at least one common characteristic. The researcher first identifies the relevant strata and their actual representation in the population. Random sampling is then used to select subjects for each stratum until the number of subjects in that stratum is proportional to its frequency in the population. For example, if we wish to estimate journey times to and from work in all the different suburbs of London we have to have a reasonable sample size in each of the suburbs. If we are sampling spatially then a simple random sample may not contain many points in certain parts of the area which are of interest. Therefore, there is a need to divide the population into groups or strata and to ensure that samples are selected from each group or stratum regardless of size and dimensions.

It should be noted that the proportions sampled in each stratum do not have to be equal. Take the example above with one stratum (area A) containing one thousand houses and another (area B) one hundred houses. Here it was decided to select 5 per cent in each stratum, that is, fifty houses in area A and five in area B. This, however, may lead to concerns that only five houses may not cover all the likely population variability; the sampling methodologies and calculations of population estimates allow us to vary the percentage sampled in the different strata, so we may decide to sample ten houses (10 per cent) in area B to give a better representation of the population in that stratum.

11.4.1.3   Sampling and Mapping Spatial Data

Many environmental and geo-based studies are concerned with the spatial distribution of a variable, such as geology, natural vegetation or rainfall, which varies continuously from place to place. For a large area it would be impossible to measure the value of this variable at every point. The aim of sampling in this situation is first of all to provide as economically as possible and as accurately as possible a description of the spatial distribution of that variable. The most likely follow-up to this procedure would be the production of a map.

In spatial sampling a major distinction can be made between random and systematic methods. The difference from nonspatial sampling is that the aim is to select points or quadrates from a continuous surface rather than items from a list. The simplest method of spatial random sampling consists of using a pair of random numbers to define a pair of coordinates (easting and northing) which can be used to locate on a map the points or quadrates that are to make up the sample.

In the stratified spatial random sampling method, the population is divided into strata and a random or systematic sample taken in each stratum. For example, suppose a geographer investigating land use/cover patterns in an area decides to sample 5 per cent of the land use/cover types within the study area. He can use the current land use/cover map as a sampling frame, that is, as a basis for selecting the sample. It would be possible to use random numbers to pick a 5 per cent sample from the whole of the register, but instead, the researcher prefers to select 5 per cent of the samples in each land use/cover type within the study area. The sample obtained in this way is a 5 per cent random sample of the map stratified by land use/cover types. The advantage of this form of spatial stratification is that it ensures an equal degree of representation of each land use/cover type regardless of size and dimensions, producing in effect a more even spatial coverage without completely sacrificing the randomness necessary for subsequent statistical testing. The use of a global random sample could result in some land use/cover types being seriously underrepresented so that important local elements of the overall pattern could be overlooked. If planning decisions were subsequently made on the basis of such a survey, this local underrepresentation could have serious consequences. Note that if a certain area of land contains more variation than another it may once again be desirable to vary the percentage sampled from stratum to stratum. Hence, this example is similar to the example in nonspatial sampling where housing density varied. As indicated, selecting the most appropriate sampling method requires an understanding of the phenomenon, the mapped object being studied and the type of spatial pattern that it is most likely to follow. Generally speaking, spatial patterns can be categorized into the following:

1. Clustered (or positive autocorrelation) distribution. The mapped objects will be concentrated in certain areas. In the case of plants this pattern is produced due to the environment in these locations being particularly hospitable to the type of plant.
2. Dispersed (or negative autocorrelation) distribution. The mapped objects will be spread out. This type of pattern is sometimes found in desert plants that compete for water, or in established forests where, in competition for sunlight and root space, the older and more successful trees will overshadow and kill off smaller and less vigorous trees of like requirements. One simple way to differentiate between clustered and dispersed patterns is by measuring the distance from a given sample to

the nearest neighbour of the same kind. This distance is usually very small in the clumped pattern, and there will be relatively little variation in this distance if the clusters are uniformly dense.

3. Random distribution. The mapped objects will be neither concentrated nor spread out in an anticipated manner. Therefore, the objects in this spatial pattern will have an equally likely chance of being at any location, regardless of other objects in the vicinity.

When analysing the distribution of spatial features (such as land uses, vegetation types and so on), measurements are taken at particular points, along lines or traverses or in small areas or quadrates and as follows:

1. Point sampling. Individual points are chosen and the feature is sampled at those points. If sampling land uses, for example, one might select ten grid square intersections on a land use map and find out the land use at each of the ten points (figure 11.1).
2. Line sampling. Lines are drawn across the map and land uses (for example) along the lines are noted (figure 11.1).
3. Area or quadrant sampling. Squares are chosen on the map or ground and the occurrence of the feature you are interested in is noted within that square (figure 11.1). Advantages of the quadrant sampling techniques are that they provide information about spatial distributions both *within* the samples (the quadrants themselves) and *between* the samples.

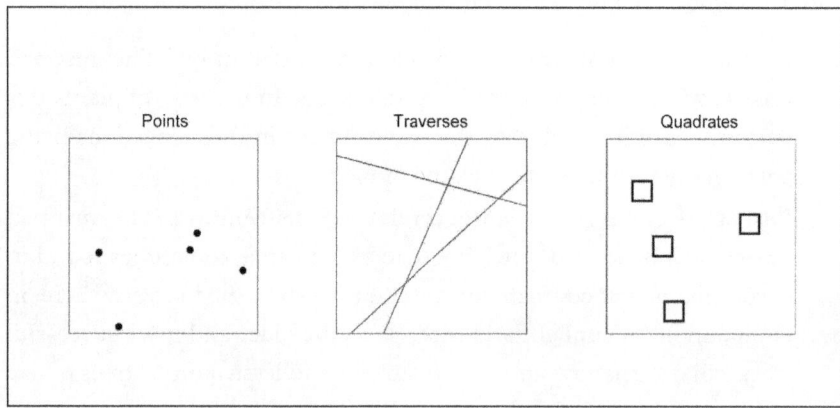

Figure 11.1. Area sampling methods.

There are several methods for deciding the location of sampling points, traverses and quadrates. The most commonly used for points, the same principles apply also to traverses and quadrate sampling, are illustrated in figure 11.2. Figure 11.2a represents the spatial distribution of pine, teak and forest within a study area.

Figure 11.2b shows a random sample of twenty points, selected by first drawing a grid over the area and numbering the grid lines. The position of each sampling point is determined by drawing two random numbers, the first to fix the position on the x axis, the second on the y axis. Where the two coordinates cross, the sampling point is located. This method is continued until sufficient points have been selected and positioned. Points that fall outside the boundary of the study area are rejected.

Figure 11.2c shows a systematic sample of points selected from the same study area by superimposing a grid of suitable dimensions over the area. The initial point is located randomly and all others determined by a fixed interval.

In a *stratified* sampling, the area is divided into subareas, within which the sample points are chosen randomly (figure 11.2d).

In terms of applying these approaches to area/quadrate sampling, the following case studies represent issues the investigator needs to take into consideration when designing sampling campaigns.

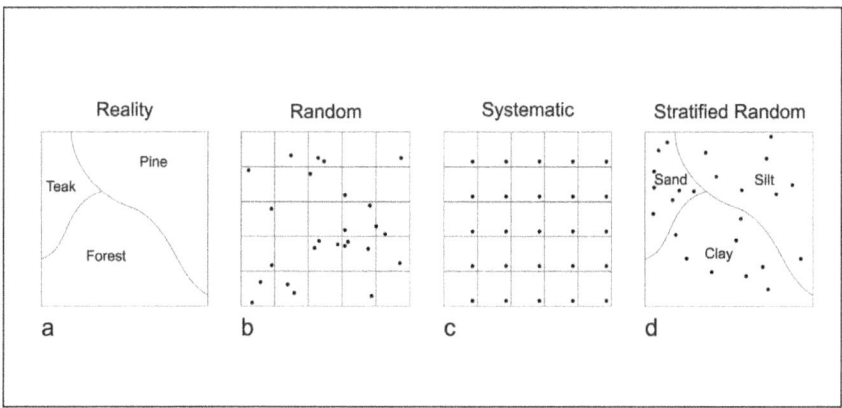

Figure 11.2. Point sampling methods.

Case Study 1

Assume that you are interested in mapping sand outcrops in a study area (figure 11.3a) and you have chosen a systematic grid sampling method to capture the data, working on the principle that the dominant class within a grid will represent the entire grid. Here the issue becomes the size of the grid in relation to the mapping object. Choosing a large grid size (figure 11.3b1) might not detect the object of interest (figure 11.3b2), while a smaller gird size (figure 11.3c1) will successfully capture the sand outcrop in the study area (figure 11.3c2). Clearly under a similar scenario particular attention needs to be given to the relationship between the smallest object being mapped and the grid size being used to map it. As a basic rule, the grid size needs to be about a third of the length or 25 per cent of the area of the smallest object being mapped.

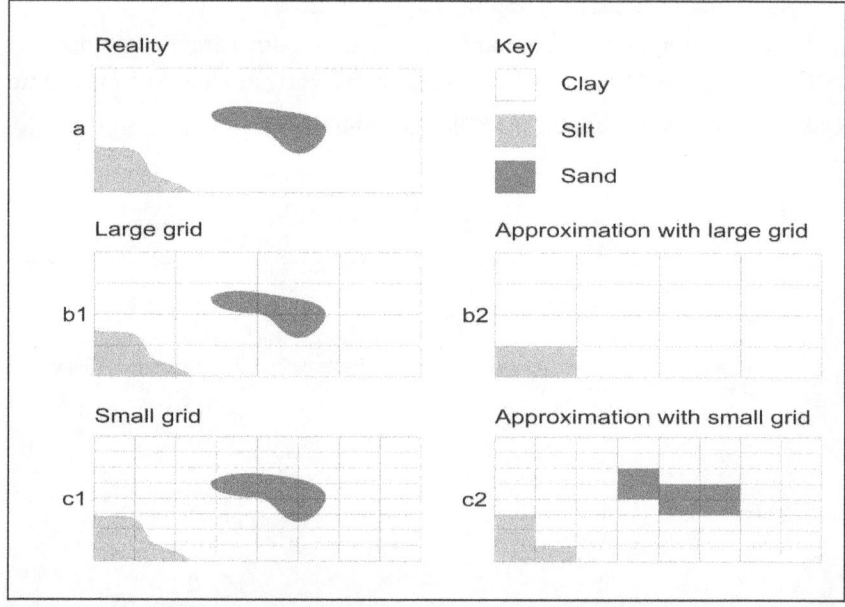

Figure 11.3. The relationship between the dimensions and orientations of an object in the field and the grid size used to map the object. Note that the large grid (b1) will not capture the sand (b2), whereas the smaller grid (c1) captures and maps it correctly (c2).

Case Study 2

Trees in an orchard are routinely planted in a square array, with 4 metres between rows and columns. If we apply quadrant samples systematically on a square grid with an 8-meter spacing, precisely twice the spacing of the trees, we could completely miss all the trees. Systematic sampling can cause all kinds of artefacts when the sample roughly coincides with a multiple of the spacing of the objects of interest. To deal with this problem, a method called systematic unaligned sampling is used, in which the sampling interval and orientation are specifically adjusted to avoid alignment with the phenomenon of interest (Congalton 1988). The stratified sampling strategy is used when we have some information about the study site. This strategy involves dividing the study region into relatively homogeneous units, and sampling each unit separately.

Case Study 3

In a programme for monitoring a group of insect pests that damage farm crops, the target area may have several different crops under cultivation. In a stratified sampling programme, it is possible to explicitly take the spatial distributions of the crops into account. We might sample more intensively in fields growing crops on which the target insects are known to inflict great economic damage, to be able to take measures as early as possible in the growing season. In contrast, we might work less in crops on which the insects are known to cause little damage. An important use of stratified sampling is seen when the geographic region has important but rare polygonal areas. Consider a programme to determine the distribution of land cover as a function of cover type. In a random sample, the number of observations of a particular type of land cover will be proportional to the area of the cover. Common land cover types will be sampled frequently, and rare land cover types may never be observed. To compensate, we can use a stratified sampling plan to make sure that we visit examples of every known land cover type, and improve our knowledge of the rare types.

11.5 A Strategy to Implement Sampling

There are a number of clear stages to be performed to carry out these types of study:

1. Definition of the population (sampling frame)
2. Decision on what to measure (including questionnaire design/data collection procedures/measurement)
3. Data collection methodology (type of data collection – observation, interview)
4. Sampling methodology design
5. Pilot study
6. Data collection
7. Data analysis/processing
8. Presentation/publication of results

11.5.1 Thinking It Through

Think carefully about your sampling method before you begin. Assuming that you chose the probability sampling approach, a checklist of the decisions that must be made when sampling will include

1. Do I need to sample?
2. If so, what is my sampling frame? Is it biased?
3. Do I need to sample spatially (on a map or on the ground)? If so, shall I use point, line or quadrate sampling?
4. Shall I use simple random, stratified or systematic sampling methods?
5. How many samples shall I collect?

It is common practice in many fields to use a *pilot study* – a rapid or preliminary look at the population of interest – before any major sampling effort. The pilot study is usually designed for three purposes:

1. It permits us to gather some information in the field, possibly from the target area. This small amount of information can be used for adjusting quadrant size, selecting the total number of samples for the principal sampling effort, testing the observational methods, and (where possible) developing some general characteristics of the study population. Such

a pilot study could permit us to choose an unaligned sampling strategy and could prevent us from being misled.
2. In the case of stratified sampling, the pilot study could provide the necessary information to develop or test the initial stratification.
3. It allows for checking of the questionnaire or data collection instrument. The pilot study permits us to check our original hypotheses about the costs and time that would be required for gathering the data, and thus avoid costly mistakes and poor data quality.

11.6   Processing the Data

This section will give some general hints on how to analyse and present the data that has been generated during the research study. This is a very large topic and depends very much on the type of investigation that has been carried out. Surveys, spatial investigations and experiments have quite different approaches and techniques for analysis, each of which needs a large textbook to be described properly. However, perhaps the most crucial stages of a research study are the design of the data collection and the actual collection. The design has been covered already and the collection follows by rigid adherence to the design strategy. If these stages are done well then a faulty or misleading analysis can always be corrected by returning to the data gathered and starting again. However, poor design and data collection cannot be corrected without restarting the whole research project.

11.6.1   Stages in Data Processing

11.6.1.1   Examination of Data

This is a continuous process from the time the first data is gathered and will involve continuous quality checking of data. The reasons for missing observations should be found and, if possible, missing data should be collected again (but if the value might have changed, for example, a plant or animal may have grown after it should have been measured, then the observation must remain missing). Impossibly large or small values should be checked for errors and if necessary be collected again, or declared missing. Values that look unlikely (even if not actually impossible) should be checked and corrected if necessary. Although a missing value is better than an incorrect one (especially if the incorrect value is very wrong), missing values do "spoil" your data collection and make the analyses less efficient and less reliable. Therefore they should be avoided if possible, or kept to a minimum if not possible to avoid.

11.6.1.2 Initial Analysis

Initial analyses will include simple techniques such as can be found in the descriptive statistics menus of statistical software. These include means, percentages, cross tabulations, standard errors and so on. They can be backed by examination of simple graphical techniques such as pie charts and histograms. If the data collection is done over a long period of time, such as a calendar year, analyses such as these can be done every month or so to give a feel for trends and type of results to be expected.

11.6.1.3 More Detailed Scientific Analysis

The data examination and initial analyses can be done using Excel spreadsheets or possibly software such as Access. However, at some stage, more powerful statistical techniques will be needed to give the results scientific validity. These statistical analyses cannot be done very well (or at all in most cases) using standard spreadsheet packages, and purpose-built statistical software such as SPSS, SAS, GENSTAT, and the like, should be used. Most of these statistical software packages can import data from Excel and other well-known spreadsheets, but it is advisable to use a statistical package from very early in the processing stages, even from data entry in most cases. There are many examples of novice researchers using Excel to enter and summarize their data in all sorts of attractive ways, but with no attempt at any proper scientific analysis. Surveys will need to look at statistical tests of hypothesis about the means of data gathered, examination of odds ratios in two-way tables (usually by a chi square test) and also fitting of regression models to examine the relationships between the different variables collected. Experiments may need to be analysed using analysis of variance techniques and spatial analysis. Many research projects will need examination of data using multivariate techniques; general linear modelling and REML are among powerful modern methods suitable for a very wide range of data analyses.

11.6.1.4 Presentation and Write-up

This should start with some attractive diagrams showing the important results and backed up with some of the initial basic statistics calculated. Beware, however, that your diagrams are not misleading or ambiguous. A diagram that looks very pretty to the uninformed eye may look absurd to the well-trained scientist.

The most important part of the results is the presentation of the more detailed statistical analyses, complete with probability values and significance tests where applicable. This is where the quality of your research output will be judged by your examiners and peers. It is also where you justify any conclusions made. This is also where your findings are likely to be challenged. If your research methodology and statistical analyses are sound, you will be able to meet these challenges. If your research methodology is sound, but your analyses are weak then you will have to re-analyse the data, correcting your errors. But if your research methodology itself is faulty, your whole project is a failure. You will have to give up or start again from scratch. So ensure that your methodology is sound and you will probably get there in the end.

Reference

Congalton, R.G. 1988. Using spatial autocorrelation analysis to explore the errors in maps generated from remotely sensed data. *Photogrammetric Engineering and Remote Sensing* 54 (5): 587–92.

Chapter 11 Activities

Activity 35

- List and explain the aims in selecting a sample.
- List and explain the factors affecting the inferences drawn from a sample.
- Develop a sampling strategy for your research by defining the relevant requirements in the following steps.
  1. Define the population.
  2. Develop a sampling plan (probability or nonprobability).
  3. Determine the sample size.
  4. Implement sampling procedures and compare critical values of sample to population.

Activity 36

Figure 11.4 shows a lake and its surrounding areas. You are an environmentalist carrying out research into the effects of suspended solids on lake habitats. All habitats within the lake have been accurately mapped using remotely sensed data and extensive filed surveys. Your task is to produce a map showing the relative magnitude and distribution of suspended solids within the lake for comparison with the habitat map. Time and money are both limited so that, in the first instance at least, you can only afford to make thirty measurements of suspended solids.

Decide on a method of sampling, and then pick thirty points inside the study area at which to take measurements. For the purpose of this exercise, measurements are made by consulting figure 11.5, which shows the suspended solids levels for the whole area. If you use a tracing of the map in your sampling procedure and place it over figure 11.5, the suspended solids levels for your thirty sample points can be read directly off the diagram.

On your map of suspended solids, using only your thirty point values, draw in isolines at intervals of 5 per cent.

USING STATISTICS TO CAPTURE AND ANALYSE THE REAL WORLD ◀ 165

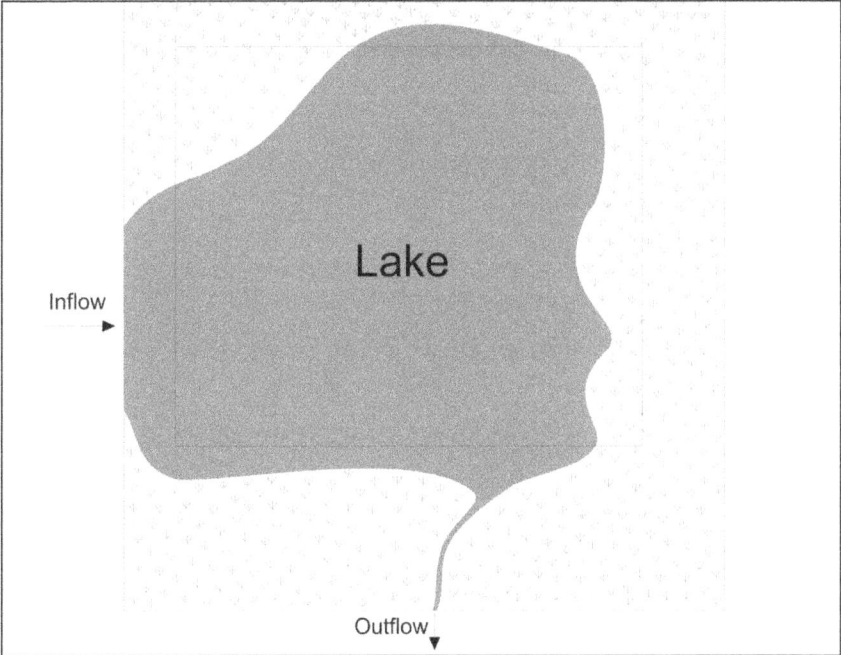

Figure 11.4. A lake, showing the boundary of the study area.

1	1	1	1	1	1	7	18	19	21	21	21	17	13	11	3	1	1
1	1	1	1	2	7	21	21	23	22	21	21	21	19	17	11	3	1
1	1	1	1	8	29	31	25	23	22	22	23	22	21	21	14	2	1
1	1	1	7	30	30	29	27	25	25	25	24	23	22	21	13	3	1
2	8	9	31	32	30	29	28	26	27	26	25	26	26	22	14	2	1
14	38	37	36	35	35	31	31	29	28	27	25	25	25	21	13	2	1
39	39	37	38	39	35	35	33	33	31	30	28	26	19	12	3	1	1
39	38	39	38	39	39	38	36	34	31	29	28	27	25	18	3	1	1
40	39	31	39	38	38	39	37	36	34	34	31	28	23	31	3	1	1
41	39	41	39	39	38	39	37	36	34	34	31	27	23	31	5	2	1
41	41	41	40	39	38	39	37	37	37	33	31	28	22	18	7	6	1
40	40	40	39	38	39	39	38	37	33	31	30	24	21	16	6	5	1
40	39	39	39	38	38	38	38	37	32	30	27	23	21	17	8	2	1
37	38	39	38	38	38	37	37	36	34	30	22	17	16	15	9	1	1
31	37	38	36	37	34	33	31	28	23	19	17	16	16	12	9	3	1

Figure 11.5. Suspended solids levels expressed as a percentage.

Hint: Work in groups and let each individual follow a different sampling method, then compare and discuss the outcome from each method.

Activity 37

Using figure 11.4:

1. Construct a grid reference system to cover the study area with intervals of 10 mm, 15 mm and 20 mm.
2. Take a reading at every second, fourth and eighth grid for all the intervals from (1) above.
3. Calculate the per cent areal coverage of various suspended solids intervals.
4. Draw graphs of estimated percentage cover (vertical axis) against sample size (horizontal axis) for all the intervals.
5. Reflect on the outcomes from (3) and (4) and draw conclusions about the necessary sample grid size for a representative sample in each case.
6. Discuss your conclusions with a peer.

Hint: Work in groups and let each individual follow a different sampling method, then compare and discuss the outcome from each method.

Activity 38

1. What is meant by spatial dependence (spatial autocorrelation)?
2. Explain how standard statistical methods handle this issue?
3. Discuss your views with a peer.

12

A Framework for Successful MPhil/PhD Research Projects

▶ SERWAN M.J. BABAN

12.1	Introduction
12.2	Reasons for Not Completing on Time
12.3	A Framework for the Successful Completion of the MPhil/PhD Project and Thesis
12.3.1	The First Year
12.3.2	The Second Year
12.3.3	The Final Year
12.4	Conclusion
References	
Chapter 12 Activities	

12.1 Introduction

The research student is expected to work relatively independently on an original research project. This process requires developing a range of skills as well as trekking through the full range of research planning, actioning, extracting conclusions and communicating the methodology and the outcomes (Baban and Sankat 2003; Wisker 2005). They are also meant to work with a research supervisor who will share their research interests and area of expertise (Blaxter, Hughes and Tight 2001).

A successful completion of MPhil/PhD thesis within regulation time requires a supervisory relationship that respects autonomy, facilitates scholarly independence and fosters academic values such as exchange of information, social responsibility, critical thinking, self-reflection and personal growth (Phillips and Pugh 1996; Mackinnon 2004). In addition, the student and the supervisor need to thoroughly fulfil their responsibilities and to work mindfully according to a planned timeframe. Unfortunately, in the majority of cases, delays and lack of completion are long-standing problems (Blume 1986) where students tend to seek extensions and leaves of absence, and take much longer than necessary to complete their projects. This phenomenon can be due to the lack of a planned and disciplined approach to research or good supervision coupled with the temptations to undertake other activities or employment during the ongoing MPhil/PhD degree programme (Cryer 2000). In other cases the students tend to have difficulty in managing their time or simply lack some essential technical, statistical, analytical or information technology skills (Phillips and Pugh 1996). In some other cases the student lacks the ability to write and to complete tasks on time; this combination is damaging, as a substantial portion of the successful completion of an MPhil/PhD degree lies in having the ability to write an in-depth and coherent thesis. Besides, almost all scientific activities carried out by the majority of professional people in their subsequent careers have to comply with and adhere to predefined time scales. Consequently not having these skills will significantly delay completion and could hamper success in professional life.

Although some institutions may have guidelines about submission dates, length and hours of supervisory work, there are few about the actual conduct of the supervisor's role. It is useful to examine this, considering the stages of the students' research efforts, the role and practice of the supervisor, and the kind of structures and systems that staff and students can set up to enable well–supervised, quality research to take place (DePoy and Gitlin 1994). Therefore, it is advisable that the training of supervisors and postgraduate students should include recognition of these facts and issues as well as some understanding of the necessary framework to manage these issues effectively. Out of such sessions have come some shared agreement and clarity of practices, awareness of problems and needs, sharing of concerns and solutions over time management, managing the stage of the project, finding and using facilities and getting along with each other (Bochner, Gibbs and Wisker 1995).

It is evident that the existence of a framework, accepted within the department or faculty, defining the stages that a student should be expected to have completed at various points in the three-year period of study, would help to reduce these delays (SERC 1992; Booth, Colomb and Williams 1995). Students need to be introduced to planning and time management at a very early stage. Students will be helped by knowing that they are expected to reach certain stages at certain times and will come to accept that part of their training is, in fact, learning how to manage their time and organize their affairs.

This chapter aims to assist with securing satisfactory progress in MPhil/PhD research by outlining the main reasons for not completing theses on time. It also offers advice and proposes a framework containing specific benchmarks, from the beginning to the completion of research, which can ensure good, steady and satisfactory progress. It is hoped that this approach will allow both the supervisor and the student to have some measure as to how the research is progressing and perhaps more importantly to introduce intervention mechanisms when progress is slow.

12.2 Reasons for Not Completing on Time

Reasons for long completion times or failure to complete (SERC 1992; Phillips and Pugh 1996; Booth, Colomb and Williams 1995; Mackinnon 2004) include the following:

1. Time, which can be characterized as

    - A gap between the expectation and the reality. All aspects of research tend to take much longer than the inexperienced supervisor and student expect.
    - A "slow start". The start to a student's research is almost always slower than the student initially expects, but even so the student is required to work hard and smart for long hours. If inadequate effort is put into the conceptualization of the problem, developing the literature survey, or such other initial activities, the result is that the remaining activities are always rushed and the research will ultimately suffer.

2. Lack of understanding of the supervision process. Broadly speaking,

there are two main aspects to supervision. First is the ability to identify and define relevant and actionable research problems, to stimulate students and foster enthusiasm, and to provide a steady stream of scientific ideas and guidance. Second is the capability to focus on the mechanics and procedures for ensuring that the student makes good progress and completes on time. The lack of either aspect can lead to delays.
3. Mismatch between student and supervisor. The relationship between a student and supervisor is a particularly close one. They start as master and pupil and ideally end up as almost equal colleagues. In these circumstances it is critical that the student and supervisor should be carefully matched taking into account such facts as whether the student is a team person or a loner, the number of students already being supervised, whether the supervisor easily handles many or few students and perhaps more importantly if the supervisor is active in the area of the research topic.

According to Phillips and Pugh (1996) students often have problems with

1. Personality factors. These include neglect by the supervisor, clash of personalities, barriers to communication arising from age, class, gender, race, or differences in approach to work.
2. Professional factors. These include a supervisor who is misinformed or lacking sufficient knowledge in the area, a supervisor with few genuine research interests or interests that differ fundamentally from those of the student.
3. Organizational factors. These include a supervisor with too many students to supervise or a supervisor who is too busy with consultancy and/or administrative work; a supervisor who is unable to manage his or her research group or number of researchers efficiently; isolation of students in departments and faculties due to inadequate arrangements, inadequate support services and provision of equipment.
4. The research topic. The student needs to be involved in the development of and have a passion for the topic (Mackinnon 2004). The supervisor may have a general idea that could be developed in various directions based on the student's background, interests and ability. Decisions regarding the choices of topic and direction need to be reached reasonably early. In some cases the supervisor is conscious that

given diligence and reasonable ability, it is highly likely that the student will complete on time. However, occasionally an exciting trend of research develops in which the outcome is more uncertain and in these cases the supervisor should have a fallback position in case some unexpected difficulty arises.

5. Working in a team. Increasingly research is carried out in collaborative teams. In these cases, it would be useful to hold regular group project supervisions during which students can share ideas, problems and questions, and supervisors can address the group about learning outcomes, length of the thesis, time, protocols, question framing, strategies, reading and so on. The potential problem in this case is not so much to set up a milestone for the project as a whole, but to clearly define the individual student's specific contribution to the work, and to make sure that not only does the student fulfil his or her "specific" contribution, but also has a clear understanding of the project as a whole. When many people are involved it is likely that there is far less chance of the student falling behind or sheering off without being noticed. The risk here is of not seeing the woods for the trees. In this case, therefore, it is almost essential for the student to be occasionally asked to explain to the group what he or she is working on currently, how much has been concluded and what are the problems foreseen for the future and to explain how this has its distinctive character and at the same time fits into the project as a whole. In order to best enable the learning of their students, supervisors need to learn how to ask open questions, how to draw out ideas and problems and how to elicit information even if the student finds communication difficult. Some of this can be facilitated by working with groups of students with similar research interests and focus.

6. Not having a critical mass. In some cases there might be only one student working in a specific area, but there will probably be a few working in related areas, whether in terms of methodology being used or in terms of subject or discipline. The sharing of key questions about procedures, systems and ideas, depending on the context, can be immensely useful for students who might otherwise feel rather isolated. Not only does a group help students to feel supported and to discuss issues, developments, problems and breakthroughs, but it can also provide the perfect opportunity for the necessary exploratory talk about

the development of enquiry, the testing of hypotheses and the sharing of discoveries. Electronic networks can aid the dissemination of skills and information and keep students in touch with each other. With this kind of communication, not only can they support each other and discuss ideas and findings and so on, but also they can keep each other in touch on issues of dates, regulations, passing the hurdle of transfer to PhD from MPhil and other such potentially threatening, often confused and ill-informed experiences.

7. Perfectionism. Some students are never satisfied, attempting to continually improve the results and unable to bring things to conclusion. Perfectionism can be a virtue, but often if a student would only write up what has already been achieved, he or she would almost certainly see more clearly whether any improvement was actually necessary, as well as the amount of effort required, or whether it makes sense to attempt that amount of work in the time available.

8. Distractions. Distraction from the main line of enquiry often causes delay. A common distraction is for a student to become obsessed with computing, with a resulting over-analysis of the experimental data, largely because of the sheer pleasure of manipulating the computer, but with inevitable delays in completing the thesis.

9. Data collection issues. Occasionally the student does not realize the inadequacy of collected data until he or she starts to write the thesis, and has to break off in order to perform a further experiment or calculation, usually resulting in a delay of at least six to twelve months.

10. Employment before completion. Often when the research is progressing well it opens up prospects for future research. A supervisor may invite the student to consider a two- or three-year continuation as a post-doctoral research assistant. Experience shows that if the student accepts, and is appointed before handing in the thesis, in the vast majority of cases the rate of progress on the thesis slows dramatically, and a delay of six months to a year is almost inevitable.

11. Resource limitations. It is important to ensure, as far as possible, that appropriate resources and equipment are made available, and that students are put in touch with the university's and wider community's research culture and activities, so they can form supportive working relationships with other research students, whether in their own field

or not. Enabling students to find support among their peers and from central resources begins to wean them away from dependency and helps them to develop autonomy in their work, without the supervisor neglecting the student's needs.

12.3 A Framework for the Successful Completion of the MPhil/PhD Project and Thesis

The existence of a structured framework is critical for the successful evolution of a research project as it sets out the stream of events, benchmarks, achievements and deliverables against a time scale. This will allow both the supervisor and the student to have some measure as to how the research is progressing and perhaps more importantly when to introduce intervention mechanisms when the research is not progressing according to the plan (Phillips and Pugh 1996; Booth, Colomb and Williams 1995; Blaxter, Hughes and Tight 2001).

The purpose of a framework is to simply guide and facilitate the student's research, to develop reliable working habits, to enable students to develop their own programme schedule and to develop the ability to make objective decisions. The framework needs to be made transparent to students by departments through meetings as well as developing and issuing written documents. The framework should include requirements for regular meetings with the supervisor and the supervisory and advisory committees, the required number of presentations and seminars per year, dates for submitting detailed annual progress reports, and the format for agreed short- and intermediate-term plans. Depending on the nature of the research work and the department, other possible requirements for inclusion are regular reports to the head of the group or department, and regular presentations to other group members, including other students. The institution can monitor the framework and students' progress through regular progress reports containing information on all of the above as well as information on meetings with the supervisor(s) and the advisory committee and the numbers of presentations or seminars given by the student.

12.3.1 The First Year

During the first year, the student will need to settle into the new environment and to develop a consistent pattern of work that is appropriate to the subject of study and research. The pattern should include learning to work hard, recognizing and accepting that completing the thesis on time will require him or her to work long hours, including possibly nights and weekends, to complete tasks within agreed timelines and ensure that his or her time is spent productively. Furthermore, the student needs to recognize the importance of systematic recording of data or theoretical calculations and the importance of keeping and maintaining a tidy, clear record of all the activities, tasks and outcomes to date.

During this year, the student will receive the formal portion of introductory instruction in whatever subjects are considered necessary and desirable for the MPhil/PhD degree. These may include theoretical and practical courses to strengthen or bridge any gaps between the student's background and the proposed research project, training in research methodology, exposure to fieldwork and so on. In this period, the literature review needs to be conducted, and the sharpness of the definition of the research topic should increase markedly. Therefore, the student should have a clear idea of the process of research, possess the necessary background information on relevant work in the literature and possess a systematic record of all that has been accomplished and attempted (Baban and Sankat 2003). Through examining completed written tasks, the student and the supervisor should know whether the student is capable of writing a coherent, connected account of the work in good English. A weakness in this area will cause the student serious distress later on and must not, therefore, be ignored.

Towards the end of this year, a decision is usually made as to whether the student is to upgrade from the MPhil to PhD degree. The student and others in the department must see this decision as objective and impartial, hence the need for a clear, transparent and well-defined process of assessment, informing the student where he or she stands and generating a reasonably objective judgement of the student's suitability for further work. Therefore, it is critical that the student should be able to gauge his or her progress at various stages and to receive timely guidance and supervision towards making improvements. Consequently, at early stages of research, it is necessary for supervisors to have frequent meetings with their students (SERC 1992). These meetings should be organized at fixed and short time intervals to discuss problems, progress and issues hindering the research. This approach will ensure that a busy supervisor meets with and is accessible to the student;

additionally it provides easy benchmarks in time for the supervisor to drive particular outcomes and to set the agenda and identify the specific deliverables for the next meeting. In terms of impartiality of the assessment for the upgrade, the process may require input from the supervisor and the advisory committee and may need to include viva voce examination carried out by at least two examiners, one of whom should be a qualified person active in research in the subject area of the project. The other should be an experienced member of staff who is familiar with the general area. This organization will examine the student on the specific details of the research by the expert and on the simple but fundamental concepts and approaches by the nonexpert.

12.3.2   The Second Year

During this stage, appropriate milestones need to be created, determining steps the student should have completed at various times in the year. It should be noted, however, that the focus is on original research where, by definition, things do not necessarily develop according to the plan. Therefore, the plan for the research project should have the flexibility to allow for dead ends and unexpected additional work, particularly in the early stage, as this is the nature of research, which fundamentally involves searching for the new, unknown and unexpected. Consequently, it is a good practice for the student and supervisor to lay out a critical path. This critical path should be reviewed at various stages throughout the year, and become more sharply defined with time. During this year and the early portion of the third year, the student should obtain the bulk of the results, which are going to form the main body of the thesis. Based on these outcomes, the supervisor(s) should determine whether the research proposal is promising and student is capable to stay on task, and deliver MPhil/PhD level work and ultimately the thesis on time. If difficulties arise with either the project or the student, then urgent steps need to taken to transfer the student to a topic more likely to produce a thesis on time, even if it is less exciting.

12.3.3   The Final Year

Setting and adhering to milestones are very important, as delays at this stage usually mean delays in the final date of submission. Questions that can be asked at this stage include: Have the original research objectives been realized? How can the outcomes be viewed in the context of previous research in the area? Does the student understand the "bigger" picture? Can the student objectively evaluate the field?

At this stage the student should have completed the theoretical and practical components of the research, completed the analysis of the data, acquired a substantial list of references and copies of the most relevant papers, and should have almost completed the presentation of results. It is advisable at this stage for the student to reread the key papers to ensure that the relationship between any previous work and his or her own is fully understood and justified. If the student's work has been carefully carried out, a likely result may be to throw some doubts on previous work. It is important to examine this carefully and to try to reconcile any differences that have arisen.

Writing a thesis is generally a matter of progressively refining chapters in the light of their internal consistency and their relationship to other chapters. This process requires time and cannot be rushed; most students underestimate the time it requires. Therefore, the writing of the first draft of the thesis needs to start early during this stage. A general introduction should be drafted as soon as possible, even if it has to have gaps. Equally it will be a great help to the student if a rough draft is written on each piece of work as it is finished. The writing on the full thesis will then be much easier. Developing a timetable of events and deliverables during the writing stage represents a critical part of a realistic framework (Blaxter, Hughes and Tight 2001). The schedule in table 12.1 shows a reasonable timetable for completion of the thesis.

A few months before the final year the supervisor(s) should spend some time with the student going over the material, with particular attention to the structure and the organization of the thesis. Finalizing a thesis is always much more time consuming than expected. Chapters have to be linked into a storyline; cross-references and "pointers" need to be inserted to keep the reader oriented to what is where and why. There should be no typing or stylistic errors, and tables, figures and references should be complete, accurate and presented correctly. Some three to six months before the final submission date, the student will benefit greatly from a mock MPhil/PhD viva. A carefully planned and implemented mock viva could reveal gaps in the

Table 12.1 A Time Frame Defining Various Deliverables during the Writing Process

Time Required (Weeks) per Deliverable	Time into Thesis Writing (Weeks)	Deliverables
4	4	Introduction
7	11	Method and results
6	17	Discussion, tables, figures, references, etc.
1	18	Consultation with the supervisor and supervisory committee
2	20	Revision of draft
3	23	Final typing, art work on figures, proofreading, etc.
1	24	Binding
Total Time	24	

student's knowledge, which may now be rectified. It will help greatly in concentrating the student's mind on the structuring of the remaining portion of the research. Most academics will be familiar with the student who has mastered all the details of a particular research project but has not realized that the external examiner may be more interested in the wider aspects of the research and its impact on the whole body of knowledge.

12.4 Conclusion

The successful completion of an MPhil/PhD thesis within regulation time requires the existence of a structured and transparent framework to set out the stream of events, benchmarks and deliverables against a time scale. This will allow both the supervisor and the student to develop reliable working habits and to have some measure as to how the research is progressing. The chapter has outlined the main reasons for failure to complete an MPhil/PhD thesis on time and suggested a framework that can ensure good, steady and satisfactory progress. The framework promotes the development of shared responsibilities and systems to inform students of formats, rules, dates, demands and expectations from supervision. It is hoped that this approach will assist the supervisor and student to detect progress and, perhaps more importantly, to know when to introduce intervention mechanisms should the research not be progressing according to plan.

References

Baban, S.M.J., and C.K. Sankat. 2003. The guide to writing and publishing research papers in peer-reviewed journals. *West Indian Journal of Engineering* 25 (2): 54–64.

Blaxter, L., C. Hughes and M. Tight. 2001. *How to Research*. 2nd ed. Berkshire, UK: Open University Press.

Blume, S. 1986. The development and current dilemmas of postgraduate education. *European Journal of Education* 21 (3): 217–22.

Bochner, D., G. Gibbs and G. Wisker. 1995. *Teaching More Students – Supporting More Students*. Oxford: Oxford Centre for Staff Development.

Booth, W.C., G.G. Colomb and J.M. Williams. 1995. *The Craft of Research*. Chicago: University of Chicago Press.

Cryer, P. 2000. *The Research Student's Guide to Success*. Berkshire, UK: Open University Press.

DePoy, E., and L.N. Gitlin. 1994. *Introduction to Research*. St Louis, MO: Mosby.

Mackinnon, J. 2004. Academic supervision: Seeking metaphors and models for quality. *Journal of Further and Higher Education* 28 (4): 395–405.

Phillips, E.M., and D.I. Pugh. 1996. *How to Get a PhD: A Handbook for Students and Their Supervisors*. 2nd ed. Buckingham, UK: Open University Press.

Science and Engineering Research Council (SERC). 1992. *Research Student and Supervisor: An Approach to Good Supervisory Practice*. Swindon, UK: SERC.

Wisker, G. 2005. *The Good Supervisor*. London: Palgrave Macmillan.

Chapter 12 Activities

Activity 39

1. List three of the most likely reasons for not completing an MPhil/PhD project and thesis on time.
2. Propose a way forward to remove all likely obstacles and difficulties, stating required action at the following levels: you and your supervisor, the department/school/faculty and the university.
3. Discuss and compare (1) and (2) above with a peer.

Activity 40

1. List and justify the activities you think should be completed during years 1, 2 and 3 in your specialized field of research.
2. Compare your list with table 12.1. Explain and justify any differences.
3. Discuss and compare (1) and (2) above with a peer.

Section 3

Writing Up Research

13

Writing a Research Proposal for Funding
A Practical Guide

▸ PETER BAVERSTOCK

13.1	Introduction
13.2	The Art of "Grantmanship"
13.2.1	Carefully Read the Relevant Documentation
13.2.2	Start Preparing Your Proposal Well before the Closing Date
13.2.3	Show Your Proposal to Others
13.2.4	Pitch the Proposal to the Expertise of the Selection Committee
13.2.5	Amount Requested
13.2.6	Keep It Short
13.2.7	Address the Selection Criteria
13.2.8	Help the Committee
13.2.9	Budgets
13.2.10	Literature Review
13.2.11	Methods
13.2.12	Publications by the Applicant
13.3	Writing the Research Proposal for a Grant
13.3.1	Title
13.3.2	Introduction
13.3.3	Statement of the Problem
13.3.4	Justification

13.3.5 Significance
13.3.6 Aims and Objectives
13.3.7 Methodology
13.3.8 Budget
13.3.9 Ethical Considerations
13.3.10 Timetable
13.3.11 References
13.3.12 Appendices
Chapter 13 Activity

13.1 Introduction

The research proposal should be a detailed written plan that outlines *what* is being proposed, *why* the research is important, *where* the research project will be carried out and *how* it will be executed. This plan and structure encourages the researcher to carefully examine and develop a clear view of the study being proposed and issues being examined, relate the research to the priorities of the region or country, ponder on new knowledge obtained and reflect on how this knowledge will serve the required purpose and who the main benefactors are.

Developing a good research plan and proposal are crucial elements for a good research project as they assist with the organization and transition from thoughts to a written form. Furthermore, in the case of multidisciplinary research projects, the process will allow team members to understand their roles. As a general rule, the effort made in preparing a proposal is directly related to the conduct of a successful research project in a timely manner. While preparing the proposal, it is critical to remember that the single most important issue to consider when preparing a grant application is that you are in a competition.

Invariably, there will be many competitive bids for the same funding pool. Therefore, it is unlikely to be sufficient that your application is good, or even excellent. It must be the best. Put another way, your failure to get funding may not be because your application was not a good one in terms of content, structure and quality but rather because yours was not the best. It is therefore absolutely essential that your application be honed to perfection. Indeed, a grant application needs to be more finely honed than a manuscript you are submitting for publication in a refereed journal. At least if your paper to a refereed journal is rejected, you can take on board the referees' comments, improve the manuscript, and send it off to another journal. With a grant application, you only get one chance. In sections 13.3 and 13.4, some general hints on the "Art of Grantmanship" are provided. But two fundamental principles override all others. The first is to start working on your proposal well before the closing date, and commit twice as much time to it as you think you need. The second is to circulate the completed proposal to as many colleagues as possible, especially people with a good track record of winning grants.

13.2 The Art of "Grantmanship"

13.2.1 Carefully Read the Relevant Documentation

Funding agencies will give a whole lot of supporting material. This should be read carefully before you begin writing your proposal. Follow the instructions to the letter. After you have finished the proposal, reread the instructions carefully to ensure you have complied with all of them. It is an absolute tragedy when an otherwise excellent proposal is rejected on technical grounds.

13.2.2 Start Preparing Your Proposal Well before the Closing Date

Most people wait until the last moment to put their proposal together. I have sat on many grants committees and I can assure you that it shows. When sitting in judgement on the proposal, you can't help thinking that if the applicant(s) did not have time to put a decent proposal together, how are they going to find the time to do all this marvellous research? As a rule of thumb, you should start working on your proposal about three to four months before the closing date.

13.2.3 Show Your Proposal to Others

Once you have a polished version of the application, send it to colleagues for comment. These should include experts in your area, as well as experts in other areas. Note that there is little point in sending *drafts* of your proposal to colleagues. What you need from them is advice on the final honing of your application – so you should send them your very best effort for comment. Moreover, you should send them your best effort at least one month before the closing date. Almost by definition, such people will be very busy, and you cannot expect them to drop everything to look critically at your proposal. And you need the time to incorporate any comments they may provide into your proposal.

13.2.4 Pitch the Proposal to the Expertise of the Selection Committee

While one assumes that any selection committee consists of eminent people, their range of expertise may vary enormously. It is essential to pitch the proposal to the level of expertise of all members of the committee. Some granting agencies send applications out for assessment to eminent researchers in the field of your proposal. Here your application would need to target an expert in the area. I once applied for funding to the "Poultry Research Advisory Committee". The committee consisted of one scientist and thirty chicken farmers. Clearly the proposal was pitched to the farmers rather than the scientist. So before putting your proposal together, take the time to phone and find out the expertise on the committee, and to find out if the granting agency sends the proposal to experts for assessment. The style of application you need to write will depend on the processes being used.

13.2.5 Amount Requested

Keep the total amount of funding requested to the usual level of funding of the granting agency, and do not accept the upper limit of funding as the amount you should apply for. While a funding agency may occasionally fund up to (say) $100,000, most of their grants may be of the order of $10,000. Often, past successful grants will be provided on the agency's website, and this will give you an idea of the average level of funding. If in doubt, check with the agency. An application for $100,000 to an agency that usually makes grants of about $10,000 will not be funded.

13.2.6 Keep It Short

A grant proposal should be concise but complete. Granting committees often must deal with hundreds of applications and a shorter application is more likely to be read fully and understood. If there is a specified page limit, stick to it – nothing irks a committee more than an application exceeding a specified length – or it is likely to be deemed ineligible. And, do not try to outsmart the committee by using a small font – that is irksome too.

13.2.7 Address the Selection Criteria

Most grants have a set of selection criteria. The committee will appreciate it if you address each of the criteria, in turn, under headings. Often applicants do address the criteria, but embed them in the context of the overall application. The committee has a high probability of missing them in this form.

13.2.8 Help the Committee

Do everything you can to make the committee's job easier. For example, if you refer to the content of a document attached as an appendix (for example, a research management plan or your curriculum vitae), give a page number. Committees like this sort of thing because it saves them time and ensures they do see the relevant parts.

13.2.9 Budgets

In budget items, do not round off to the nearest $1,000, or guess travel to the nearest one thousand kilometres. This makes it look as though you are guessing rather than providing a well-documented budget. Nothing looks worse than: "Computer, $2,000". Specify the computer you want, give a firm quote and, to be really clever, attach a copy of the quote. This indicates to the committee that you have done your homework.

Justification of the budget is an area frequently dealt with poorly in grant applications. For example, under "Personnel", you have asked for one research assistant, half-time at $30,000. It is not sufficient to say that the award rate, with on-costs, for one research assistant is $60,000 per annum. Rather, you must justify

- Why you need a person at this level (Could a technical officer or clerical officer do the same job?)
- How you arrived at "half-time"

In this regard, it is useful to do some arithmetic. For example: "I anticipate receiving 250 responses to my questionnaire. Each response takes two hours to enter into the database. Hence, total time = 250 × 2 = 500 hours = 13 weeks", and so on. For another example, under "Travel", you have said you will do twenty-two hundred kilometres. It is not sufficient to say: "The university charges 47 cents per kilometre." Rather, what the committee wants to know is precisely how you arrived at twenty-two hundred kilometres for travel. The justification of the budget should link to the justification of methods (section 13.3).

13.2.10   Literature Review

The applicant must demonstrate that he or she is totally familiar with the literature surrounding the area of research. Committees are not impressed with applications that request funding for a research assistant to do the literature review.

13.2.11   Methods

General hints on methods are given in section 13.3. From the "grantmanship" point of view, a useful hint is to have already done a pilot study.

13.2.12   Publications by the Applicant

Most granting agencies will want a list of your publications in the last five years. In the international "one-upmanship publication arena", research books are highly regarded, followed closely by refereed journal articles, and so on down to unrefereed conference proceedings. It is better to separate publications out under such headings. If you try to conceal a host of unrefereed conference proceedings or conference presentations in the list, it will have the opposite effect – they will attract the eyes of the committee and detract from your high quality outputs. Next, you will need to show your proposal to as many people as possible. Get input, feedback and constructive criticism.

13.3 Writing the Research Proposal for a Grant

The actual format of a research proposal will vary a little from discipline to discipline, and from granting agency to granting agency. However, most will have a format along the following lines.

13.3.1 Title

A good title should be short, accurate, concise, informative and comprehensible to a layperson. The title should make the central objectives and variables of the study clear to the reader/reviewer without using jargon. The title should provide *key words* for the classification and indexing of the project.

13.3.2 Introduction

The researcher needs to lay the broad foundation for the problem that leads to the study, place the study within the larger context of the scholarly literature, explain why the study is being conducted, state the problems, and justify why the investigation is needed. The researcher is required to pose clear and objective arguments and demonstrate that the "question" has a basis (grounds) for probable answer(s) and/or working hypotheses. In other words, this section needs to focus on the theoretical framework, the grounds that support the central question of the study, stating the investigator's reasoning and arguments for the attempt to find the evidence that will offer an answer to the question and/or hypothesis.

In terms of approach, it needs to be funnel-shaped, starting with the general area into which the research fits, and progressively focusing on the specific research project.

The last sentence of the introduction should read: "Therefore, the present study was undertaken to . . ." (repeat the aim).

13.3.3 Statement of the Problem

The problem statement should make a *convincing argument* that there is not sufficient knowledge available to explain the problem and its possible alternative solutions, or it should make a *convincing argument* for the need to test what is known and taken as fact, if it is called into question by new findings or conditions. This constitutes the scientific justification for the study, that is, the basis of the need for research to generate further knowledge that will contribute to existing knowledge.

These should be clear statements of the questions to be answered and should relate to the problem that is being addressed.

A logical sequence for presenting the statement would be as follows:

- Magnitude, frequency and distribution. These might include geographic areas and population groups affected by the problem, as well as ethnic and gender considerations.
- Probable causes of the problem. What is the current knowledge of the problem and its causes? Is there consensus? Is there controversy? Is there conclusive evidence?
- Possible solutions. In what ways have solutions to the problem been attempted? What has been proposed? What are the results?
- Unanswered questions. What remains to be answered? What areas have not been possible to understand, determine, verify, or test?

13.3.4   Justification

This section describes the type of knowledge expected to be obtained and the intended purpose of its application. It should indicate the strategy for disseminating and using the research findings according to the potential users of the knowledge generated. The justification, which can be included as part of the statement of the problem or in a separate section, should make a convincing argument that the knowledge generated will be useful and generally applicable within the regional context.

The issues to be dealt with here include the following questions. How does the research relate to the priorities of the region or the country? What knowledge will be obtained from the study? What is the new knowledge? What purpose will the new knowledge serve? How will the results be disseminated? How will the results be used and who will be the beneficiaries of the study? In other words, how will the results of this study be used to make a difference and how can it be used in knowledge translation?

13.3.5   Significance

The researcher should indicate how the research will refine, revise or extend existing knowledge in the area under investigation. This should be very brief, explaining to the reader why the study is "significant", in the sense of "advancing general knowledge".

If Gregor Mendel was writing his proposal, he might say: "This study is significant because if my peas work out like I think they will, then it will provide an understanding of the mechanism of heredity in all organisms, including man." He would not say: "This study is significant because it will allow pea growers to grow round and wrinkly peas." Similarly, Charles Darwin might say of his study of Galapagos Island finches: "This study is significant because it will contribute to our understanding, in a small microcosm, of how evolution by natural selection works." He would not say: "This study is significant because it will advance our knowledge of Galapagos Island finches."

The discussion of the significance of the research is a very important part of the proposal, because it really says why you are doing this research, and why the agency should fund your proposal over the others.

13.3.6 Aims and Objectives

The *aim* should be simple, and immediately *attract the interest of the reader*. A useful golden rule here is that *the aim should be described in a single sentence*. I would point out that this is often the hardest part of any proposal, and the bit that warrants the most time expended.

Objectives should be defined after the theoretical framework has been developed, and the sequence is clear between the central question and possible responses to the questions and/or working hypotheses. This should specify what kind of knowledge the study is expected to obtain. It should give a clear notion of what is to be described, determined, identified, compared, and, in the cases of studies with working hypotheses, confirmed.

13.3.7 Methodology

The methodology explains the procedures that will be used to achieve the objectives. In this section the operational definition for the variables used should be specified in detail, along with the type of variables and the ways to measure them. In addition, the methodology should consider the study design and the techniques and procedures used to achieve the proposed objectives, including the determination of reliability and validity.

In writing the methodology it is necessary to consider the processes and sequence that will be used to execute the project. It is necessary to describe the logistics for obtaining the sample, for carrying out the required measurements, for transport, for storage of specimens, for getting access into a community, for organizing focus groups and so on (if these are required for your research work). In clarifying the sequence of execution of a project there emerges an opportunity to allocate tasks, especially if the study is multidisciplinary and/or multicentred, involving more than one person. This should be sufficiently detailed to clearly indicate that you have done all the planning and that you know exactly what you are doing. Assessors of grant applications often comment that the research plan is inadequately described. In particular justify every statement you make, for example, justify sample sizes, justify sample design, justify the analytical methods, state the statistics you will use to analyse the data (see chapter 11). One area where many applicants do poorly is justifying their sample sizes. There is a large body of literature around the area of sample sizes. It would be wise to obtain advice and input on the sampling regime from a statistician. It is not sufficient to state: "A survey will be conducted." Rather you should say: "The survey form is given in Appendix 1. I will sample 50 individuals because past experience has shown that in this area, the return rate is about 30 per cent; therefore, 160 survey forms will be sent out. The 160 recipients will be randomly selected from a telephone book." It will be especially useful if you have done a pilot study. The pilot study will give the panel confidence that your proposed methodology will work. It also gives the panel confidence that you've ironed out any bugs in the logistics. And finally the pilot study will give some indication of the variance you can expect (see chapter 11).

13.3.8 Budget

The budget needs to be detailed and should include a breakdown of each item. The researcher needs to specify personnel in terms of time and rate, equipment and materials to be purchased, transport allocation for data processing, data entry and data analysis. Sometimes funding agencies may allow funds to be disbursed for academic travel, for travel to conferences, for publication. These issues will require clarification, so include them in the budget as deemed necessary. Any research proposal must be budgeted realistically, based on firm quotes that are justified. There is no point in embarking on the project unless sufficient funds are available.

13.3.9 Ethical Considerations

In most studies involving humans and animals, ethical considerations and approval from a recognized body are crucial (see chapter 8). Many journals now refuse to publish any paper or research report that does not include a clear statement on ethical approval. So in studies involving humans there must be a clear statement that informed consent was obtained and that approval was obtained from the local ethics committee. With regards to animal study, there needs to be a clear statement that the institutional review board for animals gave permission for this study.

13.3.10 Timetable

Give a realistic timetable for your project. Can it be completed in the available time?

13.3.11 References

References should include a complete list of all the articles, materials and books cited in the document. This is not a comprehensive list of all the available published work, but only a list of references as it pertains to the problems being addressed in the research protocol.

13.3.12 Appendices

These could include the data collection instrument, a copy of a survey questionnaire, the form for obtaining informed consent from humans, and the timetable, that is, the activity timetable, including the activities to be undertaken along with the expected time period required to complete that activity, either in weeks or months.

Chapter 13 Activity

Activity 41

1. Form groups comprising four to seven individuals from different faculties.
2. Spend some time discussing a common research topic that is of interest to each group.
3. Develop the outline of a research protocol using the reading material provided.
4. List the important considerations for the various subheadings of the research protocol as they pertain to the research topic of interest.
5. Discuss and present the outline of your research protocol to the class.

14

Writing a Research Report

▶ SERWAN M.J. BABAN

14.1	Introduction
14.2	Format and Structure
14.2.1	Introduction
14.2.2	Materials and Methods
14.2.3	Results
14.2.4	Discussion
14.2.5	Conclusions
14.3	Using Tables and Figures
14.3.1	Design of Tables, Graphs and Figures
14.4	Title
14.5	Abstract or Summary
14.6	References
14.7	Acknowledgements
14.8	Appendices
References	
Chapter 14 Activities	

14.1   Introduction

Researchers spend their time writing proposals, planning research, undertaking experiments, analysing data, tracing research and reading related articles. The written product is the physical form of all that occurred intellectually. Published reports and journal articles provide evidence of this dedication and is an effective way to share and exchange knowledge with the community. Therefore, a scientific report is not just an additional requirement that is needed to finalize a project; it is an important historical document that provides evidence of work, intellectual growth and contribution to the wider scientific community (Baban 2006).

The main purpose of a scientific report is to communicate. Therefore, it is important to demonstrate a clear understanding of the science being utilized by writing about it in a scientific report. Furthermore, effective communication requires an understanding of the intended audience. It is important to ensure that your intended reader has a background similar to yours before you started the project, that is, a general understanding of the topic but no specific knowledge of the details. The reader should be able to reproduce whatever you did by following your report (DePoy and Gitlin 1994). A scientific report moves from general to particular to general. It begins in the Introduction with the theory related to the experiment, moves on to the work carried out in the Methods and Results sections and returns to general ideas in the Discussion by arguing whether the results obtained are, or are not, consistent with the theory. In many cases, it may be appropriate in the discussion to comment on the suitability of the method used in the experiment (Kumar 1999).

Good scientific reports share many of the qualities found in other kinds of writing. These include presenting ideas in a logical order to facilitate the same kind of thinking, making each sentence follow from the previous one, building an argument piece by piece, grouping related sentences into paragraphs, grouping paragraphs into sections and creating a flow from beginning to end.

The report should be grammatically sound, with correct spelling, and generally free of errors. Avoid jargon, slang, or colloquial terms. Define acronyms and any abbreviations not used as standard measurement units. Most of the report describes what you did, and thus it should be written in the past tense (for example, "values were averaged"), but use present or future tense as appropriate (for example, "x is bigger than y" or "that effect will happen"). Employ the active rather than passive voice to avoid boring writing and contorted phrases (for example, "the software calculated average values" is better than "average values were calculated by the software"). The exact format of particular items within a report is less important than consistency of application. For example, if you indent paragraphs, be sure to indent them all; use a consistent style of headings throughout (for example, major headings in bold with initial capitals, minor headings in italics and so on) write "%", "per cent" or "percent" but do not mix them, and so on. In other words, establish a template and stick to it.

Figures, tables, data, equations and the like need to be used to help tell the story as it unfolds. Refer to them directly in the text, and integrate the points they make into your writing. Number figures and tables sequentially as they are introduced (for example, figure 1, figure 2, and so on, with another sequence for table 1, table 2, and so on). Provide captions with complete information and not just a simple title. Label all axes and include units. Insert a figure or table after the paragraph in which it is first mentioned, or gather all supporting material together after the reference section (before any appendices).

14.2   Format and Structure

Research reports are typically presented in the IMRAD format (introduction, materials and methods, results and discussion) (Ellertsen 2007). Respectively, these sections structure the report to articulate in the layout that this is the problem, this is the relevant background, this is the chosen approach for this study, these are the results and the results show, explain and suggest the following. There are additional minor sections that precede or follow the major sections, including the title, abstract, acknowledgements, references and appendices. It should be noted that all sections are important, but at different stages to different readers. When flipping through a journal, a reader might read the title first and, if interested further, proceed to the abstract, then conclusions, and then if he or she is truly fascinated perhaps the entire paper. You have to convince the reader that what you have done is interesting and important by communicating appeal and content in all sections.

14.2.1   Introduction

The introduction discusses the theoretical background to the investigation and places the present work in context. Introduce the problem, moving from the broader issues to your specific problem, finishing the section with the precise aims of the paper (key questions). Formulate this section carefully, setting up your argument in a logical order. Refer to relevant ideas or theories and related research by other authors. Answer the question "what is the problem and why is it important?" (DePoy and Gitlin 1994). Relevant references should be cited and the reader's attention moved from the general to the specific. The aims of the study should be clearly stated at the end of the introduction.

The introduction should be written mainly in the present tense, since you are describing a current problem and current conclusions. Details of methods and results given in the introduction should be in the past tense, and future implications based on the conclusions should be in the future tense.

The main purposes of the introduction are to

- State the research problem clearly.
- Establish your hypothesis.
- Provide justification for the work.
- State the methods and results briefly.
- State the major conclusions.

Therefore, a good introduction is expected to

- Describe the research objectives clearly.
- Provide a clear statement of the hypothesis: a foretelling statement, based on current theory, which states what you expect your experiment to reveal.
- Include some literature review, which provides general background information about what has already been published in the research area.
- Start broadly, locating the research topic in a wider context and then briefly focus on the specific research problem.
- Provide adequate information about the research area, so that readers do not need to refer to other materials to understand the research problem.
- Provide good reasons for doing the research and the questions driving the research.
- Describe how the main questions will be tackled, describe the methods used (a sentence or two is usually adequate) and briefly provide some results.

- Briefly state the major conclusions. Do not include suspense or surprise endings in the report. The findings and conclusions must be clear from the beginning.

14.2.2 Materials and Methods

This section should include all information required for an exact repetition of the research performed. Therefore, it is necessary to explain how the problem was studied by providing information on the steps followed. Depending on the kind of data, this section may contain subsections on experimental details, materials used, data collection/sources, analytical or statistical techniques employed, study area and so on. Include flowcharts, maps or tables to aid clarity. Ultimately an extensive protocol for the experiment needs to be provided so it can be repeated by others. However, it is important not to write the methods as instructions to the reader, nor present it as an itemized list.

More specifically, this section should be chronological and informative, providing details of

- The experimental design
- The controls used, including their purpose
- The data recording techniques
- Exact quantities and purities of reagents
- Technical specifications of the apparatus
- Specific methods of the sample preparation
- Accurate nomenclature
- Any subjects or samples included in the study
- The sampling protocols

Here are some tips for writing the materials and methods section:

- Do not prepare this section like a cookbook. Include the apparatus and reagents within the body of the text.
- If there are numerous specifications in the methods section, it is sometimes better to present them in a table.
- Explain any assumptions that have been made in the experiments, and give details of the units of measurement.
- Ensure that this section is not confused with the results section – do not report any findings in the materials and methods section.

- It is unlikely that the methods you are using are new; therefore, references should be cited for your techniques. If the methods are new then extensive details must be provided.
- This section is usually written in the past tense, since you have already completed the experiments.
- Brief details of the statistical methods that were used, including the reason for their choice, should also be included.

An effective way to test the articulation of this section is to ask a fellow student, friend or colleague to read it, to see if they can follow your method.

14.2.3 Results

This section consists of data and some comments that draw attention to the most significant aspects of the results, essentially answering the question, "what did I find out?" It should be kept brief and repetition of methods or results should be avoided.

Present your data in a manner that is easy to read and interpret. This is where the core of the work is presented. Thus, clarity is essential since the rest of the report hinges on what is presented in this section. Therefore, it is important to explain the actual findings, using subheadings to divide the section into logical parts, with the text addressing the study aims and linking the writing to figures and tables as the results are presented.

Interpret and analyse your data so that others can understand it. Comments on the results should be quantitative, not just qualitative; that is, any comments should be backed up with data. Ensure that your statistics are meaningful and reflect your understanding of the statistical analysis used in terms of strengths, limitations, errors and intended uses.

Provide clear interpretations for each figure and table; do not leave this to the reader. If several similar figures are involved, select representative examples for briefness and locate the rest in an appendix. Any uncertainties in measurement or calculation need also to be mentioned. Provide comments on the results as they are presented, and save broader generalizations and conclusions for later.

14.2.4 Discussion

This is usually the most important section of the report. It should include comments on the results, especially any unexpected results, essentially answering the question, "what is the significance of the research?" Therefore, it is important to discuss the significance of what has been found, in light of the overall study aims and by examining the bigger picture to conclude what has (and has not) been learned about the problem, and what it all means. The results should be compared to the standard value and be explained or justified in light of the original aims.

The main purposes of the discussion are to

- Discuss the relationships between the outcomes.
- Discuss how the results relate to the initial objectives.
- Discuss the initial hypotheses, in terms of whether the results provide adequate support for each hypothesis.
- Discuss the problems faced. Although you should always include results that do not quite fit, that is, the negative or insignificant results, never focus your entire discussion on the failings of your experiments. Never be tempted to omit or adjust your results.
- Describe the shortcomings of the research.
- Describe the implications of the research.
- Provide major conclusions, supported with evidence.
- Suggest future applications of the research findings.

The ability to explain any experimental anomalies, based on the established theories in the field, is a skill that reflects intellectual growth and maturity. Discuss how the results are similar to or different from published findings, and attempt to explain any differences, with support from references. If it is impossible to find a good explanation for the outcomes, simply admit it. It is better to admit uncertainty, rather than create poor, unsubstantiated excuses. Be careful when quoting similar findings from the literature – ensure the reader knows which findings belong to you. Discuss the significance of your findings, in terms of their potential application, or in terms of relevant future research.

14.2.5   Conclusions

The conclusions are usually included in the discussion, but they can be separated. If they are separate, the discussion should be summarized and a comment made on the success, or otherwise, of the experiment. Therefore, it is important to restate the study aims or key questions and summarize your findings using clear, concise statements. Keep this section brief and to the point.

14.3 Using Tables and Figures

Tables, graphics and photographs are placed immediately after the point at which they are first referred to in the text. The reader should also be referred (by number) to the diagrams at the appropriate time in the text and the most important features pointed out to them. Tables, graphics and photographs (called *figures*), should be numbered sequentially. In large reports with many chapters, they are sequentially numbered in each chapter (that is, for chapter 2 you will begin with table 2.1, figure 2.1).

Titles for *tables* are centred *above* the table. Titles for *figures* are centred *below* the graphic. The source of the table or figure should also be included. The source is usually in a smaller font (for example, 10 point) and aligned on the left-hand margin under a table, and under the title of a figure.

14.3.1 Design of Tables, Graphs and Figures

1. Tables

    - Arrange the tables so that similar elements read vertically, not horizontally. This will make the table easier to read.
    - Arrange tables so that the reader does not have to rotate the page to read them, that is, use portrait, not landscape.
    - Use as few vertical and horizontal lines in a table as possible.
    - Do not provide standard conditions for your experiments in a table unless they vary for the data that is included in the table.
    - Only present significant figures in a table, and ensure that there is consistency in terms of figures, notation, and symbols.
    - Ensure that units for numerical data are included in a table.

2. Graphs

    - The best graphs are the simplest graphs. The reader should be able to understand the trends illustrated in the graph.
    - If you have a large amount of data to present, can it be grouped?
    - Three-dimensional graphs should be used with caution since they

- can quickly become sloppy and confusing if they contain too much data.
- In terms of size, a good graph strikes a balance between its legibility and its size. A graph should be small but clear.
- Limit the use of colours and patterns. Most computer programmes that are used for drawing graphs offer an array of colours and patterns that can be used. If these are used excessively, the graph will look unprofessional. Furthermore, most scientific journals only publish black and white graphs; have a look at some of the journals in your field and identify how the authors present their data in black and white.

To help you choose the right type of graph, consider the following:

- Line graphs are effective for showing trends.
- Bar charts are effective for showing relative proportions.
- Pie charts are effective for showing proportions of a total.
- Combined charts are effective for showing correlations, for example, a few bar charts or line graphs may be combined, or a bar chart and line graph may be combined.

14.4   Title

The title should clearly and briefly indicate what the report is about. Therefore, it needs to be precise, concise and composed of key words. The title is never a complete sentence, and articles (a, an, the) are usually omitted. Avoid padding the title with phrases like "A study of . . ."

The main purpose of the title is to sum up your work in a single phrase or sentence. Therefore, it needs to be clear, specific and brief. First impressions are very important; therefore, a title must be prepared carefully. Scientists scan through journal article titles which they find using online journal databases. They decide which abstracts they will read based on the titles. The title should therefore sum up the experiments and findings in a single phrase, providing as much specific information as possible. A title should be worded carefully, so that its meaning is clear to most readers. Technical terms and abbreviations should only be used if they will be familiar to the readers of your report. For example, an acronym such as DNA is widely recognized and is quite acceptable in a title.

14.5 Abstract or Summary

The main purpose of the abstract is to provide a summary of the entire report for quick reading of the motivations and reasons for doing the work, as well as the methods, findings and conclusions.

The abstract should state the principal objectives and scope of the investigation, describe the methods employed, summarize the results and state the principal conclusions. A reader should be able to grasp the full scope and significance of the work reported without having to read the entire report. Thus, the abstract must be independent of the rest of your scientific report – it is a "mini report", which needs to make sense completely on its own. References to other authors or to tables, figures or text within the report should not be included. There should be no new information or ideas in the abstract that are not included in the rest of the report. A sentence or two summarizing each of the IMRAD sections should suffice. There should be no supporting material and details should be limited to just the essential message that explains what the researcher did and found out. The abstract should be written last.

The following are some tips for writing the abstract:

- Minimize the use of jargon and abbreviations.
- A sentence or a couple of phrases describing the methods is sufficient. Do not go into detail about the methods in the abstract.
- Typically, the information presented in an abstract is given in the same order as it is in the article.
- A good abstract will be brief and no more than a few hundred words.
- Abstracts are usually written in the past tense in a single paragraph.
- Because it is a condensed version of the full report, it is easiest to write the abstract last.

14.6 References

- The references should be an accurate listing of all the sources referred to in the text. Entries must conform to the conventions of the referencing system used.
- Within the text, cite references by author and year unless instructed otherwise. For example, "Comrie (1999) stated that . . ." or "several studies have found that x is greater than y (Comrie 1999; Smith 1999)".

- When citing works with two or three authors, list all the authors, and for works with more than three authors use the abbreviation et al. (note the period) following the first name, for example, Comrie and Smith (1999) or Comrie et al. (1999). Attribute every idea that is not your own to avoid plagiarism. Note that some disciplines, for example, psychology, have conventions that may differ from those described here. You should be certain you are familiar with, and use, the style of references preferred in your particular field.
- In the reference section itself, list alphabetically only the people and publications that you cited in the report (if none, omit the section). Provide sufficient details to enable a reader to actually track down the information.
- List all authors of a work in the reference list. Follow a standard format, and pay attention to consistent use of italics, capitalization, volume and page numbers, publisher's address, and so on, between the various kinds of references.

The main purposes of the references are to acknowledge sources in order to avoid plagiarism, and to strengthen your arguments with support from the existing literature.

A scientific report should be well referenced. Every piece of information that is included in your report, excluding your original data, should be referenced, preferably from peer-reviewed sources.

Your arguments will be much stronger if you can support them with references. Make sure that you include your references while you are actually writing. Tracking back to find references later on is an extremely difficult task.

14.7 Acknowledgements

The main purpose of the acknowledgements is to thank people who contributed directly to the research by providing data, assisted with some part of the analysis, proofreading, typing and so on.

Acknowledgements are optional and should not be confused with a dedication – this is not where you thank your friends and relatives unless they have helped you with your manuscript. Did you receive significant support from technicians, tutors, or other students? Were you provided with financial support? Did somebody prepare your reagents for you? Were you given essential samples or reagents? Remember, in most reports this section tends to be very brief, a few lines at the most. Identify those who provided you with the most support, and thank them appropriately.

14.8 Appendices

The appendices are considered additional material to the report, and may not be examined by the reader at all. These include, for example, raw data, figures not used in the body of the paper, sample calculations, and so on. The main purpose of the appendices is to present additional data that is too extensive to be included within the main body of the text.

References

Baban, S.M.J., ed. 2006. *Writing Up Research*. A workshop developed for the University of the West Indies, Trinidad and Tobago. St Augustine: University of the West Indies.

DePoy, E., and L.N. Gitlin. 1994. *Introduction to Research: Multiple Strategies for Health and Human Services*. St Louis, MO: Mosby.

Ellertsen, P. 2007. "IMRAD": A handy way to organize reports on scientific research. http://www.sci.edu/classes/ellertsen/imrad.html (last visited 3 August 2007).

Kumar, R. 1999. *Research Methodology: A Step-by-Step Guide for Beginners*. London: Sage.

Chapter 14 Activities

Activity 42

- List two questions that can briefly summarize the main thrust of each of the following sections: introduction, materials and methods, results, and discussion.
- Compare notes within small groups regarding the question you identified above, and seek areas of agreement within your group between the groups in the class.

Activity 43

Assume you have just completed a study involving several variables, using different methods to derive associations between the variables.

- Explain how and why the use of tables can assist you to communicate your results.
- Explain how and why the use of graphs or figures can assist with communicating your results.
- Can you envisage circumstances where you would prefer tables to graphs or figures and vice versa? Why?

Compare notes within small groups and seek areas of agreement within your group and between the groups in the class.

15

Writing to Publish in a Peer-Reviewed Journal

A Practical Approach

▸ SERWAN M.J. BABAN

15.1	Basic Issues
15.1.1	Characteristics of Inappropriate Writing
15.1.1.1	Tone
15.1.1.2	Argument Development
15.1.1.3	Organization
15.1.1.4	Presentation of Paper
15.1.1.5	Plagiarism
15.1.1.6	Spelling and Grammatical Errors
15.1.2	Distinguishing Scholarly/Refereed/Peer-Reviewed Journals from Other Periodicals
15.1.2.1	Paper-Based Periodicals
15.1.2.2	Electronic Full-Text Articles
15.2	Audience Attitude
15.3	Audience Expectations about the Article
Chapter 15 Activities	

15.1 Basic Issues

15.1.1 Characteristics of Inappropriate Writing

The following are some common, inappropriate characteristics to be avoided while writing a research paper.

15.1.1.1 Tone

In scientific writing the tone is expected not to be
- Too personal in format
- Disrespectful or sarcastic
- Preachy in its endings
- Pompous or artificially "academic" sounding
- Too chatty or colloquial

15.1.1.2 Argument Development

When developing arguments, avoid the following common errors:
- Being long-winded or even incoherent (rambling on and on without saying much of anything)
- Providing no theory/hypothesis/argument statement
- Making vague assertions
- Making statements that are inadequately supported by the citation of examples, hard data or evidence of research

15.1.1.3 Organization

The simplest structure to follow in organizing the paper is the introduction-body-conclusion format. Furthermore, some research writing tends to be too wordy or redundant. This problem can be managed through a serious and continuous effort to implement the following strategies.

Turn *being* verbs into *doing* ones. Verbs such as *is, are, were* and *has been* make writing sound dreary and ceremonial. To turn tedious writing into engaging prose, change *being* verbs into *doing* ones. For example:

Being verbs: "I *was* at the university last week, and *was* given a tour of the campus."

Doing verbs: "I *visited* the university last week and *toured* the campus."

Write accurately. Imprecise writers use extra words and syllables. Precise writers communicate the same ideas using fewer words. Therefore, during the proofreading stage attempt to look for places to substitute one word for two of them or a shorter word for a longer one.

Ask rhetorical questions. During the writing process, envisage the questions that might emerge in readers' minds. This is important because human beings are curious; rhetorical questions encourage people to continue reading. They will start looking actively for answers to the questions that were posed.

Personalize facts and figures. Engage readers by expressing numbers in human or visual terms. When readers think information affects them personally, they will pay more attention. For example:

Original sentence: "There are over four hundred car accidents due to drunk driving in the city of Birmingham each year.".

Improved version: "One in three car accidents in the city of Birmingham involve a drunk driver."

Write in the active voice. If you need to conceal the identity of the person or group involved, use the passive voice. Otherwise, write in the active voice.

Passive sentence: "At last week's meeting, it was agreed that the old software must be replaced."

Active voice: "At our last meeting, we agreed to replace the old software."

15.1.1.4 Presentation of Paper

Presentation is an important aspect of a well-written paper. Common mistakes include not including a title, page numbers, or other necessary detail.

15.1.1.5 Plagiarism

Avoid suspicion of plagiarism by citing all facts, substantial information and secondary source material.

15.1.1.6 Spelling and Grammatical Errors

Common spelling and grammatical errors to avoid include

- Sentence fragments

- Comma splices
- Run-ons and fused sentences (joining two or more sentences together with just "and" or nothing at all)
- Mixing up or misspelling simple words (confusing *their, they're, there; too, to, two; its, it's;* and so on)

15.1.2 Distinguishing Scholarly/Refereed/Peer-Reviewed Journals from Other Periodicals

Journals have played a central role in the development of science and brought about the notion of peer review. At first this was done in-house by the editor or his staff, but is increasingly done by wider groups of national or international scientists. The peer review is usually anonymous and is meant to be critical, yet contributing to the development of the author's ideas.

Periodical literature can be divided into paper-based periodicals and electronic full-text articles.

15.1.2.1 Paper-Based Periodicals

There are a number of different types of print- or paper-based periodicals that can be distinguished:

1. Scholarly journals. Scholarly journals are concerned with academic study, especially research, and they exhibit the methods and attitudes of a scholar. Therefore, the main purpose is to inform on, report or make available original research or experimentation to the scholarly world. The language is serious and is that of the discipline covered. Information presented is supported by citing references. Scholarly journals are generally published by a professional organization and contain selective advertising. They assume some similar scholarly background on the part of readers. Work published in a scholarly journal has gone through a rigorous approval and editing process in which experts in the field evaluate journal articles before they are accepted for publication. Examples include *International Journal of Remote Sensing, Applied Geography, Harvard Business Review,* to name a very few.
2. Substantive news or general interest. The main purpose of periodicals in this category is to provide information, in a general manner, to a

broad audience of concerned citizens. These periodicals may be quite attractive in appearance, be written by professionals in the field, may be published by either professional or commercial organizations and contain selective advertising of products useful to practitioners in the field. The language is intended to interest any educated audience. There is no specialty assumed, only interest and a certain level of intelligence. Articles are often heavily illustrated, generally with photographs. News and general interest periodicals sometimes cite sources, though more often do not. Examples include the *Economist*, *National Geographic* and the *New York Times*.

3. Popular. The main purpose of this type of periodical is to entertain, provide information on hobbies, persuade or sell products (their own or their advertisers), or to promote a viewpoint. Popular periodicals come in many formats, although they are often somewhat slick and attractive in appearance. They are likely to contain masses of graphics (photographs, drawings and so on). These publications rarely, if ever, cite sources, contain extensive advertising and are mainly published for profit. Information published in such journals is often second or third hand and the original source is sometimes obscure. Articles are usually very short, written in simple language and are designed to meet a minimal education level. There is generally little depth to the content of these articles. Examples include *Parents*, *Reader's Digest* and *Vogue*.

4. Sensational. The main purpose of sensational magazines seems to be to arouse curiosity and to cater to popular superstitions. These magazines often have flashy headlines designed to astonish (for example, "Aliens Abducted My Mother-in-Law"). They tend to be slick and glossy, with an attractive format, and contain numerous photos, illustrations and drawings intended to enhance the magazine's image. Sensational periodicals come in a variety of styles, but often use a newspaper format. They are written by the magazine's staff, scholars or freelance writers and generally published by commercial enterprises for profit. Their language is elementary and occasionally inflammatory or sensational. They assume a certain gullibility in their audience. Examples include the *Globe*, *Star* and *Weekly World News*.

15.1.2.2 Electronic Full-Text Articles

Researchers are often tempted to use full-text articles from the World Wide Web without determining the level of the publication. Determining if a work is scholarly is common sense but the following pointers will help with the process:

1. Identify the author. Is there an author listed? If not, chances are it is not a scholarly article. Most scholarly electronic full-text articles will include brief biographical information about the author.
2. Examine the length of the article. If the article is several pages in length then chances are it is scholarly.
3. Does the article have a bibliography, reference list, or footnotes? This is the most important criterion for determining whether an article is scholarly.

In conclusion, if the article has a bibliography or footnotes, if the article is fairly lengthy, and if the author is a researcher or professional then there is a high possibility that the article is scholarly.

15.2 Audience Attitude

Once you identify a particular journal to send your paper to, use the following worksheet to analyse its audience (that is, the likely readership profile of its subscribers) and consider the suitability of your paper for the audience in terms of approach, language and so on.

1. Audience identity (journal and readers)
    - Who is the primary audience of the journal?
    - What is the status and what are the specialties of recent authors?
    - How broad is the readership, and how wide is the circulation?
    - What is the audience's level of technical knowledge related to your subject? How specialized is the assumed audience?
    - Will the audience be familiar with concepts, procedures and language related to your subject?
    - Will any concepts, procedures or language need to be explained in more detail than others, given the technical knowledge of your subject?

- What questions will the audience be likely to have about your subject?

2. Audience attitude

    - How receptive will the audience be to your subject? Is your subject a *star* (hot, rising topic), a *cash cow* (popular, proven topic), a *question mark* (new, unproven topic), or a *dog* (failed or negative-result topic, out-of-fashion topic)?
    - Which aspect of your subject will be of most interest to your audience? (innovative technology or application, increased sensitivity or detection levels achieved, new approach to an existing technology, portability of instrumentation, robustness of equipment or method)
    - Will the audience have any probable objections to the subject? (poor experimental design, inadequate data, too expensive for practical use, too complex for use by anyone but experts, too difficult to describe without demonstration, proprietary to a business or sensitive for publication beyond "need-to-know")
    - What level of proof does the audience expect? What level of speculation will the audience reject?

15.3 Audience Expectations about the Article

- What is the average length of articles published in the journal? Is the journal likely to publish an online version of your article? If so, is that desirable?
- What is the typical arrangement of articles in this journal?
- What are the specifications for illustrations? How many tables and figures are usually included in articles published in this journal? Is the journal's graphics capability sensitive enough for your equations, maps, colour needs and so on?

Chapter 15 Activities

Activity 44

1. Examine the paper you have submitted and highlight any of the characteristics explained above.
2. Enhance the paper by following the suggestions provided and amending it accordingly.
3. Discuss (1) and (2) above with a peer and see if you can agree on the diagnoses and the enhancements proposed or if it is possible to further enhance the paper.

Activity 45

1. Analyse the audience for a journal of your choice.
2. If you had to rewrite your paper for publication in this journal how would you frame it?
3. Discuss and justify (1) and (2) above with a peer.

16

Writing to Publish in a Peer-Reviewed Journal
Developing a Checklist

▸ Serwan M.J. Baban *and* Clement K. Sankat

16.1	Introduction
16.2	A Guide to Writing and Publishing Research Papers in Peer- Reviewed Journals
16.2.1	Introduction
16.2.2	The Concept of Peer Review
16.2.3	Elementary Issues
16.2.3.1	Getting Started
16.2.3.2	Writing Styles
16.2.3.3	Grammar, Punctuation and Spelling
16.2.3.4	Developing a Rationale for the Research
16.2.3.5	Procrastination
16.2.4	The Organizational Elements of the Manuscript
16.2.4.1	Selecting the Title and Keywords
16.2.4.2	The Abstract
16.2.4.3	The Introduction
16.2.4.4	The Literature Review
16.2.4.5	The Methodology
16.2.4.6	The Results
16.2.4.7	The Discussion

16.2.4.8　The Conclusion
16.2.4.9　References
16.2.4.10　Acknowledgements
16.2.5　Illustrations
16.2.6　The Editing Process
16.2.7　The Reviewing Process
16.2.7.1　Fairness and Objectivity
16.2.7.2　Responding to Reviewers' Comments
16.2.8　The Last Hurdle
References
Chapter 16 Activities

16.1　Introduction

Writing is the best way to communicate new ideas and concepts or to describe certain principles, understanding, development or progress in a particular area of study to other interested parties locally, regionally and internationally and across time. It is accepted that the objectives of a research project are only completely met when the findings are published as a scientific paper (Lock 1984). Furthermore, publication of articles in peer-reviewed papers can benefit the authors in many ways. Such publications are likely to satisfy the criterion for promotion and career advancement worldwide, increase one's circle of professional acquaintances, and encourage ideas and responses from interested parties (Singh and Nitin 2001). Therefore, it is something of a paradox that many researchers, both experienced and inexperienced, are reluctant to write. This is understandable for the new or novice researcher, who may have little idea of what might be expected, particularly when effective mentoring is not provided.

Among more experienced researchers, a dislike for the writing experience may be due partly to a continuing lack of confidence in their abilities. Institutions of higher education and the science community in particular have acknowledged the need for publications. The huge number of papers submitted for publication in refereed and highly ranked journals reflects this. However, unfortunately, every year thousands of papers are either rejected or returned with a request for major revisions. This process often leads to researchers developing some form of insecurity and doubt about the quality of the submitted work (DePoy and Gitlin 1994). Unfortunately, very little effort is devoted to explaining that a paper can be turned down for a number of reasons other than quality of the work. These often include not targeting the most suitable journal and readership as well as the paper lacking in organization and clarity.

There has been a large increase in the number of papers submitted for publication to journals worldwide (Singh and Nitin 2001) and some argue that this is caused by institutional requirements for research ranking or for personal promotion in institutions of higher education worldwide. However, this increase is most likely caused by increasing investments in research to fuel competitiveness in countries, more funding, more researchers, more facilities and so on. This growth in research and research outputs has made it even more difficult for inexperienced researchers to publish in quality journals.

This chapter aims to assist young or more established but reluctant researchers to write papers that can convey information in an easy to understand way and stimulate the interest of reviewers and editors. Therefore, it contains guidance on the process of writing and publishing in a peer-reviewed journal. The requirements for organization, structure, argument development and the composition of various sections in a paper are discussed with the view to help novice researchers to achieve publication in journals. These issues are dealt with here and are mainly based on the views of Baban and Sankat (2003).

16.2 A Guide to Writing and Publishing Research Papers in Peer-Reviewed Journals

16.2.1 Introduction

Writing and reporting are continuing parts of the research process and should begin shortly after the commencement of a project, and continue to and beyond its completion. Ideally, research publications need to be aimed at reaching the wider academic or professional community at the highest level. This is achieved by targeting peer-reviewed journals at the international and national levels.

16.2.2 The Concept of Peer Review

Quality journals have standards for peer review whereby authors are not told who reviewed their paper and reviewers are not told who wrote the paper. In some cases, peer reviewers are informed of the identity of the authors after the manuscript is either accepted or rejected. Before they review a paper, peer reviewers are expected to observe two important considerations:

1. Confidentiality. All manuscripts are privileged communication. Reviewers are asked to refrain from showing or discussing manuscripts with anyone, except to solicit assistance with a technical point. If a reviewer feels that a colleague is more qualified to review the paper, the reviewer must first request permission from the journal's editor to pass on the paper. The review and recommendations are considered confidential.
2. Conflicts of interest. If any difficulties are anticipated in writing an objective review, reviewers are asked to return the paper immediately, unreviewed.

Once the task has been accepted, the reviewer will normally be asked to determine the merits of a manuscript and to guide a journal's editor through his or her report. The determination is based on providing answers for leading questions as well as general and specific comments on the innovation, importance for the readers and so forth, as follows:

1. Leading questions. What is the major contribution of the paper to the discipline? What are its major strengths and weaknesses, and its suitability for publication? Both general and specific comments should bear on these questions.
2. General comments.
   - Importance and interest to this journal's readers
   - Scientific/academic soundness and rigour
   - Originality
   - Degree to which conclusions are supported by the data
3. Specific comments. Reviewers are asked to support general comments with specific evidence on presentation, length, methods used, data presentation, statistical design and analysis, errors, citations and overlap with already published papers.

16.2.3 Elementary Issues

The traditional language and structure of papers are logical and detached from personal opinion. Interpretations are supported by numeric data. Effective writing demands using simple, familiar words with precise meaning rather than those that are vague. Paragraphs should be short and each one should be restricted to a single topic.

The writing process is influenced by the style and expectations of the journal that will consider the article for publication. In addition, the readership for which a paper is written determines the degree of specificity that should be included. The following are some elementary issues for consideration.

16.2.3.1 Getting Started

Examining section 16.1 will indicate clearly that planning is a very important element of the publication process. Careful planning includes the following activities:

- Defining clear and focused objectives.
- Conducting an up-to-date literature review.
- Utilizing relevant scientific methods, approaches and techniques that pay attention to detail and can be followed to reproduce the results.

Before starting to write, authors should

- o Decide on the type of the paper; for example, scientific and technical, application, subject review, or industrial development.
- o Select the level of the journal in terms of being local, regional or international.
- o Examine the readership of the journal; that is, academic, technical, professional, management or policy oriented.
- o Review a recent issue of the target journal for content, structure, style, presentation, referencing format, length and fees, if any, for page charges and illustrations, and the like.

16.2.3.2 Writing Styles

The *style* relates to how to write up the research, which may be determined by the requirements of a specific journal, the readership and author(s) preference or by a mixture of all of these factors. Therefore, the author(s) should carefully read the "notes and guidelines for authors" for the targeted journal and pay attention to the style required by the targeted journal.

The other issue related to style is *voice*, which has to do with the author's articulating and telling the story of the research. An author's voice will likely develop further with experience. However, examining and making notes on the voice used in published papers in the targeted journal can be very useful.

16.2.3.3   Grammar, Punctuation and Spelling

An essential element of the paper is communicating the work to someone who reads it. Therefore, it is important to write in a way that the reader will understand. Consequently, the use of correct punctuation and spelling, good grammar and formal style which avoids colloquialisms is essential. Otherwise, this might cause the reviewer to misunderstand or misinterpret the meaning of the work. This can also detract from the otherwise good academic merit of the paper and lead to its rejection. It is important to be mindful of serious and surprisingly common errors, which can include the following:

- Using long sentences in which the sense of what you are saying gets lost. A series of shorter, punchy sentences can advance the argument more effectively.
- Using one-sentence paragraphs. Paragraphs should contain a number of sentences on the same subject, and then lead on to the next paragraph, which will move the discussion along.
- Beginning sentences with "joining" words, such as *but*, *and* or *because*.
- Including long lists of material in the text. The paper should read as a flowing piece of text; therefore, if lists are required, they should be placed separately from the main text.
- Not understanding the full range of standard punctuation forms, including, in particular, the colon (:), semicolon (;), comma (,) and full stop (.).
- Not paying attention to spelling mistakes, sentences without verbs and simple typing errors.

16.2.3.4 Developing a Rationale for the Research

The main elements for developing a successful and effective rationale are a context, themes, progression, and linkages and references.

Context consists of the extensive understanding of the research topic, which might operate at three levels:

1. The background; for example, if the author is an engineer, the context may be engineering applications.
2. The field of study; for example, coastal engineering, sediment transport and so on.
3. The methodology used; for example, bathymetric surveys and mapping coastal currents.

In order to provide an adequate conceptualization of the research for the readers, a research paper will be expected to mention, as a minimum, two of these levels. The conceptualization is likely to form an important part of the early sections of the paper with some reference towards the end of the paper.

Themes are the key issues, concepts, questions or needs that have been identified as being of relevance and interest. These will both inform the research, so it will be evident in the contextual discussion, and help to structure the analysis and findings. They are the aspects of the field of study or discipline to which the research is contributing. These themes will need to be introduced early in the paper, forming part of its context. The author(s) will then need to refer to them throughout the main body of the discussion, as the running thread binding the paper together. A significant part of the concluding sections will have to be devoted to reflection on what the research has shown or contributed to these themes and how they might be researched further in the future.

Progression relates to how the argument is planned in stages, and how it is divided into convenient portions for the reader. Some aspects of this progression will be dealt with when referring to the use of the introduction and conclusion sections, and suggesting an early conceptualization and a later discussion and reflection.

The author will need to control the *references* rather than be controlled by them. Therefore, it is important for the author to develop an argument and apply his or her interpretation without being swamped by the references to previously published work.

The author(s) will be required to provide the summaries and linkages to determine the order in which to introduce and comment on the references, decide what else to add and how to progress the argument of the research. This will involve establishing the author's voice and the argument early on in the paper, maintaining it as the key thread running throughout while returning to a fuller evaluation of it at relevant points. As well as returning to the argument, it is common to return to a discussion of existing research, previous findings and understanding towards the end of the paper. Having introduced and critically discussed a selection of this material earlier on, they need to be related or sometimes compared to the research findings once these have been presented and discussed. This approach brings continuity and emphasis to the findings of the research paper.

16.2.3.5 Procrastination

Procrastination is a phase that most researchers go through from time to time. The basic advice to academics and researchers is to read, critically evaluate the trends in a particular subject, research and write. The point is to aim to produce some writing as regularly as possible and then work from that. The following are some suggestions for overcoming procrastination:

- Engage in focused research and development projects.
- Review relevant publications on a continuous basis as research is progressing.
- Make notes on the references read.
- Target and set a time line for publication in a particular journal.
- Draft the structure of the paper and its possible contents.
- Draft the structure for a section of the paper.
- Make a list of the points that need to be addressed.
- Aim to write a given number of words each day or week.
- Write up to the word limit, and then start to edit the paper.
- Reflect on the writing and discuss it with someone else.
- Try to write at a different time of day, or time of the week.

6.2.4   The Organizational Elements of the Manuscript

The main body of the paper is often divided into several sections and sub-sections. There should be continuity in the presentation. The style of sections and subsections should conform to the guidelines provided by the targeted journal for preparation of the manuscript. If no guidelines are available, the author should be guided by previous issues of the journal. The structure of the main sections is developed to strengthen the concept of the manuscript. The first of these supporting methods is the adoption of informative, descriptive headings for sections and subsections. The choice of these headings is important because well-chosen headings are not only an aid to the reader but also a reminder to the author(s) to keep in focus the content of each section. Well-designed and placed illustrations and tables can significantly enhance communication and the quality of presentation.

16.2.4.1   Selecting the Title and Keywords

The title of the paper needs to be brief and self-explanatory about the contents of the paper. Some journals require keywords to be provided for the paper. Normally there are fewer than ten keywords. Keywords are used for abstracting, categorization, indexing and retrieval purposes. Therefore, the keywords should faithfully describe the paper in terms of the subject, techniques and methods, geographic location, environment and so on.

16.2.4.2   The Abstract

The abstract is generally limited to about 150 words, which summarizes the essence of the information that is needed by readers. Many researchers who will not read any other part of the paper will read an abstract. Therefore, it should be entirely self-contained (Singh and Nitin 2001). Generally, there are two types of paper: review and research papers. Research papers may include reports on exploratory, testing and problem solving research. The abstract for a review paper is required to provide a road map for readers to previous research findings. For a research paper, a good abstract is expected to explain in a clear, logical sequence the scientific or engineering problem, the methodology, data collection, compilation and quality control, the main results, conclusions and the implications of those conclusions. It is difficult to compress all this information into a few hundred words, which is one of the reasons why good abstracts can be difficult to write.

One way of approaching the task is to write paragraphs to target specific information. For example, the first paragraph can focus on the introductory and background material: the aim of the project, why it is important, and the scientific background. The second paragraph can be the methodology: how to set out to do the research and the techniques used. In some cases, this may fit into the first paragraph as introductory material. The next paragraph should be the observations or measurements, primary data collection and so on. It is useful to keep the data separate from the background material and from the interpretation sections. The final paragraph ought to cover the interpretation of the results, conclusions, and some comment on the broader scientific implications of the findings (what it all means). This paragraph structure will vary depending on the structure of the work. If the paper dwells at length on methodological issues, then the abstract might reflect that, with a paragraph devoted to methodology. If the methodology in the paper is standard, then it could be absorbed quickly into the introductory paragraph. The abstract is often written last, that is, once the manuscript is completed. Frequently, journals may require a very tight abstract of one paragraph, making the task more challenging. The key here is to be succinct, with key methodology and findings presented without details.

16.2.4.3 The Introduction

The purpose here is to provide the reader with the background and aims of the paper, a definition of the problem, the background of previous work reported, including different approaches on the topic, precisely what the paper is trying to achieve and how this has been pursued (DePoy and Gitlin 1994). More specifically, the introduction is often divided into the following sections:

1. The overall aim of the paper. A clear statement of the aim should be given, as this will help reviewers and readers.
2. Scientific background and justification. These should provide the reader with the details of the topic. For example, if the aim was to make a geological identification of a structure in England, something about the geology and geological structures in England will need to be explained. This section provides an opportunity to demonstrate to reviewers the author's expertise in the field and his or her familiarity with a broad range of relevant material. It also provides the chance to set the specific

research into its wider academic or professional context. From the background material should emerge the reason for the research; in other words, the justification. Therefore, an "unknown" or an "unclear" element should arise from the background discussion. One might argue that the extent of the geological structure remains unknown, for example, or that there is controversy about oil or gas production. This "unknown" leads directly and conveniently to the next stages of the argument. If something is unknown or unclear, "finding it out" or clarifying seems like a sensible objective.

3. Specific objective of the research. When writing the overall aims it is necessary to assume that readers are not necessarily familiar with the research topic, and consequently much of the specific detail should be left out. Placing the discussion of the specific objectives after the background is recommended, as this will provide the readers with some knowledge of the subject. This section therefore aims to explain in specific terms, with reference to the issues identified in the previous section, exactly what this research is trying to achieve. It is good practice to write a section on the "Scope of the Work" as this will define the boundaries of the research and research answers. It is not expected that a research paper on a particular subject can necessarily touch on all facets of the subject.

16.2.4.4 The Literature Review

This section provides information on the work done on the topic by previous researchers. It is logical to assume that the research would have been devised after consideration of the previous literature. The aim of the work should be to build on the body of knowledge that already exists (DePoy and Gitlin 1994). It is necessary, therefore, to explain this existing knowledge and to mention the work that has led to it. Some journals may ask for both a literature review and a separate scientific background; the difference between the two should be that the scientific background provides the broad context of the work, whereas the literature review focuses specifically on previously published work and literature that are directly related to the paper. This might be work that has attempted exactly the same goals as the paper or that has been successful in the same field or used the same techniques. If the aim of the scientific background is to give readers enough information to be able to understand the *overall aims*, then the aim of the literature review is to give readers the information they need to see both the *overall aims* and the *specific objectives* in a detailed scientific context.

16.2.4.5 The Methodology

The section on methodology needs to explain the procedures followed in carrying out the research. This explanation should be sufficiently clear and comprehensive so that if other researchers wished to repeat the research in the future they could use the methodology section as an instruction manual as to how to proceed. The methodology section also assists to persuade reviewers that the author understood what he or she was doing and had knowledge of how to perform it correctly. The section on methodology is commonly expected to cover the following issues:

- *Scientific approach.* This should explain the philosophical basis and the procedural requirements of the adopted approach. For example, is the study quantitative or qualitative? Does it adopt a hypothesis-testing approach? What types of information are required to fulfil the project's aims and objectives? What are the characteristics of the research design?
- *Data collection methods.* This should explain the precise details of data collection procedures, including the measures taken to overcome problems that were encountered. Depending on whether the study involves field, laboratory or library research, this might require detailed description of experimental equipment, of field survey or sampling procedures, or of questionnaire design and implementation.
- *Data analysis methods.* This should explain the reasons for selecting particular analytical techniques, the nature of the techniques chosen, the practical effectiveness of the techniques and any problems experienced in their application to the project. It is especially important to describe any modifications made to standard procedures and why these were necessary.
- *Statistical methods.* It is often expected that the researchers also report on and justify the selection of the statistical methods used for analysing and interpreting the results.

16.2.4.6 The Results

This section reports the data that were collected by means of the procedures described in the methodology section. It is conventional practice for the data to stand alone in a section of its own. Future readers of the research can then distinguish easily between what actually happened in the field or in the laboratory and what the author(s) thought it meant. Results can be presented in a variety of ways, depending on the nature of the study and of the methodology used. Using the tabular or graphical form of presentation is the most common. A good way of getting ideas of how to present data is to study and examine published work that uses similar types of data.

16.2.4.7 The Discussion

This section will need to bridge the logical gap between the observations and the conclusions. In this section, the authors(s) need to explain clearly how the observations and/or measurements made can relate to the aims, background and scientific structure of the paper. The section on results presents the outcomes, whereas this section explains the reasons for the outcomes. The author(s) will also have to include and explain any conditions and limitations, as well as level of confidence statements in order to moderate the conclusions. The discussion needs to be separate from the results so that readers can distinguish between the "objective" element of the measurements and observations and the more "subjective" element of what the author(s) believe about those observations. A future researcher scouring the literature for data about the topic would probably be interested in the observations and not the interpretation. The discussion section may touch on the implications of the findings of the paper for previously reported work, and for professional or industrial practice, so as to give more meaning to its findings.

16.2.4.8 The Conclusion

The conclusion is expected to bring the main outcomes of the paper into sharp focus. After the abstract, the conclusion is the most read section of the paper. Therefore, the findings should be clear, concise and easy for the reader to extract. A conclusion, unlike a summary, which concentrates heavily on the results, not only reviews the results but also interprets them. The conclusion needs to list the principal findings of your research. These can be divided into the points that answer the specific questions that the paper was investigating, and some methodological or other findings that arose as a by-product of the principal line of research. In addition, there may be issues concerning the nature of the research and some ideas and recommendations concerning future research or applications. Furthermore, developmental papers will also need to identify future direction and possible applications.

16.2.4.9 References

The purpose of this section is to provide full details of all the published material that the author(s) have mentioned in the paper. A reference list is not the same as a bibliography. A bibliography is a list of publications that are relevant to your subject. A reference list contains only those items specifically cited in the text. The proper use of references helps to define the novelty of technical developments. The idea of the reference list is that if a reader wishes to go to the library and find a copy of something mentioned in the report, the list should provide all the necessary publication details. The reference list is therefore a reader service and an essential follow-up to the text. Consequently, the author(s) should communicate a substantial amount of information about the author, year, title, journal, pages and so on. The style of presentation of references depends on the targeted journal and is usually described for authors in the journal's guideline for submission.

16.2.4.10 Acknowledgements

Authors may include a section titled "Acknowledgements". This can refer to any grants used to support the research, any special technical assistance received and so on.

16.2.5 Illustrations

Illustrations should be legible; otherwise, they have a negative impact on the manuscript. The most powerful way to attract viewers is to break the monotony of the text and provide illustrations that effectively bring out the meaning of the manuscript in a vivid manner (Singh and Nitin 2001).

1. Figures. A strategic choice of illustrations, such as charts, diagrams, drawings and photographs, for the paper will greatly strengthen it. The use of colour can only be justified when a figure has more than six or eight categories. Some journals will not accept colour. The acceptable number of figures depends on the targeted journal; however, it should not exceed five or six figures. The captions should provide the overall information. It is preferable to place each figure just after its first citation in the text, on the same page if possible; otherwise, on the next page. In no case should it be placed on earlier pages. Some journals may ask for the figures to be provided separately from the text.
2. Tables. Tables are used to avoid duplication and provide substantial information such as key statistics in a compact, easy-to-follow and meaningful form. Placing the tables within the text is dependent on the targeted journal. Some journals ask that the tables be provided separately. If this is not specified, tables should be placed near where they are mentioned in the text. The acceptable number of tables depends on the targeted journal; however, it should not exceed five or six tables.

16.2.6 The Editing Process

Once the first draft is written, the "writing up" process becomes in part a process of rewriting what you have already written. Redrafting is a normal event as it enhances the sharpness of a paper and is a reflective process that enhances the quality of the paper. It does not mean that your original draft is useless, merely that the writing process takes place over a period of time, during which you will make every effort to make the paper as effective as possible and conform to the style of a particular journal. It is good practice to make notes on earlier drafts and keep the drafts for reference at later dates. Editing is necessary in order to

- Bring in new material, ideas and thinking.
- Reduce the length of the manuscript.
- Revise old sections to refer to newly drafted material.
- Change the structure, and remove any repetitions and duplications.
- Check for completeness and accuracy of data.
- Check for clarity of the basic concept and development of the argument.
- Evaluate adequacy of the approach and the solution.

- Analyse the results.

It is difficult to analyse one's own manuscript for technical contents. The best way is to stay away from it for a few days and then to have a fresh look. Give colleagues a chance to review it. Before submitting the paper, the author(s) must revisit the guidelines for preparation of the manuscript by the targeted journal and edit the paper to comply with these instructions. It is also recommended to ask a nonspecialist and detached person to proofread and to comment on the paper.

16.2.7 The Reviewing Process

Quality publications (except invited papers) are peer reviewed, often by three reviewers, before being published. This process normally takes between three and six months but can take much longer, particularly if major corrections to the paper are required. However, due to the increased desire to publish in high impact journals, the actual publication may take up to eighteen months.

Reviewers are provided with guidelines and asked to review the paper based on the following aspects and questions:

- Relevance of the paper. Is the subject matter suitable for the journal? Is the paper suitable for publication in its present form?
- The originality of the paper, rated on a scale of 1 to 5.
- Presentation. Does the paper tell a cohesive story? Is a tightly reasoned argument evident throughout the paper? Where does the paper wander from this argument? Do the title, abstract, keywords, introduction, and conclusions accurately and consistently reflect the major point(s) of the paper? Is the writing concise, easy to follow, and interesting?
- Are the methods appropriate? Current? Described clearly enough so that the work could be repeated by someone else?
- Are the statistical design and analyses appropriate and correct? Can the reader readily discern which measurements or observations are independent of which other measurements or observations? Are replicates correctly identified? Are statements of significance justified?
- Are there any errors in technique, fact, calculation, interpretation or style?
- What portions of the paper should be expanded? Condensed? Com-

bined? Deleted? Is the division between the main article and the appendices appropriate?
- Is the data well presented? When results are stated in the text of the paper, can they be easily verified by examining tables and figures? Are any of the results counterintuitive? Are all tables and figures clearly labelled? Well planned? Too complex? Necessary?
- Is the English satisfactory?
- Is the abstract informative?
- Are the conclusions sound and justified?
- Are the references adequate and correct? Have they been cited in the text?
- Does this paper report data or conclusions already published or in press?
- Comments to the journal editor.
- Comments to authors, general comments on the topic, structure, organization and specific comments on technical issues, applicability and suggestions to improve the paper.

Based on the reviewers' opinions, a large number of papers are often rejected. However, this doesn't mean necessarily that the quality of research is poor. In fact, the rejection rate could be directly linked to the demand for publication in a particular journal.

16.2.7.1   Fairness and Objectivity

If the research reported in a paper is flawed, criticism is usually directed at the science, not the scientist. Therefore, the reviewers will attempt to convince the author that
- The entire paper has been read, examined and evaluated carefully.
- Criticisms are objective and correct, not merely differences of opinion, and are intended to help the author to improve the paper.
- She or he is qualified to offer an expert opinion about the research reported in this paper.

Reviewers are well-established authorities in their field. They believe in academic service and therefore they are volunteering their time and expertise to assist others with their publications. Consequently, reviewers often aim to win the author's respect and appreciation through an informed and concise review of the manuscript.

16.2.7.2 Responding to Reviewers' Comments

Reviewers' comments can significantly strengthen the paper. The reviewers will have experience in highlighting the weaknesses of a paper and advising on how to improve it. Therefore, authors are expected to adhere to their comments and advice. If an author dismisses the suggestions of the reviewers entirely, the paper may not appear in the journal and, even if it did, the readers may have a regrettable impression of the author.

If revisions are requested, the author will need to submit a revised manuscript to the journal within a specific period, typically four to six months, depending on the journal. A cover letter to the journal's editor, which lists the major changes made to the paper (and as suggested by the reviewers), should accompany the revised paper. A manuscript undergoing revision for longer than four to six months will often be considered a new submission.

Once a manuscript has been rejected, it will be eligible for further review only if a revision was invited, or if it has been rewritten so completely that it can legitimately be called a new manuscript.

First-time authors need to be prepared for rejections and not take it personally. Therefore, once a paper has been rejected, it is advisable to wait a few days then reexamine the reviewers' comments carefully and dispassionately, then address them in an academic, scholarly manner, as necessary to bring the paper to the right level and submit it for publication in a comparable journal to the first one.

16.2.8   The Last Hurdle

The editor-in-chief is responsible for verifying that the relevant corrections, recommendations and amendments proposed by the reviewers have been complied with and incorporated in the revised version. Once he or she is satisfied that the manuscript is publishable, it is sent to the publisher. The publisher typesets the paper in the style of the journal and sends the proof to the corresponding author for verification. At this point, major revisions are not acceptable. In fact, most journals ask authors to return proofs within a few days. Nevertheless, it is advisable to ask a detached person to examine the proofs for obvious minor mistakes. The majority of journals will offer the author a number of free copies of the published paper or a softcopy in a PDF format. However, the author will be asked to sign over the copyright of the published paper to the journal. Once an author has been published, getting the next paper published should be easier due to familiarity with the publishing processes and being recognized as a published author.

References

Baban, S.M.J., and C.K. Sankat. 2003. The guide to writing and publishing research papers in peer-reviewed journals. *West Indian Journal of Engineering* 25 (2): 54–64.

DePoy, E., and L.N. Gitlin. 1994. *Introduction to Research.* St Louis, MO: Mosby.

Lock, S. 1984. Foreword. In *Research: How to Plan, Speak, and Write about It,* ed. C. Hawkins and M. Sorgi. Berlin: Springer-Verlag.

Singh, S., and K.T. Nitin. 2001. Writing and publishing a research paper in professional journals: A systematic approach. *Asian Journal of Geoinformatics* 1 (3): 87–90.

Chapter 16 Activities

Activity 46

1. Examine the paper you have submitted and highlight any of the characteristics explained above.
2. Enhance the paper by following the suggestions provided and make the amendments accordingly.
3. Discuss (1) and (2) above with a peer and see if you can agree on the evaluation and the enhancements proposed, or if it is possible to further enhance the paper.

Activity 47

1. Analyse the audience for a journal of your choice.
2. If you had to rewrite your paper for publication in this journal how would you frame it?
3. Discuss and justify (1) and (2) above with a peer.

17

Introduction to the Reviewing/Refereeing Process

▸ SERWAN M.J. BABAN

17.1	Introduction
17.2	The Review Process
17.2.1	Refereeing/Reviewing Report Form
17.2.2	Guidelines for Referees
17.2.2.1	Technical Aspects
17.2.2.2	Quality
17.2.2.3	Presentation
17.3	Ethical Issues Facing Journal Referees
Chapter 17 Activities	

17.1 Introduction

Refereeing skills are important to scientists so they can realistically assess their research and review the work of others prior to publication of their research. Journals often provide guidance on what they are interested in publishing and how the suitability of manuscripts for publication should be assessed.

Experience indicates that a potentially publishable paper should meet the following criteria. Failure to meet any one of these criteria might be sufficient to recommend rejection.

1. The motivation for the paper should be clear and compelling. Typically, the motivation will include a clearly specified research question and a

statement as to why this question is interesting. However, a paper whose primary motivation is to synthesize or even survey earlier work might also be publishable.
2. The analysis in the paper should be correct and should be appropriately rigorous given the research question and the field of research.
3. The paper must be sufficiently original to warrant publication. Typically, this originality arises from new theoretical results or new empirical findings, but it may also arise from new interpretation or synthesis of known material.
4. The paper should be well written. In particular, the logical structure of the paper should be clear, and the paper should be relatively free from errors of grammar. A skilful author can usually make an intrinsically difficult argument reasonably easy to follow, while poor writing can make even minor or trivial points hard to understand.
5. The paper should be potentially interesting to a reasonably broad group of prospective readers. These readers might be confined to a particular field within a particular discipline, but the ideal paper is one that would capture the interest of other readers as well.

17.2   The Review Process

The following are some general comments about the review process:

- Refereeing for a journal is expected to be completed within a given timeframe, usually four to eight weeks. If it cannot be completed within the specified period, it should be returned urgently to the editor, with a suggestion for an alternative reviewer, if possible. This initiative is always appreciated.
- The journal usually gives some guidance on the structure of the review, perhaps as a form to be completed (see figure 17.1).
- Some reviewers tend to make notes for the author in the margins of the manuscript. This is useful for comments on grammar and spelling. It is a matter of choice how much guidance is provided, but where the authors have had great difficulties with English, the editor will need to be informed.
- When the reviewer is not an expert in the specific field of a manuscript, he or she should define the limits to his or her knowledge. Avoid being

rude or overly harsh about the manuscript; being polite but firm is recommended.
- Reviewers should show leadership and be helpful to the author, even when the work is rejected, through attempting to suggest ways in which the work can be further developed, focused and strengthened.
- Reviewers should be particularly attentive to tables and diagrams. These should be necessary and should not repeat information already provided.

Referees are often expected to review papers within about eight weeks of receipt, allowing a turn-around time of about three months from the author's point of view. The following approach is helpful:

- When the paper first arrives (that is, within the first week) take a quick look at it. You might be able to quickly form an opinion that the paper should be rejected, based perhaps on similarity to existing work or lack of overall significance.
- If you can come to a quick decision of this type, take an hour or so to write up a short report, briefly explaining your concerns, then send it to the editor by fax or e-mail.
- If, on the other hand, the paper looks interesting and well done, then you will probably want to put the paper away until you have time to read it more thoroughly.

Referees might sometimes need to send papers back without refereeing them. Please keep the following points in mind before making such a decision:

- If you have recently had a paper published, accepted for publication, or even just advanced to the invited revision stage at a journal, the editors will expect you to do a reasonable amount of refereeing. People who use the resources of the journal without contributing to the refereeing process are considered free riders.
- If you must decline, let the editor know quickly (within a few days of receiving the paper), by fax or e-mail. The paper can be returned by regular mail.
- It is helpful to provide the names of alternative referees. Ideal suggestions are young, active scholars who might not be over-burdened with other duties and with whom the editor might not be familiar.

- If you are not competent to referee a paper in a particular area, you should return the paper and explain the reason, indicating a willingness to handle papers in your area, which you should specify clearly. Keep in mind, however, that the editor might have asked you precisely because you can provide perspective. It is helpful to the editor if you make comments appropriate to your background, even if you cannot appreciate all aspects of a paper.

Authors deserve detailed feedback in a tone that is not hostile, regardless of whether the reviewer recommends rejecting, revising or accepting their work. By agreeing to do the review, the reviewer takes on the responsibility of doing a thorough job.

Authors also have a responsibility to reviewers. Reviewers volunteer time from busy schedules to conduct comprehensive reviews, and are happy to do so for well-thought-through manuscripts. If you submit premature work, not only will you annoy your colleagues who take the time to referee, but you will gain an unsavory reputation over time. Researchers tend to work in rather small communities and reputations spread.

When a manuscript is sent for refereeing, the reviewer will typically receive a report form to complete, as well as guidelines for referees for the journal and article in question. The reviewer will also be asked to confirm that he or she is able to provide a report by the given deadline.

17.2.1 Refereeing/Reviewing Report Form

A report form is usually sent to reviewers to complete. It is divided into sections which deal with scientific quality, scientific content, accuracy and interpretation. The reviewer is asked to indicate his or her assessment of the article using the categories provided. The example of a review form provided here (see figure 17.1) represents a typical format used by scientific journals. If a reviewer is recommending rejection, then the primary reasons for the negative recommendation need to be specified. If a reviewer is of the opinion that the manuscript is competent but just not interesting enough or not important enough for a particular journal, then this opinion needs to be expressed as a part of the process. For papers where you recommend acceptance or a revision, it is helpful to say what you think is the key contribution of the paper. It is also very helpful to consider what kinds of condensation might be desirable. If a sixty-page paper contains a "nugget" of high value material that can be converted to a ten-page note, it is useful to pass that information along to the editor.

The reviewers will also need to write a report that will be forwarded to the author and a separate letter that is just for the editor. The letter to the editor needs to be clear as to the nature of the recommendation (reject, revise, or accept). Finally, the reviewer may be asked to provide comments suitable for transmission to the authors. This is an opportunity to provide guidance and advice to the authors on all relevant aspects.

Referee Form for a Journal

Paper Number:

Title:

Reviewer:

Use the following scale for your ratings THROUGHOUT this form

           Low   High
    N/A 1 2 3 4 5

RESEARCH CONTRIBUTION

Theoretical Research Contribution:

Quality of Experiments:

System Evaluation:

Overview of Hypermedia Systems or Research:

Quality of Prototype Implementation:

OTHER RESEARCH CHARACTERISTICS

Appropriate Conclusions:

Originality:

Technically Sound:

Technical Information Missing (What?):

Figure continues

CONTENT
Title Choice:
Abstract:
Introduction:
Appropriate Conclusions:
References:
Key References Missing (Which Ones?)

WRITING CHARACTERISTICS
Length:
Organization:
Clarity:
Graphics (Figures, etc.):
Needs English Editing (Y/N):

OVERALL RATINGS
Research Contribution:
Technical Content:
Originality:
Relevance:
Writing Quality:

OVERALL RECOMMENDATION:
Accept (with minor or no revisions) [ ]
Accept with major revisions [ ]
Accept with major revisions only if there is space [ ]
Reject: inadequate quality [ ]
Reject: inappropriate material [ ]
Submit to another conference/journal: [ ]

Comments for author(s):

EVALUATION INFORMATION
*** Authors will NOT see the following comments ***
Please rate your interest and/or ability to review the paper:
* Very good [ ]   * Good [ ]   * Average [ ]   * Marginal [ ]
* It was a mistake to send me this paper [ ]

Figure 17.1. Referee form for a journal

17.2.2 Guidelines for Referees

Reviewers are expected to assess manuscripts based on technical aspects, quality and presentation.

17.2.2.1 Technical Aspects

- Scientific merit: Is the work scientifically rigorous, accurate and correct?
- Appropriateness: Is the material appropriate for the journal and the readership?
- Clarity: Are ideas expressed clearly and concisely? Are the concepts understandable? Is the discussion written in a way that is easy to read and understand?
- Referencing: Is the research properly grounded in the literature? Has the author made reference to the most recent and most appropriate work? Is the present work set in the context of the previous work?
- Balance: Is the overall balance and structure of the paper good? Should the authors concentrate more on a specific area of the paper, or are there sections that are unnecessary and which could be reduced or eliminated?
- English: How is the author's writing style? Is it too "dense" to make sense? Does it keep the reader's interest? Is it too informal? Note that an informal style in itself sometimes is very effective in getting a paper's ideas across. Similarly, many authors use humour very effectively in research papers. Only if the informality or humour gets in the way should it be discouraged. (On the other hand, there are certain fields that enforce very formal writing styles, in which an informal style is deemed inappropriate.) In general, you do not need to make corrections to English in an article. It is, however, helpful if you correct the English where the scientific meaning is unclear.

17.2.2.2 Quality

- Significance: Does the article contain important new results? Is it likely to have a significant impact on current research?
- Originality: Is the work relevant and novel? Does the work contain significant additional material to that already published? If the reviewer feels that the work presented is unoriginal, it is useful for him or her to

supply references for transmission to the authors. Is this paper likely to be cited in the future?
- Motivation: Does the problem considered have a sound motivation? All papers should clearly demonstrate the scientific interest of the results. Papers should not rely solely on previous literature or novelty to motivate publication.
- Repetition: Have significant parts of the manuscript already been published? Serial publications are not encouraged and follow-up papers must contain significant additional new material to that already reported.
- Length: Is the content of the work of sufficient scientific interest to justify its length? Each article should be of the shortest length required to contain all useful and relevant information, and no longer. If reducing the length is recommended, then it is necessary to indicate specific areas where this is required and can be achieved.

17.2.2.3 Presentation

- Title: Is it adequate and appropriate for the content of the article?
- Abstract: Does it include the essential information in the article? Is it complete? Is it suitable for inclusion by itself in an abstracting service?
- Diagrams, figures, tables and captions: Are they essential? Are the tables and figures clear? Do they make sense on their own or only if one has read the text carefully? Are there too many? Would an additional table or figure help? Would an example help?
- Text and mathematics: Are they brief but still clear? If you recommend shortening the article, you need to suggest what should be omitted. Only rarely would a referee be in a position to check empirical results. Often the referee has neither sufficient time nor access to the necessary data to replicate the empirical analysis in a paper. Usually the best you can do is to convince yourself that the results seem plausible, given your knowledge of the area, and are internally consistent. One useful approach is to check some items, particularly the initial model development, and then to make sure that you can at least understand why the other results make sense. If it is very hard to follow the algebraic development in a paper, that is in itself a serious flaw in the paper.
- Conclusion: Is the conclusion significant? Is it just a rehash of the paper?

Does it provide new synthesis or insights? Does it leave the reader excited about the research, the research domain or the future? Has the author expressed the limitations of the research and of his or her approach?

17.3 Ethical Issues Facing Journal Referees

Refereeing raises ethical issues, because the anonymity of the process should not be used to reject or penalize groups or ideas one does not like. It is also important to keep the manuscript secure and although it can usually be shown to close colleagues it should not be disseminated. The reviewer should also be careful about using information presented in a submitted paper. This is best delayed until it is published, but one can certainly think on the ideas (this is one of the rewards of refereeing).

Chapter 17 Activities

Activity 48

Develop a draft paper prepared for publication in a specific refereed journal. Follow the instructions provided carefully in terms of structure (this often will require presenting information under the following sections: abstract, introduction, methodology, results, analysis and conclusions), length (often expressed as a total number of words or pages using a particular font size and line spacing), and approach. Be sensitive to readership when articulating a case (if the target is a technical journal then the technical aspects will need to be detailed, whereas this would not be the case for a journal with a focus on management, for example).

While preparing the paper, be mindful of the refereeing process and the evaluation process involved as explained in this chapter.

- Swap your draft paper with a colleague, then based on what you have learnt about reviewing in this chapter, review each other's papers.
- Attempt to evaluate the paper as
  - Suitable for publication with minimum revisions
  - Suitable for publication with major revisions
  - Not suitable for publication
- Provide feedback, justify your decision and follow this up with a round table discussion if possible to identify common mistakes and approaches available to assist with overcoming each deficiency.

Activity 49

1. Assume you are a regular referee for high-ranking international journals and during the process you were faced with the following cases. Examine each case carefully and write down your preferred approach for handling each case.
2. Discuss and justify your action with a colleague.
3. Engage in class or group discussion regarding each case.

Case 1

You were asked to read and comment on a draft paper developed by a colleague. Then, you were asked to referee the same paper for a journal. This particular journal maintains the practice of blind review, that is, preventing the identities of the authors and reviewers from being known to each other. This involves deleting the name(s) of the author(s) from the submitted paper and the identity of the reviewers from the Referee Form and any other correspondence regarding the paper being reviewed. The paper you received from the journal has been prepared accordingly.

Question: How will you proceed and why?

Case 2

A few months ago you refereed a paper entitled "ABC" for *Journal X*. Today you were asked by *Journal Y* to referee a paper entitled "XYZ". You accept the task. When the time comes, you realize that despite the title being different, "XYZ" is an only slightly modified version of the paper you already refereed for *Journal X*.

Question: How will you proceed and why?

Case 3

A few weeks ago, you received a request to referee a paper for *Journal X*. Today, you received a request to referee a paper for *Journal Y*. It is the same paper, and both journals have a policy that explicitly disallows simultaneous submissions.

Question: How will you proceed and why?

Case 4

John published an article in *Journal X*. You are writing a discussion article criticizing John's article and submitting it to *Journal Y* for publication.

Question: Should you send it to John first for his comments? Should the editors of the journal seek John's input before publishing your article?

Case 5

You are working on a paper in which you are attempting to discredit a newly formed theory on sea level rise. Despite this theory being an interesting and initially plausible scenario, there is no empirical research currently published that can defend this theory. Fortunately for you, though, you have just received and agreed to referee a paper that contains information that can strongly support the new theory. The paper is of excellent quality, certainly publishable.

Question: How would you proceed and why?

18

A Formula for Writing a Successful MPhil/PhD Thesis

▸ SERWAN M.J. BABAN

18.1	Introduction
18.2	Issues in Writing
18.2.1	Broad Conceptual Issues
18.2.2	Language Issues
18.3	How to Proceed with the Writing
18.4	Thesis Structure and Organization
18.4.1	Abstract
18.4.2	Introduction
18.4.3	Literature Review
18.4.4	Methodology
18.4.5	Results
18.4.6	Discussion
18.4.7	Conclusions
18.4.8	References
References	
Chapter 18 Activities	

18.1 Introduction

Writing is one of the most effective ways to convey ideas, concepts, principles, understanding, development, progress and findings in a particular area of study to other interested parties. In the case of the MPhil/PhD degree, it is assumed that the research is captured in the thesis. Therefore the thesis is the pinnacle of a student's research programme, and it is on the thesis that he or she will be assessed, probably in association with an oral examination or viva (Phillips and Pugh 1996). Consequently, the thesis is expected to define the problem that motivated the research, explain why that problem is important, inform on the literature of the topic, describe the new contribution, document the experiments that validate the contribution, and draw conclusions (Cryer 2000).

Writing is a continuing part of the research process; hence all MPhil/PhD students need to communicate their findings and the MPhil/PhD thesis is seen by many as the formal document that provides training for communication with other scientists. Some will even argue that writing leads to identifying gaps and aids the discovery process as it makes people think about their work in a logical and critical mode (Phillips and Pugh 1996). Thus, writing a thesis requires a student to think analytically about the structure, content, organization, grammar and style, as well as develop strong technical arguments to persuade other scientists, and to present these within the convention for formal presentations. Each statement in a thesis must be correct and justifiable in a logical and scientific sense.

If the student has difficulties with the writing processes and in communicating ideas then it is important to minimize misunderstandings and to find out as early as possible where he or she is not functioning properly. Strategies to manage these shortcomings include giving departmental seminars and conference presentations, as well as writing journal articles. Additionally, students should try to find people new to their work who will listen to their explanations or are willing to read their draft theses and tell them if they have difficulties following the arguments.

There is no uniform view across disciplines about what constitutes a satisfactory thesis, either for a degree entirely by research or for an award with a research component. This chapter in a broad sense aims to stimulate thinking and indicate topics for discussion and clarification between the students and their supervisors. More specifically, it aims to assist MPhil/PhD students with writing their thesis by providing guidance on the processes involved, as well as advice on the structure, writing up, argument development, the required composition of various chapters, and organization.

18.2 Issues in Writing

18.2.1 Broad Conceptual Issues

The following points need to be understood and adhered to while writing a research thesis:

- An MPhil/PhD thesis is expected to be both "original" and "substantial". Therefore, the research performed to support a thesis must be both, and the thesis must show it to be so.
- The scientific method means starting with a hypothesis and then collecting evidence to support or deny it. One of the most challenging aspects of writing a thesis consists of composing the evidence and associated discussions into a coherent form.
- The essence of a thesis is critical thinking, not experimental data. Analysis, conceptual, and methodological development and concepts form the heart of the work.
- A thesis concentrates on principles: it includes evaluation and clarifies the lessons learned, and not merely the facts behind them.
- A clear distinction needs to be made between a *concept* and an *instance*. A reader can become confused when a concept and an instance of it are blurred. Examples include a mathematical concept and particular software that implements it under specific conditions.
- A clear distinction needs to be made between *information* and *data*. The particulars that result from an experiment are called data. The term "information" implies that the data has been analysed, condensed or combined with data from other experiments to produce useful information.
- A clear distinction needs to be made between *cause* and *effect*. A thesis must carefully separate cause-effect relationships from simple statistical correlations. For example, even if all projects managed by group X require more time to complete than the projects managed in group Y, it may not have anything to do with the researchers, group management or facilities (the people working in group X may specialize in applications that require more time than those used by group Y).
- Inferring relevant conclusions: deduced conclusions need to be sup-

ported by evidence. Even if the cause of some phenomenon seems obvious, conclusions cannot be deduced without solid, supporting evidence.
- A clear distinction needs to be made between *commerce* and *science*. In a scientific thesis, a scientist must remain objective about the merits of an idea independent of its commercial popularity. In particular, a scientist never assumes that commercial success is a valid measure of merit (many popular products are neither well designed nor well engineered). Thus, statements such as "a significant number of manufacturers make products using technique Y" are irrelevant in a thesis.
- A clear distinction needs to be made between *politics* and *science*. A scientist must avoid all political influence when assessing ideas. Obviously, it should not matter whether government bodies, political parties, religious groups or other organizations endorse an idea. Furthermore, whether a concept is originated by a senior scientist or a first-year graduate student, it must be assessed carefully independent of the source.
- In terms of definitions and terminology, the following need to be observed:
  - Each technical term used in a thesis must be defined either by a reference to a previously published definition (for standard terms with their usual meaning) or by a precise, unambiguous definition that appears before the term is used (for a new term or a standard term used in an unusual way).
  - The introductory chapter can give the intuition (that is, informal definitions) of terms provided they are defined more precisely later.
  - All abbreviations and technical jargon need to be defined when appearing first in the thesis. Each term should be used in one and only one form throughout the thesis.
- In general, all statements in a thesis need to be substantiated either by a reference to published literature or by original work. Moreover, a thesis need not repeat the details of critical thinking and analysis found in published sources; it uses the results as fact and refers the reader to the source for further details, hence citations.
- A thesis should not make moral judgements, that is, "bad", "good", "dreadful", "obtuse" "true", "wholesome", "an ideal solution". Use "incorrect/correct" to refer to factual errors or correctness.

- A thesis needs to focus on results and not the people from whom or circumstances in which they were obtained: adhere to the plain facts. Describe the results without dwelling on your reactions or events that helped you achieve them.
- A thesis needs to be free from positive and negative self-assessment. Both of the following statements are inappropriate: "My methodology is the best . . . ", "My results are inferior . . . ".

18.2.2 Language Issues

Language seems to present a challenge during thesis writing; consequently, particular attention needs to be given to the following issues (Booth, Colomb and Williams 1995; Singh and Nitin 2001; Phillips and Pugh 1996; Cryer 2000; Blaxter, Hughes and Tight 2001; Baban and Sankat 2003):

- Style: This relates to the format for writing the thesis, which may be determined by the requirements of a specific university. Therefore, the student should carefully read the "notes and guidelines" for the targeted degree. Furthermore, to communicate ideas effectively in writing, a thesis will need to be written in a formal style, which avoids colloquialisms.
- Voice: This relates to articulating and telling the "story" of the research. The student will need to use active constructions. For example, the correct expression is "the operating system starts the device" instead of "the device is started by the operating system".
- English and grammar: The use of correct grammar, punctuation and spelling is essential for correctly communicating the work to the reader. Furthermore, readers are likely to be irritated by obvious mistakes, consequently curtailing the student's ability to communicate.
  - Expressions and sentences in a thesis must be complete and grammatically correct. Moreover, a thesis must satisfy the stringent rules of formal grammar (for example, no contractions, no colloquialisms and no slurs). The writing in a thesis must be clear and precise. Avoid expressions such as "a number of"; this could mean "some", "many", or "most". Shades of meaning are significant; the words must convey exactly the meaning intended, nothing more and nothing less.
  - Often, when long sentences are used, the argument being advanced

- Avoid the phrase "the authors claim that X". The use of the word "claim" casts doubt on "X" because it references the author's thoughts instead of the facts. If you agree "X" is correct, simply state "X" followed by a reference.
- Proofread your work for spelling mistakes and simple typing errors. It is also advisable to avoid the use of the first person, for example, "I/We will describe . . . ".

18.3 How to Proceed with the Writing

The process of writing a thesis is usually about continuously and methodically refining chapters based on their internal harmony and their connection and linkages to other chapters (Phillips and Pugh 1996). Furthermore, particular attention needs to be given to clarity, purpose and readership (Singh and Nitin 2001). This requires patience and attentiveness and simply cannot be achieved in a short time.

When developing the content of a chapter, the introductory paragraphs should indicate how that chapter relates to the rest of the thesis. According to Cryer (2000), an effective approach to attain this is to write keywords and brief notes to explain and to set the scene, the focus areas and purposes, the gap in knowledge or understanding that the chapter addresses, how the chapter fills the gap, constraints, if any, under which the work described had to be conducted and a brief overview of what is in the chapter followed by work carried out and outcomes from the work. These notes then can be edited concurrently to form the introduction to the chapter. The concluding paragraph of a chapter should indicate how its theme is carried on elsewhere in the thesis. The basic approach to achieving this is by listing some keywords or observations to explain what the chapter has accomplished, what new questions have been identified, where these questions are dealt with and what is next.

In terms of succession, it is not necessary to write the chapters of a thesis in sequence. Students often find it easier to begin by writing the chapters

(Note: the text at the top of the page continues from a previous page: "is lost, whereas a series of shorter, punchy sentences will be more effective. Furthermore, beginning sentences with "joining" words, such as *but, and* or *because* and including long lists of material in the text need to be avoided.")

that capture the research, that is, the conceptual model, fieldwork/data collection, analysis and results (Phillips and Pugh 1996). Although the draft introduction needs to be developed early to orient the thesis for the writing to follow, it needs to be finalized much later to explain how the thesis has evolved, after all the redrafts. After reading the middle chapters to verify terminology, the conclusions, introduction and, finally, the abstract need to be completed and finalized.

Once individual chapters are completed, they need to be linked to form a coherent thesis connected meaningfully with one or more story lines. Accordingly, it is good practice to word headings of chapters, sections and subsections so that they define and reflect their contents. It is advisable to keep an up-to-date content list, so the student can observe the evolving story line readily. At this stage any inconsistencies are likely to surface; therefore, this approach can save hours of writing that may later be redundant.

In terms of getting feedback from the supervisor, it is a common procedure for students to write a chapter of a thesis, submit it to their supervisors and then rewrite to accommodate comments, suggestions and amendments. However, it must be realized that the "revised" chapter has not been finished, as the story line of a thesis can never be apparent from a single chapter, and will require further modification at a later date. The approach to finalizing the last draft of the thesis needs to be that of an editorial mode. Finalizing a thesis is always much more time consuming than expected (Blaxter, Hughes and Tight 2001). The main focus of the thesis, the structure and the organization need to be examined (Booth, Colomb and Williams 1995). Chapters have to be linked, cross-references and pointers need to be inserted to keep the reader oriented, there should be no typing or stylistic errors, and tables, figures and references should be complete, accurate and presented in whatever format has been agreed with the supervisor. Particular attention needs to be paid to the abstract, contents list, beginnings and ends of chapters and the final chapter, as it is these elements that examiners tend to look at first (Booth, Colomb and Williams 1995; Blaxter, Hughes and Tight 2001).

Institutions differ in their requirements for the presentation of a thesis. The student must learn about the requirements of their institution for thesis presentation in terms of number of copies, paper size, colour and weight, fonts and/or typefaces, methods of reproduction, layout (for example, margin sizes and line spacing), pagination (for example, of front material as well as of main text), illustrations, binding, style of print on binding and so on. Furthermore, institutions and sometimes departments require a specified number of copies for their own records. It is common politeness to give a copy to the supervisor, and to acknowledge him or her formally in the thesis, along with others who have helped, and it is a favourable gesture to include a handwritten note of appreciation in the copy given to the supervisor (Phillips and Pugh 1994).

Despite technological advances, the normal practice is still for a thesis to be printed on paper rather than submitted electronically. There needs to be a title page, which normally gives the officially approved thesis title, full name of the candidate, title of the degree and name of the institution. An abstract of fewer than 300 words, a content page and possibly also a list of diagrams, plates, maps, plans and tables should normally follow this. The normal regulations are that the text should be word-processed or typed using double or 1½ line spacing (except for indented quotations and footnotes, which should be single spaced) on one side only of the page, and pages should be numbered continuously from the title page to the end, including all appendices and illustrations.

18.4 Thesis Structure and Organization

Thesis structure and organization are critical components in communicating the research and building a coherent story line. An effective method to establish a structure for a thesis is to develop the core areas of the thesis, draft the case(s), then link these together to build a progressive argument to introduce the issues involved: what research has been done to date and how effective it has been, where are the gaps in knowledge, what are the best approaches and methods available under certain physical, environmental and social conditions. This will lead to your research and need to be followed by results, analysis and evaluations of the outcomes (Booth, Colomb and Williams 1995; Blaxter, Hughes and Tight 2001). As a minimum the thesis will probably include the following elements.

18.4.1 Abstract

The aim of the abstract is to provide a short summary of the thesis. Describe the problem and the research approach. Emphasize the methodology and the outcomes in terms of original contributions. Develop some ideas regarding the usefulness of the outcome to society.

18.4.2 Introduction

The purpose of the introduction is to provide an overview of the thesis, a definition of the problem, background regarding previous work, including different approaches to the topic, precisely what the thesis is trying to achieve and how this has been pursued (DePoy and Gitlin 1994). More specifically, the introduction is often divided into the following sections:

1. Overall aim of the thesis. A clear statement of the aim should be given, as this will help the reviewers and the readers to establish a context for the research.
2. Scientific background and justification. These should provide the reader with details of the topic. This section provides an opportunity to demonstrate the student's expertise in the field and his or her familiarity with a broad range of relevant material, as well as the chance to set the specific research into its wider academic or professional context (Phillips and Pugh 1996). From the background material should emerge the reason for the research; in other words the justification. Therefore, an "unknown" or an "unclear" element should arise from the background discussion. This "unknown" leads directly and conveniently to the next stages of the argument. If something is unknown or unclear, finding out about it or clarifying it seems like a sensible objective.
3. Specific objective of the research. This section aims to explain in specific terms, with reference to the issues identified in the previous section, exactly what this research is attempting to achieve. Placing the specific objectives after the background is recommended, as this will provide the readers with some knowledge of the subject; the knowledge that was provided by the student. Sometimes it is good practice to write a section on the "scope of the work" as this will define the boundaries of the research and research answers. It is not expected that a research thesis on a particular subject can necessarily touch on all facets of the subject.

The crucially important audiences for theses are the examiners, and in particular external examiners. The examiners will expect a thesis to be well structured, organized and to be argued coherently to make the case for the solutions, conclusions or outcomes, and the like. Irrelevancies will irritate, as will having to cope with loose style and typing errors, and having to deduce meaning and conclusions. Examiners are very able and experienced in the general area, which means that background material should be as concise as is consistent with showing that the student has knowledge of it. The features that make the work significant, original and worthy of the award of the MPhil/PhD degree need to be argued cogently: each step needs to be defined; the solutions, conclusions or outcomes must be stated clearly; and all their implications identified and discussed in depth (Cryer 2000).

18.4.3 Literature Review

The aim of the literature review is to give the readers enough information to be able to understand the overall aims and the specific objectives in a detailed scientific context. Therefore, the chapter needs to provide information on previously published work that is directly related to the thesis. This might be work that has addressed exactly the same subject using the same approach as the thesis or that has worked in the same geographic location or environment, or used the same techniques and methodology (Baban and Sankat 2003). Therefore, it is logical to assume that the thesis would have been devised after consideration of the previous literature.

The chapter also provides an opportunity to demonstrate that the student has a full understanding of the background theory to the thesis subject (DePoy and Gitlin 1994). It is important to indicate that a mere encyclopaedic listing and description is not sufficient. Evaluations, which determine the professional judgement of the student, are an essential requirement (Phillips and Pugh 1996).

18.4.4 Methodology

This chapter needs to explain the procedures followed in implementing the research. This explanation should be sufficiently clear and comprehensive so that if other researchers wished to repeat the research in the future they could use the methodology section as an instruction manual as to how to proceed (Baban and Sankat 2003). The methodology section also assists to persuade the readers that the student understood what he or she was doing and that he or she had knowledge of how to perform it correctly (Booth, Colomb and Williams 1995; Phillips and Pugh 1996; Cryer 2000; Blaxter, Hughes and Tight 2001). More specifically, this chapter is commonly expected to cover the following issues:

1. Scientific approach. The chapter should explain the philosophical/conceptual basis and the procedural requirements of the adopted approach. The student needs to develop a "theme" that ties together all his or her arguments. It should provide answers to the questions posed in the introduction at a conceptual level. For example, is the study quantitative or qualitative? Does it adopt a hypothesis-testing approach? What types of information are required to fulfil the project's aims and objectives? What are the characteristics of the research design?
2. Data collection procedures. The chapter should explain the precise details of data collection procedures, including the measures taken and the assumptions made to overcome problems that were encountered. Depending on whether the study involves field, laboratory or library research, this might require detailed description of experimental equipment, of field survey or sampling procedures, or of questionnaire design and implementation.
3. Data analysis methods. The chapter should explain the reasons for selecting particular analytical techniques, the nature and the merits of the techniques chosen, the practical effectiveness of the techniques and any problems experienced in their application to the project. It is especially important to describe any modifications made to standard procedures and why these were necessary.
4. Examining and justifying the selection of the quantitative and the qualitative methods selected and used for analysing and interpreting the results.

18.4.5 Results

This chapter describes the results of the investigation that provide evidence in support of the thesis. Usually experiments either emphasize proof-of-concept (demonstrating the viability of a method or technique) or efficiency (demonstrating that a method or technique provides better performance than those that are already in use).

This chapter must be separate from the previous chapters. It is conventional practice for the data to be presented in a separate chapter. Future readers of the research can then distinguish easily between what actually happened in the field or in the laboratory and what the student thought it meant. If the methodology was recorded correctly and was satisfactory, future researchers may choose to use the data and the observations even if they are not interested in your interpretation (Baban and Sankat 2003). If the results are clearly presented, the reader should be able to assess them and to evaluate the conclusions deduced from them. The reader might choose to reach a different conclusion from the same results. Results can be presented in a variety of ways, depending on the nature of the study and of the methodology used. Using the tabular or graphical form of presentation is the most common. A helpful technique for getting ideas about how to present data is to study and examine successfully completed MPhil/PhD theses from relevant faculties, departments and disciplines. See chapter 14 for further pointers.

18.4.6   Discussion

This chapter will need to bridge the logical gap between the observations and the conclusions. Here, the student needs to explain clearly how the observations and/or measurements made can relate to the aims, background and scientific structure of the thesis. The student will also have to include and explain any conditions and limitations, as well as statements regarding the level of confidence in order to moderate the conclusions (Phillips and Pugh 1996; Blaxter, Hughes and Tight 2001). The results chapter presents the outcomes, whereas this chapter will need to explain the reasons for the outcomes. The discussion needs to be separate from the results so that readers can distinguish between the "objective" element of the measurements and observations and the more "subjective" element of what the student believes about those observations (Baban and Sankat 2003). A future researcher scouring the literature for data about the topic could probably be interested in the observations and not the interpretation. The discussion will also need to explain the implications of the findings of the thesis on professional or industrial practice, so as to give more purpose to its findings. See chapter 14 for further pointers.

18.4.7 Conclusions

The conclusion is the final stage of the logical argument that the thesis presents. The conclusion is expected to summarize what was learned, how it can be applied and to bring the main outcomes of the thesis into sharp focus (Cryer 2000; Blaxter, Hughes and Tight 2001). Furthermore, the thesis will also need to identify future direction and possible applications. The conclusion needs to inventory the principal findings of the research. These can be divided into the points that answer the specific questions that the thesis was investigating (the aims and objectives), some methodological or other findings that arose as a by-product of the principal line of research. In addition, there may be issues concerning the nature of the research and some ideas and recommendations concerning future research.

18.4.8 References

The purpose of this section is to provide full details of all the published material that the student has mentioned in the thesis. A reference list is not the same as a bibliography. A bibliography is a list of publications that are relevant to your subject. A reference list contains only those items specifically examined by the student that have been cited in the text (Blaxter, Hughes and Tight 2001; Baban and Sankat 2003). The proper use of references helps to define the novelty of technical developments. A significant proportion of the background element of the thesis can be reduced with proper citation of the references. The idea of the list is that if a reader wishes to locate a copy of a reference cited in the thesis, the list should provide all the necessary publication details. The reference list is therefore a reader service and an essential follow-up to the text. Consequently, the student should communicate a substantial amount of information about the author, year, title, journal, pages and so on. The style of citation of references depends on institutional requirements.

References

Baban, S.M.J., and C.K. Sankat. 2003. The guide to writing and publishing research papers in peer-reviewed journals. *West Indian Journal of Engineering* 25 (2): 54–64.

Blaxter, L., C. Hughes, and M. Tight. 2001. *How to Research*. 2nd ed. Buckingham, UK: Open University Press.

Booth, W.C., G.G. Colomb and J.M. Williams. 1995. *The Craft of Research*. Chicago: University of Chicago Press.

Cryer, P. 2000. *The Research Student's Guide to Success*. Buckingham, UK: Open University Press.

DePoy, E., and L.N. Gitlin. 1994. *Introduction to Research*. St Louis, MO: Mosby.

Phillips, E.M., and D.I. Pugh. 1996. *How to Get a PhD: A Handbook for Students and Their Supervisors*. 2nd ed. Buckingham, UK: Open University Press.

Singh, S., and K.T. Nitin. 2001. Writing and publishing a research paper in professional journals: A systematic approach. *Asian Journal of Geoinformatics* 1 (3): 87–90.

Chapter 18 Activities

Activity 50

1. List five of the most relevant conceptual issues that need to be understood while writing a research thesis in your specialized field.
2. Discuss and compare these with a peer.

Activity 51

1. List three of the most important issues that concern you during the writing process.
2. Discuss and compare your list with a peer and attempt to suggest reasonable solutions for all the issues identified.

Activity 52

1. Before you read the information in this chapter, how would you have organized your thesis?
2. Compare the structure and organization of your thesis with the proposed arrangement in section 18.4.
3. Discuss and compare (1) and (2) above with a peer.

Contributors

Serwan M.J. Baban is Vice-Chancellor, University of Kurdistan-Hawler, Federal Region of Kurdistan, Iraq. He was formerly Professor of Environmental Geoinformatics, Head of the School of Environmental Science and Management, and Director of the Centre for Geoinformatics Research and Environmental Assessment Technology at Southern Cross University, Australia. Prior to this he was the Chairman/Dean of the School for Graduate Studies and Research, University of the West Indies, St Augustine, Trinidad and Tobago. He has published extensively in national and international journals, international conference proceedings, and chapters in books, as well as consultancy reports. He is the editor of *Enduring Geohazards in the Caribbean: Moving from the Reactive to the Proactive*. Baban is a member of the editorial board and an academic referee for a wide range of international, regional and national journals.

Peter Baverstock is former Pro Vice-Chancellor and Vice President Research, Graduate Research College, Southern Cross University, Australia.

Bill Boyd is Professor in Geography, School of Environmental Science and Management; Associate Dean (Teaching and Learning), Division of Health and Applied Sciences, Research Director, Centres for Geoarchaeology and Palaeoenvironmental Research and Cultural Heritage Management, Southern Cross University, Australia.

Bruce Lauckner is Manager, Research and Development, and Biometrician, Caribbean Agriculture Research and Development Institute, St Augustine, Trinidad and Tobago.

David Lloyd is Senior Lecturer, Protected Area and Coastal Management, and Manager, Bundjalung Site Audit and Assessment and Cultural Mapping Project, School of Environmental Science and Management, Southern Cross University, Australia.

Patricia Mohammed is Senior Lecturer, Centre for Gender and Development Studies, and Chair, School for Graduate Studies and Research, University of the West Indies, St Augustine Campus, Trinidad and Tobago, West Indies.

Clement K. Sankat is Pro Vice Chancellor and Campus Principal, University of the West Indies, St Augustine, Trinidad and Tobago, West Indies.

www.ingramcontent.com/pod-product-compliance
Lightning Source LLC
Chambersburg PA
CBHW031310150426
43191CB00005B/158